Teaching *The Moral Leader*

T0300346

This book is a comprehensive, practical guide to help instructors integrate moral leadership in their own courses, drawing from the experience and resources of the "The Moral Leader," an innovative leadership course taken by thousands of Harvard Business School students over nearly twenty years. Through the close study of literature, including novels, plays and historical accounts, followed by rigorous classroom discussion, students confront fundamental moral challenges, develop skills in moral analysis and judgement, and come to terms with their own definition of moral leadership and how it can be translated into action.

The detailed and hands-on nature of the guide makes it possible for instructors, with or without a specialized background, to replicate the Harvard Business School course or to integrate moral leadership into an existing course. The guide presents flexible class plans, easily adaptable to a wide variety of business and academic topics. It suggests how to adapt the course to other settings, provides supporting materials, and reviews the approach to teaching "The Moral Leader," enabling instructors who are intrigued by teaching through literature to build confidence in their ability to adopt this uniquely powerful pedagogy.

An accompanying student textbook, *The Moral Leader: Challenges, Tools, and Insights*, also available from Routledge, focuses on class preparation and the context of each work, helping students address questions like: What is the nature of a moral challenge? How do people "reason morally"? How do leaders – formal and informal – contend with the moral choices they face? How is *moral leadership* different from leadership of any other kind? Struggling with these questions, both individually and as members of a vibrant learning community, students internalize moral leadership concepts and choices, and develop the skills to pursue it in their careers and personal lives.

Sandra J. Sucher is Senior Lecturer at the Harvard Business School. She brings to "The Moral Leader" the kind of real world understanding of effective leadership development that comes from decades of experience as a high level corporate executive.

Teaching
The Moral Leader

A literature-based leadership course

A guide for instructors

Sandra J. Sucher

Routledge
Taylor & Francis Group

LONDON AND NEW YORK

First published 2007
by Routledge
2 Park Square Milton Park Abingdon Oxon OX14 4RN

Simultaneously published in the USA and Canada
by Routledge
711 Third Ave, New York, NY 10017

Routledge is an imprint of the Taylor & Francis Group

© 2007 Sandra J. Sucher

Typeset in Minion and Bell Gothic by
Florence Production Ltd, Stoodleigh, Devon

British Library Cataloguing in Publication Data
A catalogue record for this book is available from the British Library

Library of Congress Cataloging in Publication Data
Sucher, Sandra J.
    Teaching "The Moral Leader": a literature-based leadership course
    a guide for instructors/Sandra J. Sucher.
        p. cm.
    Includes bibliographical references and index.
    1. Leadership – Moral and ethical aspects.   2. Social ethics.   I. Title.
    HM1261.S83 2007
    174′.4–dc22   2006038497

ISBN10: 0–415–40065–1 (pbk)
ISBN13: 978–0–415–40065–7 (pbk)

Contents

CONTENTS

Preface

I began planning this book after my third time teaching "The Moral Leader" at the Harvard Business School, a thirteen-week two-hour seminar with MBA students devoted to moral decision-making and leadership through the study of literature and history. Literally thousands of students have taken "The Moral Leader" at the school since the 1980s. The course works to further the skills students are seeking, skills that will enable them to become effective leaders of organizations.

I do not take the development of leadership skills lightly. I spent more than twenty-five years as an executive myself, briefly in the world of nonprofit organizations, and then, after earning an MBA from Harvard Business School thirty years ago, in a career in service businesses – fashion retailing, and mutual fund and brokerage financial services. I have served as chairman of Boston's Better Business Bureau, been a corporate director several times, and have had the questionable fortune to be on the board of an organization that had to be taken over by government regulators. The corporate world is my world, and my search since joining the faculty of Harvard Business School some eight years ago has been to connect theory with practice in the classroom.

The school's dominant pedagogy is case-method teaching, a format that gives students the opportunity to explore situations they may encounter, always with an emphasis that moves from understanding to action. A case class is centered on action questions – *What should Mr or Ms X do?* or *What would you do in this situation?* – and the ability to rehearse decisions may very well make the difference between success and failure in many of the situations students will face.

A course like "The Moral Leader" complements case-method teaching (and lecture-based pedagogies as well), but its aims are quite different. Instead of focusing students on what they might do themselves, they are led on a deep dive into the world of *others*, forced to understand how it is that someone other than themselves has apprehended a situation they found themselves in and has decided to act.

Anyone who has tried to lead even the smallest group understands that, while we may not know precisely what we should do ourselves, many of the most puzzling mysteries of management center on the nearly inexplicable actions of others. "The Moral Leader" uses literature as its source material; the novels, plays, stories, and histories train students to see the world, fully, through someone else's eyes.

"The Moral Leader" is about more than this, of course. It is called "The *Moral* Leader" because it is designed to help students explore their own notions of morality, to get to know themselves and their own ideas through their reactions to the characters and situations they read about, and through interacting with other students whose views are different, often shockingly different, from their own.

Moral and ethical problems abound in organizations because they serve multiple interests; they are baked into the reality of organizational life. The literature and historical accounts used in "The Moral Leader" allow students to examine moral action through the lens of others' actions. Unlike a case-based discussion, they see beyond the situation to how it is worked out, and this perspective on cause and effect, on action and impact, takes students from speculation of what might happen to a consideration of what did happen and why. The classes thus provide a laboratory for understanding how morally charged situations develop and are shaped through action. The opportunity to see a situation all the way through is essential, providing students with the impetus to refine, validate, or revise their own processes of moral judgment.

The course is also an elaboration on leadership, built with a strong focus on skills I believe allow leaders to master themselves in morally charged situations. These include the abilities to recognize different types of moral challenge, to understand how to reason a path through a moral problem, and to appreciate what moral leadership looks like when it is demonstrated by real people, leaders who must make moral decisions under conditions of responsibility for others.

Organizations offer few if any opportunities to develop these skills or even to practice the dialogue of moral debate they depend on. Yet we have daily evidence of how crucial such skills are to organizational leadership, and with increasing globalization, vast changes in the life sciences, and conflicting pressures from developing, emerging, and developed economies the situations leaders face will grow only more complex over time.

I also have come to believe that the course is intense, powerful, and practical precisely because it does not focus solely on problems situated in contemporary organizations. Instead, the readings take students far and wide, back thousands of years, and deep into other cultures. Effective leadership requires intimacy and breadth, the ability to connect oneself to oneself and to connect to others. This is a life-long search with boundaries that stretch well beyond any particular organization or assignment, well beyond, in fact, the professional careers that any of us pursue. A course like "The Moral Leader" allows students to develop self-awareness and a hunger to understand the broader world they live in. The curiosity and self-knowledge they gain is a powerful combination, one I believe will serve them well in all the roles they will play.

I am not alone in appreciating how valuable literature and underlying philosophy can be to the study of leadership. Organizations such as the Aspen Institute and the Hartwick Institute for Humanities in Management till this soil in the US, as do the instructors who have written of their own experiences and insights, such as Robert Coles, who introduced "The Moral Leader" to Harvard Business School, and my colleague Joe Badaracco, whose 2006 reflection, *Questions of Character: Illuminating the Heart of Leadership through Literature*, will be valuable to anyone with an interest in the topic. Many scholars link literature and philosophy more generally, including Martha Nussbaum, Wayne Booth, Louis Pojman, and Burton Porter, and there is a growing literature that focuses on a related connection between philosophy and film.[1]

Teaching "The Moral Leader:" A Literature-Based Leadership Course aims to augment these efforts by providing a thorough, hands-on guide for instructors who are intrigued by the topic of moral leadership and by the approach of learning through literature but who want to understand how these actually work in the classroom. *The Moral Leader: Challenges, Tools, and Insights*, the companion student textbook, furnishes additional background and conceptual material to guide students in their learning.

Throughout my executive life I have been concerned with processes – the way that work is done, as a principal tool for understanding and improving organization performance. Teaching, I have found, is little different, so an explication of how to design, facilitate, and teach this type of course is, I believe, as important to successful adoption as appreciating the theories and insights into learning, leadership, and moral decision-making it is based on. All of this is described in the book that follows.

NOTE

1   A review of selected theoretical atecedents to "The Moral Leader" is covered in Chapter 2, and the philosophical underpinnings of the course are described in Chapter 8 and Chapter 14. Additional sources you may find helpful include: the philosophy reader by Louis P. Pojman and Lewis Vaughn (eds), *The Moral Life: An Introductory Reader in Ethics and Literature*, New York: Oxford University

Press, 2006; Burton F. Porter, *Philosophy Through Ficction and Film*, Upper Saddle River, NJ: Pearson Prentice Hall, 2004; Christopher Falzon, *Philosophy Goes to the Movies: An Introduction to Philosophy*, New York and London: Routledge, 2002; and, Cynthia A. Freeland and Thomas E. Wartenburg (eds), *Philosophy and Film*, New York and London: Routledge, 1995.

Acknowledgments

Since Robert Coles' introduction in the 1980s, "The Moral Leader" has been taught by a succession of instructors at Harvard Business School (not many – all supremely capable, all passionate about the course), and each has put his, or her, own unique stamp on the course.

The course I describe draws on this illustrious past, and I am grateful to Robert Coles, Mary Gentile, Scotty McLennan, and Joe Badaracco for warmly and generously sharing their favorite stories, approaches, and (for Mary) her clear view of what this project could mean to other instructors and (for Joe) his entire file of background notes and the opportunity to watch a complete semester of the course being taught.

Mary and Joe have offered guidance on the development of this book (I was even told I had a "moral obligation" to see the project through), as have a number of other colleagues at Harvard Business School who have provided feedback on the manuscript. They include Lynda Applegate, Regina Bento, David Garvin, Willis Emmons, Matthew Kumar, Lynn Paine, and Tom Piper, and the members of Technology and Operations, my home unit, especially Charlie Fine (on loan from MIT), Bob Hayes, Deishin Lee, and Noel Watson, who were particularly helpful in letting me see the course through the eyes of instructors who teach a very different discipline. I am grateful, as well, to Srikant Datar, Jan Hammond, and Roy Shapiro, who initially offered me the chance to become involved with the course.

This version of "The Moral Leader" is my own, developed with Barbara Feinberg, my long-time collaborator, a student of history and philosophy whose skill as a course designer has enriched every aspect of the undertaking. I am grateful to Barbara for her irreplaceable contributions to and unflagging enthusiasm for the entire Moral Leader project, which made its completion a surer bet than I would have counted on. The project represents my best attempt to make good on the potential of this distinctly valuable approach to student learning.

My thanks as well to two extremely able research associates: Joshua Bellin, whose outstanding research, writing, and adaptations enabled the student textbook to take its current form, and Bianca Buccitelli whose organizational skills, common sense, and good counsel helped bring "The Moral Leader" projects to fruition.

The Division of Research at Harvard Business School supported this project over several years. I am grateful to the research directors for their support, and to Francesca Heslop, my editor at Routledge, who championed the project and saw from the start how it could enhance the art of teaching leadership, and Simon Whitmore, who helped bring the project home.

You will find excerpts from my own classes throughout this book as well as in "conversations" that relate student comments in every class chapter. You will thus see how integral the students of "The Moral Leader" have been to the evolution of the course. There would be no course without the students I have learned along with; they continue to surprise, delight, and teach me. To them all, I am grateful.

I am dedicating this instructor guide to my family. To my parents: Gerald Sucher (1920–2005) – for telling great stories, and Jean Sucher (1922–2006) – for showing me how they are lived. To Susan and Stuart, and Mark and Jane, for help through good and hard times. To Richard, who has encouraged every twist and turn of my career; and to Libby and Andrew, who make me proud of being a parent every day.

Chapter 1

Introduction

Every year since the 1980s, a hundred or more Harvard Business School students have taken a literature-based course on moral leadership called "The Moral Leader." They find its combination of powerful material and guided discussion compelling and challenging to their own assumptions, beliefs, and questions. When I was asked to develop my own version of the course, I became convinced that others would find that combination as gratifying as I have, and thus the idea of this guide for instructors, and its companion student text, took root.

Teaching "The Moral Leader" has been written for people concerned with the intersection of leadership and complex situations involving moral and ethical stakes – instructors of management, organizational behavior, philosophy, education, medicine, engineering, and the list can go on. As instructors with such concerns, you may be searching for ways to engage students in issues of moral leadership, to build capabilities in that arena. It has also been written for those intrigued by harnessing the power of literature itself: each of the texts and corresponding class plans shows how students' learning can be both broadened and deepened through exposure to the rich, profound, diverse, and ageless human preoccupation with morality found in such readings.

For all of you, whether you adopt "The Moral Leader" in whole or in part, or seek inspiration for integrating literature into other approaches to learning (see Appendix 1), this guide aims to provide hands-on suggestions. *Teaching "The Moral Leader"* addresses how learning through literature is done: how such a course is structured and how learning is integrated; how class sessions based on literature are organized and facilitated; and the practical details of how class participation and papers in such a course might be evaluated and graded. In sum, my goal is to equip you to take on the challenge of introducing the topic of moral leadership into your own classrooms.

THE "MORAL LEADER" COURSE: OVERVIEW

The power of "The Moral Leader" course stems from the use of prize-winning novels, short stories, plays, biographies and autobiographies, and selected supplementary readings that enable discussion to be focused and cumulative. (Chapter 3 expands on this point.) The aim is for students to develop their own workable definition of moral leadership – through their preparations for class, their participation in discussion, and in a final paper. The course does not provide a pre-existing definition of either "moral" or "leadership" but guides students towards their own discovery of meaning.[1] Thus, student discussion is structured, as the following sections (and this entire guide) make clear. And it is graded, for this is an academic endeavor that incorporates the same rigor (and grading) as any other Harvard Business School course. As is the case with any course, and particularly one on this topic, learning does not ipso facto translate into action. "The Moral Leader" does not guarantee moral leaders.

The course does, however, reflect a commitment to educating the *whole student* – the adult who will make choices in a variety of venues, often with responsibility for others as well as for himself or herself. These other people may be family members, fellow citizens, investors, customers, patients, clients, suppliers, regulators, board members, or members of the organizations, industries, and professions that students will join as their careers develop.

The reading list for the course is international in scope, appealing to students through fictional and historical accounts set in the US, Great Britain, Nigeria, Japan, Thailand, Greece, Antarctica, and Italy. Students read about challenges faced more than two thousand years ago and ones as recent as September 11, 2001, by actors in times of war, peace, and unsettling periods in between. The varied settings, times, and situations reinforce the universality of moral challenge and the requirement for students, future leaders – and for all of us – to develop abilities to describe and analyze moral problems, to think them through, and to act (see Table 1.1).

The texts are arranged in a flow of thirteen two-hour sessions, divided into three modules – Moral Challenge, Moral Reasoning, Moral Leadership – that move students through an exploration of the topic of moral leadership. The flow highlights a succession of questions that constitute the modules of the course: *What is the nature of a moral challenge? How do people "reason morally"? What do these look like when they are undertaken by leaders – individuals who must make decisions under conditions of responsibility for others?*

These are not necessarily literary questions, or philosophical ones (except for that of moral reasoning), or ones that derive from any particular school of leadership studies. They are, instead, the kind of practical questions that

Table 1.1 The Moral Leader readings

Reading	Setting	Format
Module I: Moral challenge		
Endurance:Shackleton's Incredible Voyage Alfred Lansing	Antarctica, 1914	Historical account
Antigone Sophocles	Ancient Greece	Play
Blessed Assurance Allen Gurganus	1940s America	Novella
Things Fall Apart Chinua Achebe	Nigeria, early twentieth century	Novel
Module II: Moral reasoning		
Trifles Susan Glaspell	Rural America, early twentieth century	Play
Principles of Biomedical Ethics Tom L. Beauchamp, James F. Childress		Text excerpts
The Sweet Hereafter Russell Banks	Contemporary America	Novel
The Remains of the Day Kazuo Ishiguro	Britain between world wars	Novel
A Man for All Seasons Robert Bolt	Sixteenth-century England	Play and movie
Module III: Moral leadership		
The Prince Niccolò Machiavelli	Sixteenth-century Italy	Treatise
The Secret Sharer Joseph Conrad	1890s off the coast of Siam	Short Story
Truman and the Bomb	Second World War, beyond	Text excerpts
Just and Unjust Wars Michael Walzer		Text excerpts
Personal History Katharine Graham	1970s America, recalled	Autobiography
A Good Life Ben Bradlee		Autobiography
American Ground: Unbuilding the World Trade Center William Langewiesche	Post-September 11th USA	Eyewitness account

students ask themselves as they wrestle with the reality of moral decision-making and worry about their ability to make good, morally satisfying decisions when they are in leadership roles.

In addition to the literature, background readings on moral philosophy are offered, sparingly, at points where students have struggled for clarity and are grateful for models of moral reasoning and decision-making. These readings also provide reassurance: students, and the instructor, are hardly alone in their exploration.

Module I: Moral Challenge

The Moral Challenge module lays the groundwork for the course, introducing students to situations with clear moral and ethical stakes, where they are able to examine how people behave when faced with a moral challenge. The four texts illustrate what is to many students a surprising concept: moral challenges are not all the same – there are *types of* moral challenge, and each one suggests a different set of strategic responses. For example, most students have not considered the difference between a "right versus wrong" challenge and a challenge of "competing rights" in which each position is morally defensible, and what this difference might imply for action. Students learn how to describe the particular tensions each type of challenge presents, and are able to examine the strategies – some successful, many not – that characters in the stories devise to resolve them.

Module II: Moral Reasoning

Better able to appreciate the various types of moral challenge they may encounter, students then move to the Moral Reasoning module, where they will explore how people actually think these challenges through. The four texts are laid out in a progression that steadily broadens and deepens students' understanding of what moral reasoning consists of, and of how it works. Beginning with reasoning from moral theory, the stories layer on additional ways that people reason about their challenges, including reasoning that flows from their history and life situation, reasoning from an established system of beliefs and values, and reasoning that encompasses multiple bases of morality – the ability to consider and attempt to make good on multiple moral duties and ideals.

Module III: Moral Leadership

In the third module, students build on their understanding of moral challenges and of moral reasoning by examining what moral decision-making and action look like under conditions of responsibility for others. The module on Moral Leadership is designed to help students explore what distinguishes moral leadership from leadership in general, and even what distinguishes it from good and effective leadership. The module focuses on protagonists who have been awarded (or have taken) formal responsibility for an entity of some kind – a state, a ship, a business – and who face moral tests as part and parcel of their leadership responsibilities. The module sets out to create an expectation for students that moral leadership is part of normal, everyday leadership work, something to which they might aspire or even be expected to perform when they become responsible for established groups and institutions.

The module is structured around two sets of leadership tasks – a pair of twinned challenges that leaders face – exercising authority and earning legitimacy. The challenges are woven through each text in the module, with an emphasis that flows increasingly from authority to legitimacy. Along the way, students encounter leaders who must balance the benefits and harms of the decisions they make, who must decide whether to take a stand to defend a cherished moral principle, and who earn the right to lead without the benefit of designated authority.

USING THIS GUIDE

The next two chapters allow you to get a sense of the course as a whole. The first is a brief review of learning through literature from the perspective of various advocates that places "The Moral Leader" course in a broader theoretical context. The following chapter details how learning is integrated into the course, how sessions are facilitated, and how class participation and student papers may be graded.

The thirteen class plans, which make up the major chapters of this book, are written in the spirit of Harvard Business School teaching notes – as documentation from one instructor to another, with as much detail and as many tips about potential pitfalls and important learning opportunities as it is possible for me to convey.

Class plans describe the learning objectives of each session – the themes and questions it is designed to raise – and include introductory comments that may help you start the session. Each class has its own designed discussion path, with corresponding student assignment questions, and detailed plans, including challenge questions and exercises, for you to use to lead students through the class. The class plan chapters also include samples of student dialogue from my own classes that illustrate what conducting each discussion, using the path outlined, might sound like.

Those interested in possibly introducing works of literature into their own courses will find that the lesson plans and other core materials provide realistic and actionable examples of how to work with literature. For this second audience, I have also prepared additional appendix materials. These include thoughts on how to adapt the course approach and modules, and suggestions of how specific texts might pair with or be used to enhance the teaching of other subjects. You will know, better than I, which pairings might make sense – the suggestions are meant to stimulate connections.

In addition, *Teaching "The Moral Leader"* also has a student text and a website.

The student textbook

The companion student textbook, *The Moral Leader: Challenges, Tools, and Insights* (Routledge, 2008), prepares students to participate in the course. It includes guidance for how to read the material in a course like "The Moral Leader" – how to read literature for the lessons it provides, and how to prepare for class participation. Module introductions provide brief theoretical background on the concepts of Moral Challenge, Moral Reasoning, and Moral Leadership, laying out how these have been viewed by, for example, philosophers, social scientists, and those who study the practice of ethical decision-making.

Each session is documented for students in its own chapter. Since the readings span thousands of years and multiple cultures, there is also brief background material on the historical and social context of each of the novels, plays, and historical accounts used in the course. These vary widely, covering topics as diverse as village life in pre-colonial West Africa (for Chinua Achebe's *Things Fall Apart*), to religious practice in the American South (for *Blessed Assurance*, by Allen Gurganus), to women in business in the 1970s (for the class on *Washington Post* publisher Kay Graham). The background materials put students, and the instructor, on a relatively level playing field of knowledge, from which any of them can contribute insights that go beyond the information provided. Students have told me that the background materials give them confidence in their ability to analyze and assess the actions of characters who inhabit worlds vastly different from their own.

There are also biographical notes on each of the authors, assignment questions, and brief introductions to the themes and questions suggested by each text, providing students, in total, with a robust perspective on areas to focus on in their preparation.

The website

"The Moral Leader" website, maintained by Routledge, offers additional materials, including downloadable outlines of the question flow of each class, and summary comments that could be used or handed out to students. "The Moral Leader" project will evolve through feedback and interaction, and I look forward to learning about similar ventures, and to suggestions for materials that a community of interested instructors and students would find helpful.

CAN *ANYONE* TEACH THIS COURSE?

While rigorous in process and thorough in its coverage of the intended purpose of each class, the course does not require formal background in ethics, literary analysis, or leadership studies. Moreover, no one is an expert in all the situations, formats, themes, and materials found in "The Moral Leader"! The course, in fact, is designed to be *kind* to the instructor, whose role is one of being a prepared discussion leader. Rather than imparting a specific body of knowledge, you insist on rigor from students in their preparation, assertions, arguments, and debates. In this you will be aided by the course's architecture, the detailed class plans, and the techniques for addressing complex topics, all of which are described in this guide.

There is a profound joy that comes from helping students learn through literature. You will have a chance to engage students in topics of evident importance and concern, using materials of exceptional quality and depth, through a rigorous process of guided learning; quite simply, it is worth an experiment.

NOTE

1 Because course learning emphasizes ongoing and cumulative engagement with a variety of material focused on "what is moral," no explicit definition of morality, or ethics, is introduced at the outset. Rather, through written assignments, class discussions, and supplementary readings, students derive a sense of what is moral that is both individually meaningful and has real-world application to them. See Appendix 2 for more information on this topic.

A literature-based leadership course

Chapter 2

Learning through Literature

Why is literature such a powerful source of learning? There is in fact an entire literature on this question, and in this chapter I'll highlight some suggested answers that have been most helpful to me in understanding what happens when students individually read, then communally discuss, rich, complex material. This is a highly personal editing, sorted by author, and looks at literature and learning from various perspectives. While these authors refer, in various ways, to the power of literature (or, in shorthand, "stories"), in fact they are talking about the *engagement* of students and literature. It is that process that unleashes the power.

ROBERT COLES

"The Moral Leader" course was introduced to the Harvard Business School in the 1980s by Harvard psychiatrist and educator Robert Coles as part of his own exploration of the use of literature for student learning about moral questions and action. The business school was just one of Coles' stops. He introduced literature-based learning first to Harvard undergraduates and then to graduate students in Harvard's schools of medicine, law, architecture, politics, divinity, education, and design.[1] The rationale, validated through these experiments and recorded, movingly, in Coles' 1989 reflections in *The Call of Stories: Teaching and the Moral Imagination,* is that literature can be used for personal discovery about moral matters because it *gets inside students* – they take and make it their own. Coles describes what this taking and making are for – and how they work.

> Novels and stories are renderings of life; they can not only keep us company, but admonish us, point us in new directions, or give us the courage to stay a given course. They can offer us kinsmen, kinswomen, comrades, advisors – offer us other eyes through which we might

see, other ears with which we make soundings. Every medical student, every law student, or business school student, every man or woman studying at a graduate school of education or learning to be an architect, will all too quickly be beyond schooling, will be out there making a living and, too, just plain living – that is, trying to find and offer to others the affection and love that give purpose to our time spent here. No wonder, then, [characters] can be cautionary figures to us, especially to us doctors, can be spiritual companions, can be persons, however "imaginary" in nature, who give us pause and help us in the private moments when we are trying to find our bearings.[2]

Students are aware of this power and of the role that the literature takes in their lives, as the following student comment from Coles' text illustrates:

"Who is this Stecher?" a student of mine at Harvard Business School asked, referring to the central figure in William Carlos Williams' trilogy, an immigrant who eventually rises high socially and economically. The student – to our fascination in that class – was intent not only on an intellectual summary. "He's a mass of words, I suppose – what we read in a novelist's book. But to me Stecher is – oh now, part of me! What do I mean? I mean that he's *someone*; he's a guy I think of. I picture him and can hear him talking. And he looks different to each one of us, and the way he talks is different for each one of us, because each of us has our own accent. He's inside us, and so is Gurlie [his wife]. I can see him walking, or working, or climbing those stairs to his apartment, or eating – and listening to his wife, as she pushes him to get out there and climb the ladder. Williams' words have become my images and sounds, part of me. You don't do that with theories. You don't do that with a system of ideas. You do it with a story, because in a story – oh, like it says in the Bible, *the word becomes flesh*."[3]

What are students doing with this literature – with what gets inside them? In a course like "The Moral Leader," literature is not useful – and valued – because it provides answers (although it may at times do just that), but because it raises questions, puts a name and a face on a situation that may be exotic or familiar, and introduces students to what the future, their future, might hold as moral actors in a world of moral challenge. And the marvelous strength of stories is that they have a life of their own, a life that imbeds itself and keeps on influencing the student and her learning long after the story is read, discussed, and initially digested. As Coles puts it:

The whole point of stories is not "solutions" or "resolutions" but a broadening and even a heightening of our struggles – with new protagonists and antagonists introduced, with new sources of concern or apprehension or hope, as one's mental life accommodates itself to a series of arrivals: guests who have a way of staying, but not necessarily staying put.[4]

WAYNE BOOTH

Coles is not alone in his advocacy of literature as a particularly powerful source of learning about moral action, or even for how literature is taken in by students. Literature scholar Wayne Booth extends the point, arguing that we are inseparable from the stories we read.

But anyone who conducts honest introspection knows that "real life" is lived *in* images derived in art from stories . . . Indeed, our imitations of *narrative* "imitations of life" are so spontaneous and plentiful that we cannot draw a clear line between what we *are*, in some conception of a "natural," unstoried self, and what we have become as we have first enjoyed, then imitated, and then, perhaps, criticized both the stories and our responses to it.[5]

Booth advances his argument, asserting that because stories have such a profound influence on us they can shape our character:

A commonplace has it that by the age of thirty, the character has set like plaster, and will never soften again. Another one says, "Give me a child until the age of six, and I care not what influences him afterward." No doubt some early "fixings" are necessary in every life, but for most of us our character – in the larger sense of the range of choices and habits of choice available to us – changes, grows, and diminishes largely as a result of our imaginative diet.[6]

MARTHA NUSSBAUM

Just how this "imaginative diet" works on us is taken up by Martha Nussbaum, law professor and interpreter of Aristotelian philosophy. To Nussbaum, literature offers two connected roads in to moral sensibility and competence. First is its ability to depict particular contexts – not just to depict them, but to teach the detailed *seeing* that moral judgment and moral action require. In *Love's Knowledge: Essays on Philosophy and Literature*, Nussbaum asserts "the priority of perceptions, [or] priority of the particular".

In these essays, and in the novels, much is made of an ethical ability that I call "perception" after both Aristotle and [William] James. By this I mean the ability to discern, acutely and responsively, the salient features of one's particular situation. The Aristotelian conception argues that this ability is at the core of what practical wisdom is, and that it is not only a tool toward achieving the correct action or statement, but an ethically valuable activity in its own right.[7]

How does engaging with literature do this? "The point is that in the activity of literary imagining we are led to imagine and describe with greater precision, focusing our attention on each word, feeling each event more keenly – whereas much of actual life goes by without that heightened awareness, and is thus, in a certain sense, not fully or thoroughly lived."[8]

Literature does not just fully and more carefully describe situations, events, and actions than we may do ourselves in the self-narration that we create as we experience such things, it also provides a window into the emotions, the internal life of actors. Following Aristotle, Nussbaum asserts that "[w]ithout feeling, a part of correct perception is missing."[9] Emotions are an integral part of practical wisdom and moral reasoning, and a guide to moral truths.

> Good perception is a full recognition or acknowledgement of the nature of the practical situation; the whole personality sees it for what it is. The agent who discerns intellectually that a friend is in need or that a loved one has died, but who fails to respond to these facts with appropriate sympathy or grief . . . doesn't really, or doesn't fully, see what has happened, doesn't recognize it in a full-blooded way or take it in . . . the emotional part of cognition is lacking.[10]
> . . . The emotions are themselves modes of vision, or recognition.[11]

From these and other arguments, Nussbaum concludes, like Coles, that literature has much to contribute to the education of students bound for professional lives, or any kind of active life in which moral decision-making will be called for. She says:

> Where the teaching of moral reasoning is concerned, the Aristotelian conception will strongly endorse recent American efforts to make this a central part of education in medicine, law, business, and in undergraduate education more generally. But here again distinctions need to be made. The sort of moral reasoning recommended by the Aristotelian will be clear, well argued, theoretically rich. But it will also make large demands upon the imagination and the emotions. It will be very far from a large course in formal decision theory, or in the principles of economic rationality (as these are most often

portrayed). It will at all times encourage the student to attend closely to the heterogeneity of life. And course materials will include works of literature that enrich and develop the sense of life, expressing, in their own attention to particularity and their richness of feeling, elements of the Aristotelian conception. It will include as well the deep and rigorous study of alternative moral conceptions, in order to give the student a clearer sense of the available choices. All this will be in the service of promoting the student's ability to choose a general conception of the good life, and to perceive, in practice, what this conception requires. At every stage in the process, the student would continue to refine her abilities to reflect and perceive in and about concrete cases, perhaps again through continued contact with works of literature and history.[12]

GARY KLEIN

These psychological, literary, and philosophical justifications for the use of literature to document and explore moral action are augmented by another argument, one based on the observation of people engaged in decision-making in natural settings, i.e., in real life. Gary Klein, a US-based researcher in naturalistic decision-making, examines how individuals make decisions in highly charged situations – military commanders in harm's way, firefighters on the job, nurses in hospital neonatal units. Klein's organization, which has been conducting such studies since the 1980s, identifies various powers that individuals come to rely on for decision support, such as intuition (defined through their studies as pattern-matching from prior experiences) and mental simulation, imaginary run-throughs of planned actions used to check their feasibility.

Storytelling has emerged as one of the powers routinely employed by decision-makers.[13] Klein's organization has found – not surprisingly – that stories are used to transmit values and lessons (the power they have for others); stories also serve as a way that individuals have of making sense of events and even to solve problems related to them (the power they have for ourselves).

A story is an encapsulated view of a situation: economic, and therefore tractable – something we can get our arms around and make sense of, unlike the disjointed flow of reality that we would otherwise face. "We like to hear good stories retold. What is more interesting is our need to *tell* stories, again and again. Each telling helps us understand more about the lessons embedded in the story."[14] This is learning by group as well as individual analysis and reflection, a central feature of a course like "The Moral Leader," and, evidently, a common method of learning for those with a strong need to do so, like Klein's nurses, firefighters, and members of the military's fighting forces.

15

ENGAGING WITH LITERATURE IN *THE MORAL LEADER*

An animating principle of "The Moral Leader," originating with Robert Coles, is that literature is perhaps uniquely helpful to students intent on learning about moral leadership because of its ability to embrace their emotions as well as their intellect – hearts as well as minds. Thus, moral reasoning as presented in the course is not a purely cognitive activity,[15] and the emotive force of powerful "stories" provides students with a realistic experience (even if fictional) of the complexities of individuals facing moral challenges and attempting to come to terms with them. Moreover, literature exerts its influence not only in the moment but also on into the future, when students face situations analogous to what they found in their reading and recall how "characters" behaved. As well, as students reflect on (and perhaps reread) what they first encountered in the course, they discover that, as they have changed, so have the meaning and significance of the material. Overall, engaging with literature encourages the kind of situation awareness – attention to detail, to context and to circumstances – essential to moral judgment and, ideally, to moral action.

NOTES

1   Robert Coles, *The Call of Stories: Teaching and the Moral Imagination*, Boston, Mass.: Houghton Mifflin, 1989, pp. xvii–xviii.
2   Ibid., p. 159–160.
3   Ibid., p. 128.
4   Ibid., p. 129.
5   Wayne C. Booth, *The Company We Keep: An Ethics of Fiction*, Berkeley, Calif.: University of California Press, 1988, pp. 228–229.
6   Ibid., p. 257.
7   Martha C. Nussbaum, *Love's Knowledge: Essays on Philosophy and Literature*, New York: Oxford University Press, 1990, p. 37.
8   Ibid., p. 47.
9   Ibid., p. 79.
10 Ibid., p. 79.
11 Ibid., p. 79.
12 Ibid., pp. 103–104.
13 See Chapter 11, "The Power of Stories," in Gary Klein, *Sources of Power: How People Make Decisions*, Cambridge, Mass.: The MIT Press, 1998, pp. 177–196.
14 Ibid., p. 179.
15 See, for example, Joshua D. Greene, R. Brian Somerville, Leigh E. Nystrom, John M. Darley, and Jonathan D. Cohen, "An fMRI Investigation of Emotional Engagement in Moral Judgment," *Science*, 2000, vol. 293, 2105–2108.

Chapter 3

Course Design, Facilitation, and Grading

That sounds fascinating. But how do you teach *this course?*

As the previous chapter made clear, the sheer engagement with literature offers insight, particularly when individual reading is combined in discussion with similarly prepared people. On one level, then, the literature itself is the instructor. It would be impossible to have a class on, say, *The Prince* that did not evoke a powerful exchange of ideas and consequent learning. "The Moral Leader," however, has a broader agenda than the insight gained solely from such engagement. It has *objectives* built into the design of the course, reflected in the arrangement of readings, the questions that each session raises, and the conscious attempt to expand and deepen learning from one session to the next. At the end arises a general understanding of the moral leadership landscape such that students can begin to define their own "moral leader" meaning within it.

At the Harvard Business School, "The Moral Leader" is taught in thirteen two-hour sessions that meet once a week in a seminar or small-group setting.[1] A seminar consists of a class of twenty-five students at HBS; in other institutions, the class size will probably be considerably smaller. Class plans, described in general below and then detailed in the individual class session chapters, have been set for *one and three-quarter hours*, to allow them to be used by instructors in courses or programs that meet either for two-hour or one-and-a-half-hour sessions. See also Appendix 1, which discusses how the course can be adapted to other settings and situations.

This chapter describes how "The Moral Leader" course works; in conjunction with the subsequent chapters that dig into individual sessions, you will find that the course is indeed teachable. We shall look at details of how classes are facilitated and end with a discussion of grading and papers.

LEARNING OBJECTIVES

"The Moral Leader" is designed to enable students to explore the rich material of the course – extraordinarily fine literary and historical stories of moral challenge and leadership – both broadly and deeply. Armed with background about the wider historical and social environment from the student textbook, students are guided through a detailed analysis of the circumstances of the characters, focusing on the individual situations and problems they face. Ultimately, students build capabilities in moral analysis and moral judgment, which helps them towards the goal of personal discovery and insight into their understanding of moral leadership.

The texts have been chosen for their thematic relevance at both macro and micro levels. There are obvious segues from one reading to another, but there are also more subtle connections (these are explicated in the teaching plans that follow). This sophisticated flow allows students to make sense of increasingly complex topics that build to an understanding of moral leadership – what it entails, and how it is demonstrated. Table 3.1 shows the broad themes evoked by the texts; these themes anchor the course and its learning and are described in detail in the class session chapters.

Moral analysis

The course's design aims at having students create a set of analytical skills that prepare them to exercise moral leadership. These include the ability to identify what constitutes a situation with moral or ethical stakes, and the related ability to identify and distinguish types and categories of moral problem. These skills evolve as the course unfolds, and significantly, as they emerge, there are opportunities, built into various sessions, for them to be practiced – in class. Not only are there specific questions about identifying the morally salient features of a particular situation – bounding the problem so it can be worked on without losing sight of important complexities and ambiguities, and how to characterize objectively the different sides of a dilemma and the positions that various parties take. There are also opportunities to re-imagine situations that are seemingly intractable in the material but could be recast. (Thus, how would it be possible for Creon and Antigone to find common ground?)

These are not abilities that students necessarily come to class with, and the class plans allow students sufficient airtime to offer up their own analyses, have them challenged, and expand and refine them.

Table 3.1 *The Moral Leader themes*

Session	Theme
Module I: Moral Challenge	
Endurance	Survival: The challenge of right versus wrong
Antigone	The challenge of "right" versus "right"
Blessed Assurance	The challenge of a moral dilemma
Things Fall Apart	The challenge of new principles
Module II: Moral Reasoning	
Trifles	Reasoning from moral theory
The Sweet Hereafter	Reasoning from personal perspective
The Remains of the Day	Reasoning from a moral code
A Man for All Seasons	Reasoning from multiple moralities
Module III: Moral leadership	
The Prince	Exercising authority
The Secret Sharer	Earning legitimacy
Truman and the Bomb	Balancing benefits and harms
Katharine Graham	Taking a stand
American Ground	Assuming leadership

Moral judgment

The course also gives students the opportunity to learn how to exercise moral judgment – the ability to assess the moral soundness of actions, motivations, rationales, and consequences. This, too, is a skill learned in discussion, and it is only through the repeated ability to articulate and defend a judgment, and to have that judgment challenged (usually by a peer), that students learn how varied moral judgments can be, how well-intentioned, reasonable people can take widely differing views, defend them ably, and still not agree on a single conclusion. These insights are thinly earned through spectator learning, in which students learn from watching others' arguments; maximum learning requires the ability to have *my* judgments articulated and challenged – not once, but throughout the course, so I can learn, *and demonstrate that I have learned*, what constitutes reason, evidence, and the compelling use of moral logic.

Personal discovery

The course is designed also to allow students to extrapolate from the texts to broader discussions that connect directly to their own experiences, incoming mental models, and burning questions. The classes are enriched by discussion blocks in which students are given the opportunity to describe situations in which, like the protagonist, they faced a certain type of moral challenge, to explore imaginative alternatives to choices protagonists make (and then to ask why these options were not evident to the characters at the time), and to connect the material in the stories to their own, often unarticulated constructs (*What is my moral code?*). These exercises push students beyond the material in the novels, plays, and historical accounts to personal discovery, a sound goal for a course which has as its central aim preparing students to explore what they believe moral leadership consists of.

STUDENT GUIDANCE

The student textbook, *The Moral Leader: Challenges, Tools, and Insights* (Sandra J. Sucher, Routledge 2008), prepares students for active and informed participation in the discussions and the course. The heart of this preparation is a particular approach to reading, *reproduced here entirely from the student text*. This framework reinforces the approach taken to class facilitation, as described below.

READING THE MATERIAL[2]

> *The point is that in the activity of literary imagining we are led to imagine and describe with greater precision, focusing our attention on each word, feeling each event more keenly – whereas much of actual life goes by without that heightened awareness, and is thus, in a certain sense, not fully lived ... So literature is an extension of life not only horizontally, bringing the reader into contact with events or locations or persons or problems he or she has not otherwise met, but also, so to speak, vertically, giving the reader experience that is deeper, sharper, and more precise than much of what takes place in life.[3]*

This topic may be unexpected and puzzling because it provides suggestions on how to read. But, in fact, you have already in your educational career honed your skills at various types of reading, ranging from literary analysis which may focus on the careful hunt for symbol, theme, and use of language, to the type of reading skills associated with executives: the ability to skim, pick out important points, do some (but not exhaustive) analysis, and come to a point of view – grounded in data and analysis – that you can defend.

In "The Moral Leader," the materials we read include fiction, history, biography, autobiography, and plays, in several instances complemented by extracts from philosophical and ethical writings. These works require yet another approach to reading, analysis, and judgment-formation. While different, however, it is no less rigorous and disciplined than other approaches.

The following reading framework will help you engage in the material of the course and prepare yourself for class discussion. This framework operates at two levels.

LEVEL 1: READING FOR REACTION

The first level is what we'll call *reading for reaction* – often visceral reaction – to the story and characters and the decisions they make, or, for the philosophical writings, to the nature of the arguments that are being laid out. Part of the pleasure of this course is the uniformly high quality of writing we are treated to, and this writing can grab our attention, and our emotions, in very powerful ways. It is critical for us to know what grabs us – what strikes us as compelling, or angering, or dismaying, or inspiring – since these emotions give us pointers for what we want to focus on as we look at the texts in more detail. The philosopher Martha Nussbaum, author of the quote above, observed that emotions are themselves modes of vision, or recognition.[4] So, as you are reading and reacting, you are monitoring your reactions – so that you can eventually understand *why* you respond the way you do.

But "The Moral Leader" is not a great-books course. We are here to learn from these works, not only to react to them. There are assignment questions for each class that ask you to engage in particular analyses, interpretations, and judgments, as well as in personal connections. These questions imply that you do more than just read for reaction. The questions benefit from the next level, where we do the work necessary to learning.

LEVEL 2: READING FOR DEPTH AND LEARNING

The second level is *reading for depth and learning*. At this level you are examining the material carefully from three perspectives: description, analysis, and judgment.

Description

While description sounds easy enough, in "The Moral Leader" it means getting into the mind of a character or the heart of an argument – people (and ideas) that are, or may be, very different from you and your own ways of thinking. The questions you ask of yourself are: "Do I really understand this person or this point of view? Could I articulate what makes this person tick? Could I expound on this idea?"

This particular skill, the ability to understand other people and other ideas, is probably one of the most important capabilities you can acquire in making you effective in organizations. As I'm sure you know from your own experience, nearly all of the meaningful work you do will involve your ability to engage other people and their ideas, so focusing on careful description – the ability to get inside other people and their ideas – is critical.

Because the material in "The Moral Leader" is varied, not every character you meet or every idea you encounter will be immediately "likeable." Indeed, you discovered this when you reacted to the material. But the process of description asks you to enter fully into the general context and specific situations of characters, and to appreciate the complexities of the ideas presented. In contrast to reaction, where you yourself were (viscerally) responding, in description, you are essentially taking yourself and your reactions out of the equation.

Analysis

The analysis perspective asks you to make sense of what you read, looking at the characters, actions, context, and ideas in a more conceptual way. Where description asked you to imagine yourself as someone else or to understand other viewpoints, the abstracting process of analysis helps you to examine what's going on and how arguments unfold. Analysis begins your search for the reasons why certain situations develop the way they do, why people behave in certain ways and not others, what makes arguments different from one another.

Much of the work we do when we analyze is *pattern recognition*, looking for noteworthy or surprising trends in available data, or for specific, identifiable types of situations, actions, or modes of reasoning. In "The Moral Leader" we aim to expand the number and kinds of patterns that you recognize and can draw on for analysis.

For example, you will start to develop an understanding of fundamental types of moral problems. Being able to characterize a situation as belonging to a class of moral problem (for example, problems of conflicting rights) is a first step in wrestling the problem to the ground, a way of making it more tractable. You will also be exposed to different moral theories, or perspectives, from which to engage in moral analysis, judgment, and decision-making. Over time, you will begin to recognize strands of these moral perspectives in the justifications that characters offer for their actions – another pattern to look for that helps you understand how they are thinking and deciding.

These approaches will augment the analytical skills and instincts you bring to the material and will increase your ability to analyze the texts we study. The assignment questions for each class will build on these general skills, and will focus them on particularly important issues to examine and to understand.

Judgment

The third perspective is judgment, the hardest of all to come to *after* description and analysis. That is, we are all tempted to "judge" right off the bat. This course emphasizes, however, that judgment is what we do last. After allowing yourself to react to what you've read, then delving into a deeper understanding of what you've read – only at this point are you truly ready to make a judgment. "Judgment" is your best-considered evaluation of characters and their actions, of ideas and their implications – on the basis of having done the work of reaction, then of description and analysis.

Good judgment – judgment that others will consider and feel compelled to respond to – requires careful preparation. The most persuasive judgments are those that come packaged with reasons – well laid out arguments, supported by data of various kinds, that explain how you arrived at this position and not some other. As you flesh out your arguments, you will find that you challenge your own thinking, clarifying, refining, and helping you understand the nature of the judgments you make.

SUMMARY OF READING FRAMEWORK

You'll find this course much more rewarding if you become aware of reading at both of these levels: reading for reaction as well as reading for depth and learning. Discipline in reading this way assists in class discussion because you will be clear on the perspective you are speaking from.

- Is your comment a description – an attempt to help us really (i.e., objectively) understand a character and her situation and context – or an idea?
- Do you have a way of interpreting events or actions or characters or arguments that helps us see the material in a clearer and richer light – in short, are you analyzing?

■ Are you judging – speaking from the vantage point of your own prior description and analysis, and your values, experience, and considered beliefs?

FACILITATING CLASS DISCUSSION

In *Education for Judgment: The Art of Discussion Leadership,* an explication of the Harvard Business School case-teaching method, C. Roland Christensen describes his view of a learning community. It describes in both general and practical terms the environment aimed for in "The Moral Leader":

> In a true learning community ... diverse backgrounds blend and individuals bond into an association dedicated to collective as well as personal learning. The students seem interested in one another and the academic assignment for the day. And their discussion has the open-ended quality of exploration. Speakers not only present points of view but test and modify their ideas; instead of doggedly defending personal conclusions, they listen to one another with interest, not fear. Differences of opinion produce inquiries, not disputes. Working as a unit, the class learns to value measured progress without expecting instant gratification.[5]

How does an instructor instill in a class the value of "measured progress" and a tolerance for less-than-immediate gratification? A first critical element is an understanding on the part of students that they are on a collective journey. However, belief that learning is a process requires more than a simple declaration (or even vehement insistence) from the instructor that the promise of learning will be fulfilled over time. Instead, I have found that students will believe and cooperate in such an endeavor if the architecture of ideas that the course is built on makes sense to them and satisfies their intuition that, "Yes, this is a logical way to go after the learning objectives" that have been described.

Course modules: course architecture

The modules of "The Moral Leader" constitute the course's architecture. They are laid out as straightforward topics reflecting practical underlying questions.

Module I: Moral Challenge

■ What is the nature of a moral challenge?
■ Are there types of challenges or are all moral challenges the same?

Module II: Moral Reasoning

- What are people doing when they "reason morally"?
- Is moral reasoning purely cognitive? What else is involved in deciding about problems with moral or ethical stakes?

Module III: Moral Leadership

- What do moral challenges and moral reasoning look like when leaders are involved?
- How is moral leadership different from leadership of any other kind?

The modules provide a structure for student progress. It makes sense to students first to examine fundamental concepts such as moral challenge and moral reasoning before applying them to leaders, individuals who act under conditions of responsibility for others. While other architectures certainly are possible, the modules help students and the instructor clearly understand the path they will take through the literature in light of the course's end point: determining one's own meaning of moral leadership.

Class plans

The discussion paths for each class provide a second level of structure. Here, too, students are asked to be patient and to hold their fire – talking about the books and their reaction to them in a flow that will enable the themes and lessons from each story to be explored in a careful and rigorous manner. Class plans vary, but largely follow a structure that adheres to the student framework for reading (as provided above, and in the student text). Students actually experience the power of a method – describe, analyze, judge – that reinforces the importance of leaders' coming to judgment only after the hard work of description and analysis has been completed.[6]

While topics for each session are prompted in student assignment questions, the discussion flows for class may not correspond directly to the order of the students' assignment. The discussion paths described in the class plans have emerged over multiple iterations of the course and provide a logical flow, but one that always has elements of surprise or challenge built in. Typically, these have been stimulated by the comments of individual students or the reactions of a specific group. They enrich the class designs, giving them a liveliness that only comes from careful listening to and collaboration with students. In the class plans for individual sessions, I note some of these divergences.

25

Class roadmaps

I have found that it helps to lay out a roadmap of topics to be covered in each class, usually writing this on the board. This is an adult way to work with students, enabling them to exercise self-control and to become partners in the learning process. For example, for the class session on *Antigone*, Sophocles' classic story about a conflict between two "rights," the posted discussion flow is as simple as:

- Understanding the conflict
  - Positions of Antigone and Creon
  - Antigone and Creon – as people
- Judgment
- Moral alternatives

Board plans

As a course in which active facilitation is the instructor's primary concern, boards play a limited but still important role. I generally do not record student comments on the blackboard, as I would in a case-based course or for a technical subject. But after considerable experimentation I realized that students find it useful to have a visual image to focus on that illustrates the central themes and tensions in the class. So, in the *Antigone* class, the board image (which in this case I would create from student discussion) would look like Figure 3.1. Students are able to anchor their comments to the image – and do so, often gesturing to the relationship that is drawn.

General guide to facilitation and an example

The details of facilitation are laid out in the class chapters that follow, each of which features a comprehensive plan for how to conduct the session. The purpose of each discussion block is described, as is its relationship to the class plan as a whole. Instructors are armed with support and challenge questions for class debates, with exercises that draw students into a more personal connection to the material and topics, as well as with detailed questions that push students to careful descriptions and analyses of the stories' characters, their decisions, and the consequences of actions they take.

While the questions are written as if it is the instructor who will serve as interlocutor, the goal for the course, accomplished sooner than you might expect, is for students to challenge each other's positions and logic, requiring deeper defenses, uncovering inconsistencies, and providing counter-factuals – what-if scenarios to test and strengthen opinions. Instructors facilitate the session by laying out the main subjects of discussion and by pushing students

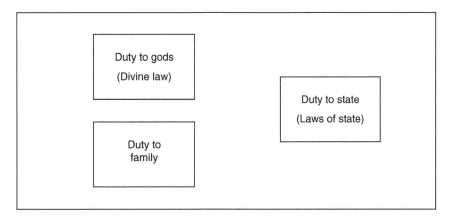

Figure 3.1 Antigone *board plan*

through probes that keep the discussion on track while moving them more deeply into the material.

As with other types of facilitation, the goal for most of the class session is participant exploration. There is time at the beginning and end of class for instructors to frame issues and to summarize main lessons, and there are teachable moments (moments in which a central point of discussion can be summarized) in each class session. *But by and large the instructor is both leading and following the discussion,* helping students to channel their comments into productive inquiry, and then to reflect on where that inquiry has led them. Such discussions, while controlled, are also often quite surprising. I have never left a session in which I was not challenged with a new point of view, or impressed with the clarity with which students hear and test each other.

Individual students – and the class as a whole – increase in skill and openness as the course develops, and the last class is substantially different from the first, with more intense exchanges and well-defended arguments over moral issues and leadership concerns.

An example of facilitation

Here is an example of the kind of internal narration and "just in time" adjustment to class dynamics that goes on (at least for me) as I teach in this facilitative mode. I experienced this situation while teaching the eighth text studied in the course, *A Man for All Seasons,* Robert Bolt's play about Thomas More's conflict with Henry VIII (the conflict over the King's divorce of Catherine of Aragon and the eventual split of England from the Roman Catholic Church). I, the instructor, am talking to myself:

This is unexpected. Every other time I have taught *A Man for All Seasons*, the students have been extremely moved by More – "A man of conscience;" "This is what it looks like to stand on principle;" "I'm inspired!" But today's class is taking off on a new direction.

"This strong a commitment to religion makes me nervous." "There are a lot of terrorists who would believe as strongly as he does."

The connection between a strongly held belief and terrorism had come up earlier in the course in the discussion of *Antigone*.

So I ask: *This reminds me of the discussion we had during* Antigone. *Some of you drew a similar analogy between Antigone's commitment to the law of the gods and extreme (and dangerous) religious belief. Are there any differences between Antigone's convictions and More's?*

The probe works. Students begin to draw some lines of demarcation:[7] "More believed in the law as well as religion – he just had to choose in the end."

"[Unlike Antigone] More tried to explain why he believed what he did – he says that the supremacy of the [Catholic] Church in England is promised in the Magna Carta and in the King's coronation oath." "He's not as blindly stubborn as she."

Important insights begin to emerge from the students as they reflect on the comparisons between the two characters: "A person can believe – strongly – in religion *and* the law;" "Holding strong convictions is not exactly the same thing as stubbornness;" "Even strong beliefs – even *religious beliefs* – may need to be explained to make them comprehensible to others;" "Reason and conviction can coexist, at least in some people."

These moments represent a true partnership between the instructor and the students. They are what make teaching a course like "The Moral Leader" so stimulating – a chance to live on the edge of interaction and response in a way that is highly satisfying to instructors who are passionate about connecting to their students.

Hints and tips

The general guidance offered here is augmented in the chapters that follow with specific advice for each class session. In addition to these very specific guides, there are a few situations that can be addressed more generally. I have struggled with such moments myself, and aim to help you learn from my (and others') experiences.

Variations in student groups

Of course, even with the same class plans and readings, student groups work together quite differently. Some groups are quiet, hard working, and generally collaborative – preferring to agree more often than to disagree. While not aiming toward consensus judgments per se, these groups seem more interested in validating all opinions and in providing room for a gradual process of getting to know each other through the material. Other groups, frequently with stronger individual personalities, can feature dramatic recurring debates between what comes to be seen as predictable positions or lines of reasoning. The students in these classes relish sparring, and particularly enjoy the parry and thrust of argument.

The class plans are robust to both general types of groups, with challenges and probes to encourage debate among collaborators, and requests for personal disclosure and connection to the material to help more adversarial groups appreciate the sides of classmates that do not come out in their routine exchanges.

When discussion falters

There will be times when the class plan, no matter how well tested or successful in the past, does not seem to be working with a particular group. The class plans feature different types of discussion formats, and sometimes all that is required is to move from a block where a group is stuck to a different topic and type of inquiry.

Occasionally I have asked students for their views on the problem they seem to be having with a particular discussion. This is tricky, since a discussion that appears to be slow-paced from the front of the room may be simply the result of students thinking hard and considering how they want to respond to a question that has been posed.

But if several different approaches do not seem to engage students, then an inquiry as to the nature of the problem may be in order. One class, for example, focused on a character that students simply didn't like. When I engaged the resistance and asked students to discuss it (*We're usually so talkative in here, but we can't seem to get any traction today*), it opened the class up – and we were able to move on, energized, in fact, by the "digression."

Such moments are not frequent, but they should be expected given the powerful texts, topics covered, and close-to-the-bone discussions about moral problems that the course is based on.

Instructor neutrality

The texts in this course feature topics of race, class, cultural differences, and religious conviction, as well as morally profound decisions such as the use of the atomic bomb by US President Harry S. Truman – not surprising for a course on moral leadership, but none the less topics that most of us do not routinely entertain in our classes or executive sessions. Christensen's description of a learning community includes important pointers for instructors who will teach material like this. Of the students in such a community, he writes: "Instead of doggedly defending personal conclusions, they listen to one another with interest, not fear. Differences of opinion produce inquiries, not disputes."[8]

I have been asked what instructors need to do to create such a productive climate, one in which students feel free to debate serious and even troubling issues, and where they are not afraid (or are less afraid than they might normally be) to express their views with candor. My general answer, shared by others,[9] is for the instructor to maintain a stance of personal neutrality when such subjects are up for discussion.

I learned this lesson early in my career, when I was being trained to conduct educational sessions for senior school administrators who were concerned about student recreational use of drugs. My clinical supervisor (a psychiatrist and psychoanalyst) advised that when asked by the (usually far older) program participants if I used drugs myself I was to explain carefully that there was no way that I could answer the question. If I answered, *Yes*, then those who viewed drug use (and drug users) as reprehensible would disregard any information from me that would follow. But if I answered *No*, then others would conclude that I didn't know what I was talking about.

Instructors facilitating courses like "The Moral Leader" are in a similar relationship to their students as I was to the school administrators: we need to create a climate in which personal views can be openly expressed. But, where school administrators might be concerned about possible bias on my part, at least they were not being graded. So it is even more important for courses taught in academic settings to be facilitated from a stance of neutrality to protect the space that students need to explore their own positions and disagreements, particularly about the more divisive cultural and moral debates in the course.[10]

STUDENT "MENTAL MODELS" AND THE "MORAL LEADER" CLASS CARD

Students are no strangers to problems with moral or ethical stakes, and they come to "The Moral Leader" with their own ideas about what constitutes a moral problem, how moral reasoning works, and what a demonstration of moral leadership might look like. These ideas vary from highly conscious perspectives that students appear to have thought long and hard about and can articulate easily, to (more commonly) less well elaborated ideas about the workings of moral problems, the mechanics of moral or ethical problem-solving, and the dynamics of moral leadership.

Mental models

Some researchers define these incoming perspectives as *mental models*, and describe learning as a process of comparison and construction: "When we encounter new material, we try to comprehend it in terms of something we think we already know. We use our existing mental models to shape the sensory inputs we receive. That means that when we talk to students, our thoughts do not travel seamlessly from our brains to theirs. The students bring paradigms to the class that shape how they construct meaning."[11] A way of tapping into these is with the "class card," described below and detailed in Appendix 2. This brief activity has value for instructor and student alike.

The "Moral Leader" class card

Before the third class session, students are asked to create a "Moral Leader "class card, a brief, ungraded assignment that requires them to document their incoming definitions of the main concepts of the course. The rationale is for students to understand their own mental models, the baseline of ideas that they will build on, refine, and revise as the course unfolds, culminating in their end-of-term paper. The questions that the students are asked to respond to are simple:

1　How would you define Moral Challenge?
2　What does Moral Reasoning consist of?
3　What does Moral Leadership mean (or suggest) to you?

None the less, students report significant difficulty in putting into words these intuitive (but often not yet clearly defined) concepts. The exercise validates the course as a personal search, and highlights the central goal of helping students develop their own workable definition of moral leadership by the course's end.

I find the cards a helpful introduction to the students, an early indication of their thoughtfulness, rigor, or honest confusion. Students may come to class with similar ideas or others that it is helpful to tease out and to build into discussion. Extracts from student class cards, found in Appendix 2, illustrate the kinds of ideas that students bring with them into the course.

EVALUATING STUDENT PERFORMANCE

Students are evaluated throughout the course on the basis of their participation in class discussion and at the end through an assessment of their course paper.

Class participation

Active class participation is the norm in "The Moral Leader," and evaluation of participation is a critical input to the student grade. To grade students, I distinguish between grading *students' ideas* and their *ability to articulate and work with their ideas and those of others.* The learning environment needs to be one of acceptance and tolerance, given the nature of the material and the personal and moral judgments that are the focus of the course. Because of this, while the ideas expressed by students are of course important, it is equally important to look for signs of increasing clarity and sophistication in their arguments, and for greater candor and thoughtfulness in their debates.

There are always ethical considerations in any discussion-based course,[12] and in a literature-based course like "The Moral Leader" that digs deeply into students' engagement with the material there is a particular obligation to provide opportunities for people with different levels of ability to develop their own conceptions of moral challenge, moral reasoning, and moral leadership, and to articulate these ideas through class participation. A seminar-sized group makes it possible for students to speak as often as they want, but more quiet students and those whose ideas are less well accepted by the group still may need to be encouraged to participate, and frequently.

It took me several years to develop an approach to grading class participation that I felt was *reliable*, i.e., producing roughly similar evaluations of similar comments over time, and *appropriate*, i.e., reflecting the kinds of skills, abilities, and performance attributes that students demonstrate in a discussion-based, literature-based course.

For example, a particularly important element in grading class participation in a course based on personal reflection like "The Moral Leader" is "meta-cognition," the ability of students to "think about their own thinking."[13] Students display a range of incoming capabilities and can become more proficient at meta-cognition over time. The grading template would assign a low score to a student who "treats their own views as fact; does not separate opinion from fact;" medium or baseline to a student who is "aware of own thought patterns and opinions;" high to a student who can provide an "excellent description of own thought process; can change point of view knowingly;" and highest to a student who "offers novel, well fleshed out frameworks."

I scan the detailed grading template as I consider each student's participation in the class that just occurred, giving them a composite score that takes all of their comments and the relevant grading categories into account. The template serves as a memory jogger, ensuring that I use the same yardstick for each class and for each student. See Table 3.2. for the participation grading template.

The course paper

The purpose of the course paper is for students to clarify – and chronicle – their own understanding of moral leadership as it has evolved during the course. Advised to find a protagonist that interests them personally, students choose a diverse set of subjects for the paper, ranging from classic works of fiction such as Henrik Ibsen's play *A Doll's House* and F. Scott Fitzgerald's *The Great Gatsby*, to contemporary works by authors such as Edward P. Jones, whose novel *The Known World* depicts black slave owners at the time of the US Civil War. Students can also use biographies or histories as their source material, and many choose contemporary or near-contemporary figures, from Thabo Mbeki's stance on HIV/AIDs to Anwar Sadat and the Middle East peace process.

The assignment has three parts:

■ *A description of a situation* (or a few) in which the student believes the protagonist has demonstrated moral leadership
■ *Analysis of why they believe this* – the reasoning behind their assumptions, and their assessment of the decisions and actions of the protagonist
■ *Reflection and lessons* – implications that the student draws from the protagonist/situation and the course that inform their understanding of moral leadership, what it consists of and what it entails

I ask students to review their topic with me in advance, to avoid subjects or literary works that may prove unworkable in the confines of the paper's (roughly) fifteen-page limit and purpose. While the variety of student paper topics poses the predictable challenge of assessing the quality of student analysis and reflection among works of differing levels of complexity and scale, it is endlessly fascinating. See Appendix 3 for the detailed assignment, bibliography offered to students, and paper grading template.

Table 3.2 Class participation grading template

Element	1–3	5	7	9
Textual analysis	Error or incomplete reading	Correct grasp of facts	Identifies patterns or themes	Novel or very well crafted interpretation
Influence of comment	Distraction	Maintains flow of discussion	Adds new layer or larger question Class picks up on contribution	Sets new direction for discussion Class picks up on and follows contribution
Logic/coherence	Hard to follow Inconsistent Incoherent	Clear Consistent	Ability to lay out strands of argument and evaluate them	Excellent ability to lay out argument and evaluate it
Argumentation	Harsh Personal attack Inappropriate persistence	Direct, clear response to other On-point rebuttal Good defense of point of view with back-up data	Clear depiction of novel or well-structured point of view Ability to escalate/deepen argument	Direct engagement Helps others clarify their views or change them
Meta-cognition	Treats own views as fact; does not separate opinion from fact	Aware of own thought patterns and opinions	Excellent description of own thought process Can change point of view knowingly	Offers novel, well fleshed out frameworks

Linking/continuity	Repeats points without realizing/ acknowledging Misses obvious links in material or comments	Knowingly maintains flow Acknowledges links in material or comments	Good summary: draws strands of discussion together Creates links across works or class sessions	Excellent synthesis of discussion Creates links across works or class sessions
Application of course concepts/ frameworks	Misuse of concepts No use of concepts	Use of frameworks within discussion as expected	Appeals to frameworks even when not expected Attempts to master frameworks through application	Helps others understand frameworks or concepts Brings new or novel dimensions or interpretations to concepts
Personal experience	Inappropriate theme Inappropriate level of detail	Appropriate theme Appropriate level of detail	Illuminating: helps others see new angle or understand in more depth	Changes way that class thinks about topic

WHAT FOLLOWS

The remainder of this book explores individual classes, how they are structured in themselves and how they link to previous sessions and anticipate those that follow. At the same time, I have attempted to write the class chapter plans to be individually valuable (and usable) and also to suggest how they can be regrouped in various ways (see Appendix 1).

NOTES

1 Larger-size class formats, designed to be taught and facilitated differently, can also be highly successful, as demonstrated by the experience over more than ten years of my colleague Joe Badaracco, whose course for 100 students was consistently well subscribed and deeply appreciated by the students who took it.

2 Harvard Business School Case #605-027, revised August 23 2006. Copyright © 2006 by the President and Fellows of Harvard College.

3 Martha Nussbaum, *Love's Knowledge: Essays on Philosophy and Literature*, New York: Oxford University Press, 1990, pp. 47–48.

4 Ibid., p. 79.

5 C. Roland Christensen, "Premises and Practices of Discussion Teaching," in C. Roland Christensen, David A. Garvin, and Ann Sweet (eds), *Education for Judgment: The Artistry of Discussion Leadership*, Boston, Mass.: Harvard Business School Press, 1991, pp. 19–20.

6 In fact, studies of stereotypical thinking suggest that immediate judgment may be an enduring factor in moral analysis – see the fascinating results of the Harvard University "Project Implicit," which measures unconscious bias (https://implicit. harvard.edu/implicit/, accessed 12/12/06). Related studies suggest, however, that immediate judgments can be tempered by time and the opportunity to reflect on one's immediate reaction – see William A. Cunningham, Marcia K. Johnson, Carol L. Raye, J. Chris Gatenby, John C. Gore, and Mahzarin R. Banaji, "Separable Neural Components in the Processing of Black and White Faces," *Psychological Science*, 2004, vol. 15, no. 12, 806–813. "The Moral Leader" provides students with an opportunity to practice the second, more reasoned approach throughout the course.

7 I will draw on discussions of students in "The Moral Leader" throughout this book. I am grateful to all of the past participants in the course who it has been my privilege to lead, and whose comments I combine into the dialogues represented here. I have melded together comments from different class sessions in the dialogues to provide a representative sample of opinions offered – a sense of the issue as it can be discussed – rather than a word-for-word recounting of any particular class and its views.

8 Christensen, op. cit.

9 Instructor neutrality does not imply a lack of guidance or direction for discussion; see Robert F. Bruner, *Socrates' Muse: Reflections on Effective Case Discussion Leadership*, Boston, Mass.: McGraw-Hill Irwin, 2003, p. 45, for a description of

the fully neutral facilitative "traffic cop" who cedes all responsibility for learning to students. It is, instead, deliberate silence from the instructor on her own moral judgments of issues discussed, a refusal to make students into "converts" of the instructor's views; see Joyce Garvin, "Undue Influence: Confessions from an Uneasy Discussion Leader," in Christensen, op. cit., p. 276. See also, J. Jeffrey Auer and Henry Lee Ewbank, *Handbook for Discussion Leaders*, New York: Harper & Brothers, 1954, p. 68, for a typical warning to leaders to refrain from attempting to facilitate discussion on subjects on which they have strong personal or professional convictions so participants can make progress in an atmosphere that is free from (leader) prejudice.

10   Instructor neutrality is equally necessary in executive sessions and settings, and may be even more so, because executive participants often carefully monitor their participation, keeping in mind their organizational role and the possible reputation risk of expressing controversial views too candidly.

11   Ken Bain, *What the Best College Teachers Do*, Cambridge, Mass.: Harvard University Press, 2004, pp. 26–27.

12   See David A. Garvin, "A Delicate Balance: Ethical Dilemmas and the Discussion Process," in Christensen, op. cit, pp. 287–303, for a description of the ethical dilemmas discussion leadership poses for the instructor.

13   Bain, op. cit., p. 25.

Moral Challenge Class Plans

Moral Challenge Module Map: Themes and Learning Points

Central theme	Text and setting	Storyline	Learning points
Survival: the challenge of right versus wrong	*Endurance*, by Alfred Lansing Antarctic, 1914	How Ernest Shackleton saved the members of an Antarctic exploration expedition	Impact of context / situation Burden of leadership Tactics of leadership Mixed motives
The challenge of right versus right	*Antigone*, by Sophocles Ancient Greece	A clash of competing "rights" in which neither side yields	Action driven by principle Benefits and drawbacks of strongly held beliefs Moral alternatives
The challenge of a moral dilemma	*Blessed Assurance*, by Allan Gurganus 1940s America	A young, white insurance collection agent is torn between helping his black clients and his need for employment	Moral awareness Exploitation Conflicting moral duties
The challenge of new principles	*Things Fall Apart,* by Chinua Achebe Early twentieth-century Nigeria	An Ibo clan confronts the arrival of Christian missionaries and British colonial authorities	Differences in world view Navigating a changing terrain Strategies for response

Chapter 4

Endurance: Shackleton's Incredible Voyage

Survival: the challenge of right versus wrong

SHACKLETON'S AVERSION to tempting fate was well known. This attitude had earned for him the nickname "Old Cautious" or "Cautious Jack." But nobody ever called him that to his face. He was addressed simply as "Boss" – by officers, scientists, and seamen alike. It was really more a title than a nickname. It had a pleasant ring of familiarity about it, but at the same time "Boss" had the connotation of absolute authority. It was therefore particularly apt, and exactly fitted Shackleton's outlook and behavior. He wanted to appear familiar with the men. He even worked at it, insisting on having the exact same treatment, food, and clothing. He went out of his way to demonstrate his willingness to do the menial chores, such as taking his turn as "Peggy" to get the mealtime pot of hoosh from the galley to his tent. And he occasionally became furious when he discovered that the cook had given him preferential treatment because he was the "Boss."

But it was inescapable. He was the Boss. There was always a barrier, an aloofness, which kept him apart. It was not a calculated thing; he was simply emotionally incapable of forgetting – even for an instant – his position and the responsibility it entailed. The others might rest, or find escape by the device of living for the moment. But for Shackleton there was little rest and no escape. The responsibility was entirely his, and a man could not be in his presence without feeling this.[1]

ENDURANCE: THEMES AND QUESTIONS

What is moral leadership?

Endurance does double-duty, introducing the question that frames the course, "What is *moral leadership?*", as well as the first module on Moral Challenge. Many students will be familiar with the story of Ernest Shackleton's 1914 voyage, in which he saved himself and twenty-seven men who volunteered for one of the last great polar explorations: a land crossing of Antarctica. The story of the crew's 497 days on sea and ice and Shackleton's successful rescue of those marooned on Elephant Island has been reenacted on film and on television, documented in diaries, historical accounts, and websites, and even served as inspiration for a US school for leadership development.

Despite Shackleton's heroic actions, when asked whether he demonstrates *moral leadership* many students hesitate, unsure for a variety of reasons that emerge from the story and that are explored during discussion.

That Shackleton displays leadership – even excellent leadership – is abundantly clear. He shows flexibility, shifting the definition of success from crossing Antarctica to saving his crew, but it is the numerous decisions made during the twenty-one-month ordeal – when to leave, when to stay, when to attempt action, and when to resist the urge to act – that provide students with a view of **the burden of leadership: what moral decision-making looks like under conditions of responsibility for others.** The apparent contradiction of Shackleton's actions – "Old Cautious" paired with breathtaking audacity – offers an important lesson about risk management: One must be cautious most of the time to be able to take risks when they are truly necessary.

Endurance also reveals the fine print of leadership, the type of reasoning and gestures both large but especially small that excellent leaders, well suited to their task, use to earn the respect and willing compliance of their followers. Shackleton's insights into the psychology of the crew as individuals and as a group are particularly striking to students, most of whom have never been close enough to effective organizational leaders to appreciate the very personal nature of a leader's relationship to his followers when that relationship is well thought through, understood, and acted upon. The theme of **legitimated leadership, of respect earned and re-earned through action**, will echo through the course.

The role of context in moral decision-making

Endurance also compels students to consider **the critical role that context plays in moral challenges, the way it defines and limits the set of choices moral actors can elect.** The historical account by Alfred Lansing is rich in detail: the depiction of the physical context of the challenge posed to Shackleton and his crew is palpably, gut-wrenchingly clear, from the shrieking sounds of the ship, *Endurance*, as it is hammered by the ice that destroys it, to the storms that nearly defeat Shackleton and his small band of rescuers on their voyage to South Georgia Island in search of a seaworthy ship to save the remainder of the crew.

Students discover that **fortune or luck plays an important role in determining the outcome of decisions made and actions taken.** Leaders can act, but they often cannot control conditions that can make the difference between success and failure. The Shackleton story is humbling, and this important perspective on leadership – **the requirement to act within an uncontrollable world** – is introduced and also carries as a theme through the course.

Survival: a challenge of right versus wrong

Shackleton faced the challenge of survival for himself and for the twenty-seven volunteers who manned his expedition. **What responsibilities do leaders face when their own lives are at stake, and when the lives of those who are in their keeping are at risk? What is permitted? What is required? What is prohibited?**

Certain options seem entirely indefensible from a moral point of view. Shackleton couldn't, for example, join forces with the most skilled navigator and, taking the sturdiest of the three small ships that were part of the party's stores, make off to effect his own survival.

Other options are less clear-cut than this first example of a right-versus-wrong challenge. Must Shackleton aim to save the entire crew, or is he permitted to pick and choose, favoring those with the most to contribute to the salvation of a group? Could he leave behind an injured sailor, whose continued presence may risk the survival of all the others?

In this first class students are required to defend their judgment of what is right, what seems wrong, and what falls somewhere in the middle, depending on the circumstance. *Endurance* thus allows students to examine various *right-versus-wrong* conflicts, and it sets the stage for the remaining three stories in this module, in which more complex types of moral challenge are presented.

What does morality consist in?

Students hesitate in describing Shackleton's actions as a demonstration of moral leadership because they are unsure how to define morality.

The story encourages at least four different interpretations of the term "moral"; through it, students are introduced to a more multi-faceted view than many initially considered. In *Endurance,* **morality is demonstrated by action** – Shackleton's act of saving the crew. **Morality is also demonstrated by adherence to moral principle** – in this case, to a principle of equality that requires saving all of the crew, rather than just the strongest and most able. **Morality can appear to be demonstrated by consequences** – all of the crew, and Shackleton himself, survive. **Finally, the text raises the question of whether morality requires moral motives** – a conviction that actions are undertaken for moral purposes, rather than, for example, for personal gain or reputation enhancement.

Shackleton's actions pass all but the last test, and it is on that basis that many students discover the cause of their concern and hesitation. The story raises the question of **whether a leader's motives must be wholly moral in order to earn the label moral leadership, or whether mixed motives are allowable.** This debate has implications for how practically and realistically students think about moral leadership; it will weave through the course and, for many students, reach resolution in the last class.

STUDENT ASSIGNMENT

READING: *Endurance,* by Alfred Lansing.

1   Was Shackleton a moral leader? How do you know?

CLASS PLAN OUTLINE: DISCUSSION BLOCKS

1   What Impact Does the Environment Have on the Challenges Shackleton Faced? (15′)

2   How Would You Evaluate Shackleton's Leadership? (20′)

3   Is Ernest Shackleton a Moral Leader? (40′)

4   Leadership Lessons from Shackleton (15′)

CLASS PLAN OVERVIEW

Endurance is one of the simplest tales studied in the course, selected as the initial class for that reason, and for the way that it simultaneously introduces students to a particular type of moral challenge – a right-versus-wrong dilemma – and to the broader course question of what moral leadership consists in. As the introductory session of the course, discussion is planned for only one and a half hours to give time for start-up administrative activities, including a course overview. I usually do my course overview very briefly at the end of class, after students have experienced the type of discussion and interaction the course will feature.

Describe, analyze, judge

Students will initially be unsure how to participate, as is common in any discussion course. The class plan follows a general structure for collaborative discussion that builds on the student reading model of first reading for reaction and then reading for depth and learning. The class plan focuses students on three tasks: describe; analyze; judge. The flow sets a rough template for succeeding sessions and represents a process lesson in itself: we are not prepared to judge until we have done the hard work of describing and identifying with the character's situation, and then analyzing important facts, events, actions, and themes.

Students are grounded (and often reassured) by a review of the class plan roadmap (see roadmaps and board plans at ends of chapters throughout), which describes the flow of discussion topics. The discussion flow moves from description and an analysis of the impact of the Antarctic context on Shackleton's challenge, to an analysis and assessment of Shackleton's leadership, to judgment of whether, in the students' view, Shackleton has demonstrated moral leadership.

I have found several techniques helpful in teaching students how to keep their comments on point: restating the discussion question to make sure it is clear; asking students to hold comments that relate to later topics until the topic is addressed (and then calling on them in those discussions); using the roadmap to show them where, in the flow, their comment will fit.

The first class (and often the next one or two) requires more guidance than at times feels comfortable or appropriate in a course that depends on students' willing and candid participation for success. I have found, none the less, that early discipline offered in a friendly manner and with a clear rationale (*"We'll make much more progress, and have better discussions, if we can work together on this"*) pays off in discussions that satisfy both students and the instructor. This is not a free-for-all or a hunt in an uncharted wilderness, but a rigorous and disciplined process for engaging in in-depth discussions about topics that matter.

1 EVALUATING THE IMPACT OF CONTEXT (15′)

In "The Moral Leader," students learn to distinguish the overall context of a character – the general environment and its distinguishing characteristics: point in time, location, historical forces, political forces – from the particulars of the situation and immediate choices that the character faces. Decision theory researchers refer to this facility as *situation awareness*, and it is essential to moral decision-making. *Endurance* presents a particularly memorable example of the role of context and paves the way for a more nuanced exploration in the classes that follow of the relationship between context, choice, and action.

A way of opening the discussion

In this course we shall work on being able to identify with the contexts, and situations, of the characters we study. Researchers in decision theory refer to this capability as "situation awareness," and it is essential to moral decision-making.

Questions driving the discussion are in bold

Has anyone been in a physical environment similar to that faced by Shackleton and the *Endurance* crew? Describe the environment: What is it like to be in this kind of environment – how do these conditions affect you?

The discussion of context begins with a question designed to help students empathize with the plight of Shackleton and the crew of *Endurance*, an important task given the alien nature of the environment and the dire situation facing the members of the stranded ship. Some students will have stories of having had to endure extreme cold and wet, or heat and dryness, or having found themselves laboring under an uncertain outcome in a rugged terrain. The question asks students to enter imaginatively into a setting in which the vagaries of the physical environment, ordinarily a matter of nuisance rather than survival, become determining actors in a drama in which they can envision themselves.

Students will often speak to the need for vigilance and the emotional toll that harsh physical settings can exact on the members of groups trapped in them; one student with mountaineering experience shared the awareness of never knowing, when he put his foot down, whether below him would be ice, water, or air. Students also may give voice to the moments of beauty and wonder and physical challenge that are part of the motivation of searching out such environments in the first place.

In a group of students in which none could claim relevant experience, they were able clearly to imagine the context: "It would be an uncertain environment – not in your control." "There would be vast whiteness everywhere you look – and endless wet." "There'd be no privacy."

From the standpoint of any leader (not yet Shackleton in particular), what are the leadership challenges of a context like this? What impact does this environment have on the challenges a leader would face?

The setting is one of vast cold, of course, thousands of miles by sea from the nearest known outposts of human activity and assistance. But crucially for the story is the unpredictability of the environment, in which leaders are subject to forces far greater than their own. This discussion usually yields the insight that in this environment it is only with luck, in addition to skill and fortitude, that a leader can hope to find success.

How much responsibility should leaders be charged with in such a setting? Should they be held responsible for what the ice does – or just for their own decisions and what they can control?

Some students argue that it is not fair to hold a leader accountable for results in a capricious environment over which he has no control; leaders can only be assessed on the basis of what they try to accomplish. Preparation matters, as does careful management of resources (including human resources) – these are things that a leader can be evaluated on.

Others will argue strenuously that consequences matter, particularly for those in leadership roles, and especially if the leader is responsible for putting the crew in the risky position to begin with. The fact that 5,000 applicants applied to participate in Shackleton's Antarctic adventure may be raised here; his crew was voluntary and not coerced into their precarious position. Most students maintain, none the less, that even with a group of willing and eager participants leadership confers ultimate responsibility, regardless of the setting.

Is this an easy situation to be a leader in? A hard one?

Most students make the straightforward argument that it is very hard to be a leader in this kind of environment, pointing out the length of time of the ordeal (twenty-one months), the vast uncertainty of climatic forces, both seasonal patterns and the impact of weather changes from one moment to the next, the physical isolation of the stranded crew, their limited and diminishing resources, and increasing levels of strain and physical toll on physical assets and the men all make for a harrowing context in which to lead.

Some students make an interesting counter-argument, however, that a leader in this kind of situation faces an easy leadership challenge: few and relatively clear choices; ready measures of success and failure; general motivation of all to get out of the situation alive.

You may want to probe and ask, **If you were allocating 100 percent of the challenge – how much of it is made easier by having a clear goal?** Students rarely give more than a 25 percent weight, leading to the following block, in which they are asked to assess how well Shackleton managed the remaining 75 percent of the challenge.

2 EVALUATING SHACKLETON'S LEADERSHIP[2] (20′)

Students enjoy the analysis of the many talents that Shackleton displays as a leader. Eager for models of leadership to emulate, they find useful lessons about how an effective leader actually behaves.

How do you assess Shackleton's leadership in handling this situation? What did he do well? What aspects of Shackleton's leadership strike you as most effective?

Tenacity

Endurance presents leadership in one of its more familiar modes – a strong, commanding, charismatic individual who does what's right, does it against all odds, and sets a powerful example. But Shackleton's leadership style is more complex than is usually depicted in Hollywood movies or in many books. Students are struck by the quality of Shackleton's leadership, first and foremost by his tenacity, the sheer grit that is needed to lead the group to victory, however that has been defined.

Sense of responsibility

Second, students note Shackleton's sense of responsibility. While he worked hard to make sure that others had time off from the rigors of their collective ordeal, Shackleton was incapable of forgetting his position and the responsibility it entailed. Always alert to danger, he managed some miraculous saves – plucking at least one crewmember out of the icy waters after the ice floe they were on cracked. That rescue was characteristic of the vigilance he maintained throughout the trip – an important example for students of the responsibility that comes with leadership.

Resolute confidence

A third attribute students identify is what could be called *resolute confidence*. Shackleton kept his own counsel, withholding any expression of concern or dismay, and maintained steady optimism that they would in fact survive. US President Franklin Delano Roosevelt had a term for this ability; he described it as "public confidence, private doubt." And it couldn't just be bravado: Shackleton's confidence had to survive the scrutiny of experienced seamen who were far from naïve about the conditions they faced. Moreover, Shackleton had to be honest with himself and with the crew about the risks and choices he was making, since he needed the crew's active participation at each phase of their long and difficult journey.

Shackleton obviously has the respect of the crew – why? What has he done to earn their respect?

In the group and apart from it

Shackleton's particular style of leadership was most evident in his relationship to his crew. As others have pointed out,[3] Shackleton can be seen as a transition point, somewhere between the battering ram that we usually think of as a heroic leader and the group-minded leader of the modern management press. One insightful student observed that Shackleton was both in the group and apart from it. He had the ability genuinely to know (and seemingly care about) the needs of his crew. Shackleton had very high emotional intelligence ("emotional sensitivity"); he engaged in an endless series of deft, careful moves to manage the morale of his crew. It takes a confident leader to make as much mental room for other people's needs as Shackleton did, and he represents a new and different model from the hierarchical leader many students imagine.

Earning and re-earning respect

What particularly distinguished Shackleton was his ability to earn and re-earn the confidence of the crew. Students point out that Shackleton's leadership was characterized not by one defining moment, but by thousands of such moments over the twenty-one months of their journey. Many are impressed by the way that Shackleton led by example; he does not ask crewmembers to do anything he would not (or did not) do himself. He earned the crew's confidence by providing them with enough food, by moving them in what frequently appeared to be the right direction, and by guiding them in activities that usefully or at least entertainingly passed the time. Shackleton's "public confidence" was a reality that members of his crew believed was justified and in which they could trust.

The crew call Shackleton "Old Cautious," but clearly this is a man who is willing to take on extreme risk. How do these characteristics work together?

Risk management is at the heart of exploration, and students find in Shackleton an exemplar of the art of taking risks intelligently. He is supremely aware of how uncertain his environment is and how quickly circumstances can change. Shackleton seems to operate with the understanding that extreme risks require extreme caution: it is only through the exercise of caution most of the time that one is capable of taking bold moves, risky moves, when necessary. The constant attention to discipline and the ferocious attention to morale created a group that was capable of nearly instantaneous response – a critical ability that enabled the crew to survive.

3 IS ERNEST SHACKLETON A MORAL LEADER? (40′)

The final question allows the strands of the course debate to be laid out, and it is generally a lively discussion. You will ask students to take a position on Shackleton's leadership, and can take a vote to allow the positions to be made visible. Challenge questions are provided to help you push students to articulate and clarify their thinking, but many of these are questions that students will ask each other. An important objective in this discussion is to help students express their largely inchoate definitions of what constitutes a moral decision or moral action – what moral principle or rationale they can infer about Shackleton's actions, even if that principle is not explicitly laid out in the text.

So we have stark choices, a decisive person who manages the crew well and has their respect, but is Shackleton a moral leader? In what ways are his actions a demonstration of moral leadership?

Probes for "Yes" position

In my experience, a majority of students vote that Shackleton is a moral leader, but then have a hard time defining exactly why he qualifies for that title. It seems obvious that saving people is a morally worthwhile act, but exactly what is moral about it is harder to articulate.

Are you bringing a pre-definition to this? What is your definition of morality?[4]

Students offer competing definitions: morality is demonstrated through *moral actions*; morality is *acting consistently with moral principles*; morality will *yield positive consequences* for affected parties; morality *requires positive intent* or the *pursuit of a morally worthwhile goal*. Students are frequently dismayed that there is no single definition they can all agree on, and some appear to envision a fairly horrible semester ahead of them, with hours spent in theoretical debate. Much of the discussion that follows is meant to be stimulate and to reassure, allowing students to begin to grapple with these definitions by working them out in the context of the *Endurance* story.

To begin this exploration, students can be asked to differentiate: **Were Shackleton's actions moral because he decided to save the crew, or was it because he decided to save the *whole* crew?** You can also ask students what they can infer about the moral principles that were guiding Shackleton: **What is the moral justification for his decision – why save everyone?**

One response that often emerges is that Shackleton seems motivated by the principle of *equality*: all members of the crew have a right to live, even the ones who he didn't like and who didn't pull their own weight.

In this context, students often debate whether Shackleton actually had a choice in saving the crew (or, at least, in attempting it), pointing to the mores of the British, which prompted a student to ask whether it was moral "if I just do what is moral according to the norms of my society." Another responded, "Yes – if they are moral norms. Even if Shackleton is only saving the crew because British society would expect it of him, it's still a moral action."

What would your judgment have been if Shackleton had tried to save just some of the crew? And, further, Would someone who is a good leader necessarily decide to save the whole crew? Is there a different logic that another leader might apply in this situation?

Many students acknowledge that another leader might have considered shedding weak or ill crew members who would limit the group's flexibility and consume rations needed by others. They point out that another leader might have considered doing away with troublemakers, knowing how important discipline is in such a precarious situation.

Some also hypothesize that another leader might have maximized his own chances for survival by taking only the most able-bodied and skillful men on the *James Caird*, the boat that was used by Shackleton for his 800-mile journey across open water to obtain a larger boat to rescue the remainder of the crew. An argument could be made that, if the *James Caird* did not make it, the crew waiting on Elephant Island would never be rescued.

Students realize that these are more than just hypothetical decisions. A leader with a different take on success and a different view on how to get there could justify each and every one of these actions.

Why do you think Shackleton wasn't compelled by this logic?

Students who characterize Shackleton as a moral leader will point to his prior actions. In *Endurance* we learn that Shackleton stopped his second exploration just ninety-seven miles from the South Pole because he didn't believe he could reach his destination without loss of life. And once again, in this third expedition, students see Shackleton redefining success as survival. The concept of consistency is introduced in this discussion, and students begin to lay out the expectation that moral actors behave in ways that are consistent with past actions, and with their moral principles.

What would have happened if some of the crew had died – would you still judge this as a demonstration of moral leadership?

A similar debate emerges over the question of whether Shackleton would be judged a moral leader if some member of the crew had died. One student noted, "Our judgment is colored by how well this all turned out – that's why we think he acted morally." Students ask themselves how they would have judged Shackleton if he had tried to save the whole crew but failed.

This discussion allows you to ask students about the role of consequences in their definition of morality. **Are acts only moral when they have morally positive consequences?** You can also ask them to link their comments to the first part of the class in which they pointed out how uncertain the environment was that Shackleton operated in. **Is it fair to evaluate Shackleton's actions by consequences when luck plays such an important role in what happens?** The class will usually divide between students favoring a utilitarian point of view that evaluates moral actions on the basis of positive outcomes, and those who judge Shackleton, instead, by how they interpret his intent. As one put it, "You can't decide if an act is moral without considering the motive of the actor."

Is exploration a moral goal?

Some students will argue that Shackleton is a moral leader because exploration is a moral goal, a "reflection of the human spirit" and the search for knowledge that moves societies and whole civilizations forward. Other students will debate this point, claiming that the goal of exploration and the risks it entails come close to an "immoral act." They hold Shackleton responsible for putting the crew at risk, arguing that, while some men had experience in discovery expeditions, many did not; some crewmembers were in no position to judge the risk they were signing up for. Students will also challenge the goal of exploration, asking "Who cares whether anyone crosses Antarctica on foot?"

All of what you describe seem to be good leadership activities, but in what ways are they moral?

A final argument is that what was moral was not what Shackleton did but how he did it. Students justify this position by referring to the activities detailed in the prior discussion of Shackleton's leadership: the selection criteria that Shackleton used in hiring his crew; his management of the group's morale with respect to food, work, play, and the management of time; his strategic assignment of individual men to the small boats and tents they lived in while stranded; his tactical decisions.

Other students will challenge this line of reasoning, arguing that "good and effective leadership includes these things." They will assert that saving his crew was an integral part of Shackleton's role as leader, and that the decisions for how he treated the crew were driven more by external events and shaped by expedience.

Probes for "No" position

Let's specify this. When you say Shackleton is not moral, what are you saying about his leadership: Is he amoral (not acting for moral purposes)? Is he immoral (actively seeking to do harm or to avoid responsibility)? What, exactly, is missing – what would make this moral leadership in your view?

Students in the *not a moral leader* camp will base their attack largely on their interpretation of Shackleton's motives. They claim that Shackleton's motives for the rescue, like those that inspired the expedition, are self-serving. These students see Shackleton as a "publicity-seeking opportunist" with an eye on the main chance; "He saved the crew because that was the only way he could save his reputation as a leading explorer."

Other students will be less harsh, stressing, instead, that Shackleton was driven by expedience: he saves the whole crew because of the negative impact on morale if some crewmembers were left behind, and because he can't predict in advance who would be helpful to the rescue effort.

53

It may be fair to characterize Shackleton's actions in saving the whole crew as expedient – a calculated act. But are expedience and morality necessarily at odds: Why can't an action be both practical and effective *and* moral?

Students will sometimes raise this question themselves, "Why are these opposed? Why can't Shackleton want to make money *and* do good?"

This debate about Shackleton's various motives is crucial. In my experience most students come to the course believing that moral action requires pure and unconflicted motives, and evident self-sacrifice, to count. The origins of these beliefs are many, but one of the goals of the course is to begin to help students situate moral decision-making and action in a real-world context of complex situations in which real people, not saints or sinners, are engaged. This means that motives will nearly always be mixed and more subtle questions need to be asked: not whether mixed motives exist, but whether the presence of moral motivation – the desire to benefit or not harm another – is evident, and in what degree.

In the real world it is expected that people will act in ways that redound positively upon themselves; the pursuit of positive consequences from one's actions is not ordinarily a cause for disapproval. Students can be challenged by asking: **What, if anything, is different about decisions with moral or ethical stakes?** What standards are they using to evaluate moral decisions and the people who make them?

4 LEADERSHIP LESSONS FROM SHACKLETON (15′)

You will want to provide students with some closure after this long and at times difficult debate. Asking them about the leadership lessons they took from Shackleton provides an opportunity for students to return to a topic that is easier to discuss, that builds on the prior debates, and that allows them to draw some of the strands of the discussion together.

It's clear that we are not going to come out with a consensus decision about whether Ernest Shackleton demonstrated moral leadership – that's not the purpose of this discussion, or of any of the others we shall have. But we have had a good airing of the different arguments for and against this judgment. Let's think more broadly in closing the class: What lessons about leadership did you learn from Ernest Shackleton?

Students report a wide range of lessons from the discussion. For example, some comment on Shackleton's resilience: his ability to make a decision; see it fail; and then have the confidence to make another decision. Others remark on the length of time he carried the burden of leadership – twenty-one months – and the impact of small decisions made day after day. The question also provides a transition to the instructor's assessment of Shackleton's leadership and summary of the class, which then appears more as one viewpoint among many than as a final and authoritative opinion.

The *Endurance* discussion is the beginning of the group's collective exploration of the moral domain. It is hard work and students' frustration is at times visible when definitions of morality do not come readily to hand, or, worse, when multiple definitions are suggested. Your summary comments can help students see how far they have come in this first discussion. And, while you can acknowledge the frustration, you do not want to eliminate it entirely since it is an important motivation for the classes that follow, creating urgency for students to come to terms with how they define moral action, moral reasoning, and, eventually, moral leadership.

Summary comments for instructors, a course introduction, and an outline of the discussion flow can be found on the "Moral Leader" website: www.routledge.com/textbooks/9780415400640

Role of context

Evaluation of Shackleton's leadership

Is Shackleton a moral leader?

Leadership lessons

Figure 4.1 Endurance *roadmap*

Evaluation of moral leadership

Moral act?

Moral principle?

Moral consequences?

Moral motive?

Figure 4.2 Endurance *board plan*

NOTES

1　Alfred Lansing, *Endurance: Shackleton's Incredible Voyage*, New York: Carroll & Graff, 1999, pp. 85–86.

2　The analysis of Shackleton's leadership draws heavily on Joe Badaracco's class discussion and lecture on *Endurance*, "The Moral Leader," Harvard Business School, 1999.

3　Ibid.

4　Looking forward into the course, it is useful for instructors to know that the readings for class five, the introductory class of the module on Moral Reasoning, include a description of various moral philosophies. (See the assignment from Beauchamp and Childress' *Principles of Biomedical Ethics*, class five.) I have found this reading to be particularly compelling because it is written for practitioners in the field of biomedicine and thus provides a rich, context-specific description that students can absorb. By this class, students will have immersed themselves in four different types of moral challenge, and will be ready to engage with this more theoretical material as an aid to their learning.

Chapter 5

Antigone

The challenge of right versus right

> ANTIGONE: There is no shame in honouring my brother.
> CREON: Was not his enemy, who died with him, your brother?
> ANTIGONE: Yes, both were brothers, both of the same parents.
> CREON: You honour one, and so insult the other.
> ANTIGONE: He that is dead will not accuse me of that.
> CREON: He will, if you honour him no more than a traitor.
> ANTIGONE: It was not a slave, but his brother, that died with him.
> CREON: Attacking his country, while the other defended it.
> ANTIGONE: Even so, we have a duty to the dead.
> CREON: Not to give equal honour to good and bad.
> ANTIGONE: Who knows? In the country of the dead that may be the law.
> CREON: An enemy can't be a friend, even when dead.
> ANTIGONE: My way is to share my love, not share my hate.
> CREON: Go then, and share your love among the dead. We'll have no woman's law here, while I live.[1]

ANTIGONE: THEMES AND QUESTIONS

The role of principle in moral decision-making

Antigone continues the module on Moral Challenge, a module that lays out fundamental moral problems and allows students to examine and assess strategies that are used to come to terms with them. Sophocles' play is used to explore **the role of principle in moral decision-making and action.**

The challenge of right versus right

Antigone is a particularly apt choice because it confronts students with the problem that good, worthwhile principles aren't necessarily singular. Moral decision-making would be relatively easy if all that was required in a given situation was discerning the right thing to do. *Antigone* upsets this comforting model, illustrating that in the same circumstance people can be governed by very different moral justifications and action-guiding principles. The play brilliantly depicts **the problem of competing "rights,"** pitting Antigone's **filial loyalty and duty to the laws of the gods** against Creon's **duty to the state and its stability** in the wake of a brutal civil war.

Antigone begins the students' long march to understanding the troubling issue of **complexity,** a necessary feature of moral awareness, reasoning, action, and leadership. Creon's confrontation with Antigone lays bare the inconceivability of the other's point of view. How can we think so differently? And, if both points of view have merit, how are they to be accommodated?

Loyalties and duties

The themes raised in the play will be echoed later in the course. **Loyalty to family** is evident in *Blessed Assurance,* the novella featured in the class following *Antigone,* and in *The Sweet Hereafter* in the second module. **Loyalty to god's law** is a central feature in *A Man for All Seasons,* Robert Bolt's play about Sir Thomas More.

The **importance of the state** as the stable house within which private individuals can pursue their lives is also a recurring theme, raising questions, as in *Antigone,* about the **particular duties and obligations of a head of state** and the **limits that should be put on actions taken in the name of a larger civic and political entity.**

The theme of **leadership duties** is woven throughout the last module on Moral Leadership, beginning with the class on Machiavelli's *The Prince,* moving through the class on Harry Truman and the decision to use the atomic bomb at the close of the Second World War, and culminating in the decision by Kay Graham and members of the *Washington Post* to pursue what became known as the "Pentagon Papers" and the Nixon Watergate scandals.

Like presidents and kings, organizational leaders are responsible for the maintenance of a "state;" the definitions and limits on power depicted in the course's readings illustrate leadership challenges students may face as their own careers progress.

Action driven by moral principle

Antigone illustrates what action driven by moral principle looks like. The genius of the play is in the **inescapable humanity of its characters.** Antigone's heroic defiance in the name of filial love is paired with what could arguably be interpreted as cruelty to her sister. Creon's defense of the imperatives of the state is mocked by his refusal to credit any opinion other than his own, least of all the wishes of the elders, individual members, and general polity of Thebes.

The play illustrates the power and limitations of strongly held beliefs – the intransigence, willful blindness, and unwillingness to engage that can characterize individuals who act on principle. This characterization extends the theme of **mixed motives** surfaced in *Endurance,* forcing on some students a conclusion that neither of these characters, even if driven by moral motives, is particularly admirable.

Moral alternatives

What can be done in the face of such differing views? The apparently intractable conflict between Antigone and Creon allows a singular feature of the class to emerge – an exploration of moral alternatives. While students may have studied *Antigone* before, this exploration takes the discussion to a new level of practical application.

Two questions prompt students to exercise their **moral imagination**. In the first, they are asked to solve the problem between Antigone and Creon – to come up with a solution that takes into account the interests and convictions that each brings to the problem of Polynices' burial. Students find that they are able to come up with solutions that might, in fact, work. This exercise introduces students to the concept of **moral alternatives**, the view that our initial considered judgment and plan for addressing a situation need not be our last.

The ability to identify alternatives raises a question in turn: What is it about Creon and Antigone that prevents them from coming up with these trade-offs and compromises? Students are asked to describe **the attributes of a person who, even in the face of strongly held values and beliefs, would be able to make negotiated choices.**

They develop a portrait of a reasoning, reasonable individual, able to see multiple sides of an issue, a character very like Haemon, Creon's son and Antigone's betrothed. The exploration creates a new hypothesis to take into the course about the **attributes that might be useful and perhaps even necessary to someone looking to lead a morally responsible life.**

Both of these exercises present students with a view of moral decision-making and action as something much closer to real life than they at first imagined, a practical endeavor in which well-intentioned individuals can engage.

STUDENT ASSIGNMENT

READING: *Antigone*, by Sophocles (in *The Theban Plays*).

1 Please consult the table of contents. Read the "Introduction," "The Theban Legend," "The Legend Continued," "The Legend Continued," and the play, *Antigone*.

2 How are Antigone and Creon different? How are they alike?

3 What *really* is the conflict between them?

4 Assuming you could, how would you resolve it? Be prepared to defend your position.

CLASS PLAN OUTLINE: DISCUSSION BLOCKS

1 Laying Out the Conflict (25′)

2 Are These Positions Inherently in Conflict? (10′)

3 Characterizing the Protagonists (20′)

4 Passing Judgment: Which of These Positions Is More Compelling? (25′)

5 Are There Alternatives? (25′)

CLASS PLAN OVERVIEW

The *Antigone* class reinforces and makes more explicit the pedagogy used in the introductory class on *Endurance*. "The Moral Leader" is designed to enhance students' ability to analyze a problem with moral or ethical stakes. Dilemmas encountered by fictional or historical figures provide the focus for this evolution, but many students bring to these problems the same tendency toward immediate judgment and instantaneous reaction that they often use in confronting moral problems in their own lives.

Class plans are designed to push against this inclination, asking students to first establish a basis for understanding the facts of the situation ("What is really going on here?") which they then analyze, looking for patterns and root causes ("Why is this happening?"). Armed with this more powerful and nuanced appreciation, students are then asked to evaluate elements of moral significance – actions taken, their consequences, the rationales for action, and the actors' motivation ("How do I judge these things?").

The fundamental principle, of course, is that better decisions and better outcomes are achieved when understanding precedes judgment.

INTRODUCTION

A way of opening the discussion

As you know, the primary materials in this course are works of literature and history. These works have been chosen because they bring us much closer to moral challenges as they are really lived. We see real characters, wonderfully depicted. We also get the benefit of enormous intelligence and wisdom in the choice of situations that are documented, and in the perspective that the authors have on those situations. Nowhere is that more clear than in today's work.

It is helpful as we start to recall that Sophocles was writing in a different literary tradition from the one we are used to. The literary scholar and philosopher Martha Nussbaum provides an evocative description of the context:

> *Before Plato came on the scene the poets (especially the tragic poets) were understood by most Athenians to be the central ethical teachers and thinkers of Greece, the people to whom, above all, the city turned, and rightly turned, with questions about how to live. To attend a tragic drama was not to go to a distraction or a fantasy, in the course of which one suspended one's anxious practical questions. It was, instead, to engage in a communal process of inquiry, reflection, and feeling with respect to important civic and personal ends. The very structure of theatrical performance strongly implied this. When we go to the theater, we usually sit in a darkened auditorium, in the illusion of splendid isolation, while the dramatic action – separated from the spectator by the box of the proscenium arch – is bathed in artificial light as if it were a separate world of fantasy and mystery. The ancient Greek spectator, by contrast, sitting in the common daylight, saw across the staged action the faces of fellow citizens on the other side of the orchestra. And the whole event took place during a solemn civic/religious festival, whose trappings made spectators conscious that the values of the community were being examined and communicated. To respond to*

these events was to acknowledge and participate in a way of life – and a way of life, we should add, that prominently included reflection and public debate about ethical and civic matters.[2]

The elements of the story were known to the audience, in this case:

Antigone, a daughter of Oedipus, King of Thebes, by his mother Jocasta, buried by night her brother Polynices, against the positive orders of Creon who, when he heard of it, ordered her to be buried alive. She however killed herself before the sentence was executed and Haeimon, the king's son, in love with her and unable to obtain her pardon, killed himself upon her grave.[3]

In this civic/religious festival, the audience came to see what interpretation the poet had applied to a well-known story, what lessons to ponder and consider. The response to the play was so positive that at its first representation the Athenians awarded Sophocles the government of Samos. The tragedy was then presented 32 times at Athens without interruption.

1 LAYING OUT THE CONFLICT (25′)

You begin the class by asking students to put themselves into the minds of Antigone and Creon. What is asked for is description, not judgment – **What are they doing? Why? What rationale do they provide for their actions?** I have found it useful to characterize the task as laying out the *positions* that Antigone and Creon are taking. It is important to signal that, while we are looking at actions, we are mostly concerned with arguments. Why behave this way? What justifies these decisions?

This is a more complex analytical task than it at first appears, since Antigone and Creon are motivated by different principles, objectives, and goals. It is helpful to start with Antigone as the more sympathetic character, but the trick to this discussion – and there is one – is to build a solid base of understanding and appreciation of the events that drove Creon to establish an edict against the burial of Polynices. This is an important introduction to the role and responsibilities of public leadership, and, with some prompting, students find themselves describing both the civil war (the precipitating event) and Creon's theory of governance. You will find that students move seamlessly from description into judgment, so it is important to establish the contract for this (and other) discussions by asking students to hold off evaluation until a clear picture is developed of Antigone's and Creon's points of view.

Questions driving the discussion are in bold

What position is Antigone taking in relation to Creon? Let's start with actions. What, exactly, has she done?

You begin the discussion of Antigone by asking students to review the actions Antigone has taken. Students appreciate (or, at least, acknowledge) the depth of conviction Antigone displays in translating her beliefs into consistent, concrete, and highly dangerous activities. Students identify the following acts: Antigone attempts to bury Polynices at night; she stands up to Creon in direct confrontation; she refuses the help of her sister Ismene; she is, at the end, willing to die for her principles.

Why does she do these things?

This review leads naturally to the follow-up questions of *why* Antigone is willing to take these risks and to make this sacrifice. Student responses will range from the ethical, "Why would anyone willingly sacrifice themselves for another?," to the psychological, "She seems to be consciously seeking death – why? Is she just in love with the picture of her own self-sacrifice?", to the historical, "This is what ancient Greeks would have done because of how seriously they viewed funeral rites." Students probe distinctions: "Is Antigone *willing* to die, or does she *want* to die?" And some see Antigone as progressing in conviction as the play's action unfolds: "She begins with some uncertainty, but through her encounters with her sister, and especially Creon, she seems to become increasingly sure of her decisions."

What lies behind Antigone's position? What principles is she drawing on and arguing for?

You can help focus the discussion by asking students to channel these responses into a description of the *position* Antigone is taking in response to Creon's edict – the rationale she offers for her actions and the principles she draws on and argues for.

Students recognize that Antigone makes two arguments. First, she is bound to act as she does because of filial duty – duty to her slain brother. Second, Creon's actions are an offense against the "unwritten unalterable law" of the gods that specify what the living owe to the dead.

Students can be pressed to sketch the limits of each of these rationales:

Is sacrificing oneself to bury a family member within the boundaries of ordinary filial piety? Why does Antigone believe that this extreme demonstration of filial devotion is required?

And, regarding the laws of the gods for treatment of the dead:

What is this duty based on? Is this duty owed to anyone or does it pertain just because Polynices is Antigone's brother?

Two rationales emerge in response. First, Polynices *deserved* to be buried – he has a right to commemoration and to the rituals that provide solace to the souls of the dead. Second, Creon *does not have the right* to dominate the sphere of the transcendent – some laws are beyond the reach of man and even of man's rulers.

Why does Creon object? Why did he make his edict?

Here, too, you start with the facts, asking students why Creon established an injunction against Polynices' burial. This will stimulate a review of the events that precipitated Creon's edict – a brutal civil war led by Polynices against the city of Thebes – and relationships: Polynices is not just Antigone's brother and a rebel but Creon's nephew as well – a member of his own extended family who took up arms against him.

What is the rationale for Creon's position? What principles is he defending?

You then ask students to describe the rationale for Creon's action – the position he is taking. Most will recognize that Creon is fulfilling the role obligations of a civic leader, driven by duty to the state and rooted in the requirement to promote and maintain order.

How does Creon define duty? According to Creon, what is the duty of citizens? What does Creon believe is owed to Polynices?

You can ask students to flesh out other elements of Creon's philosophy of governance: how he sees the duty of citizens and why civic order and respect for law are so important to him. Thus prompted, students will defend his actions and the need to establish order in a city torn by civil war. It is also useful for students to consider what Creon believes is owed to Polynices. One student responded that, in Creon's view, "Polynices is owed what any other traitor would deserve, and even less because the rebellion he led against Thebes was also a rebellion against his own family."

Is that it? Are there other motives at work?

If it has not emerged by this time, students will discuss Creon's perhaps justifiable family fury – betrayed first by his nephew Polynices, and now, again, by his niece and future daughter-in-law, Antigone.

2 ARE THESE POSITIONS INHERENTLY IN CONFLICT? (10′)

The next brief discussion is designed to dispel the idea that Antigone's and Creon's conflict is a foregone conclusion – that duty to state, to family, and to the gods are intrinsically in conflict.

Are the principles that Antigone and Creon defend truly irreconcilable? Are duty to state, to family, and to the gods inherently in conflict?

We know, of course, that Antigone and Creon fight – literally to the death – for their respective positions. Yet students recognize that there is no reason why these duties should necessarily conflict. One student pointed out, "In a well-ordered society, the laws of state flow from and correspond to the cultural understanding of divine law." Another observed, "Under other, perhaps more fortunate circumstances, the laws of state are structured to allow observance of duties to family, to religion, and to the state, without having to sacrifice one for the other." Some students disagree: "There will be conflicts: as soon as someone breaks laws of the state – family law kicks in." Yet, even where there is conflict (as in a case cited of one brother protecting another by refusing to disclose where the first brother is hidden), most students agree that such conflicts are the exception, rather than the rule, in states with sound laws and governance.

Why are they in conflict here?

Students respond that it is Creon who sets up the conflict by creating a state-based, man-made law that makes a three-fold violation: of religious law – the law of the gods; of family law – the natural duties and mutual obligations of the family unit; and of civil law – the feelings of the living polis for one of their own. But while Creon's actions created this conflict, it was Antigone's response – her unwillingness to yield to his "unnatural law" – that drove the conflict to the limit.

3 CHARACTERIZING THE PROTAGONISTS (20′)

The analysis of the conflict between Antigone and Creon is completed with a discussion of the nature of the two as individuals. Students will have made observations about the character and personality of Antigone and Creon in the prior discussions. This block is designed to allow them to elaborate on those early observations and to flesh out some hypotheses about the role that personality (the self) plays in the conflict between the two.

What is it about Antigone and Creon – as individuals – that created this conflict? In what ways are they similar?

Students are quick to point out the many ways in which Antigone and Creon are similar: their characters are drawn to the same sharp edges; they share a common vehemence of expression and belief. "They both had reasons for their actions. These were considered judgments – not rash." The discussion can be deepened by asking: **Is there the same weight of conviction on both sides?** Antigone is willing to defy Creon openly, knowing she will die. "She expresses the kind of conviction that my sixteen-year-old sister would demonstrate." Creon, for all of his willingness to defy the polis of Thebes and the gods, does not appear, until the story's end, to understand that his actions could lead him to harm.

Students also can be asked to flesh out the similarities in how the two behave, for example, toward family members. They point out that Antigone's dismissive treatment of her sister, Ismene, parallels Creon's similarly dismissive treatment of Haemon, his son.

Who is the real rebel here?

Students will observe that both take the law into their own keeping; but, while Antigone breaks civic law, Creon, as has been seen, breaks multiple laws – of the elders, of the living polis, of the gods.

Why couldn't either of them give in?

This final question on similarities will yield descriptions of the mutual intransigence that the two characters share. A more sophisticated student observed that the conflict between them is a clash of "existential freedoms" – neither can yield without falsifying his essential being.

In what ways are they different?

The differences between Antigone and Creon are obvious: female versus male; young versus old; private versus public; pious versus (at least initially) uncaring. Surprisingly, except for the last category, students often gloss over these differences, perhaps because it is not politically correct to point to differences that stem from gender or age. *Antigone* scholar George Steiner observes, however, that it is the very presence of these fundamental conflicts (and others – the conflict of the living versus the dead) that makes the work so enduring.[4]

You will want to press students on the impact gender has on this conflict: "It is unthinkable for Creon to yield to a woman;" students also point out that Creon castigates Haemon for being blinded by lust. And they should also be asked about the impact on the conflict of age: "Creon couldn't yield to youth – to Antigone *or* to Haemon."

The prejudices expressed by Creon are an integral part of his objections and rationale, as is Antigone's awareness of the lives she is forgoing – bride, wife, mother. The conflict between the two is shaped as much by these differences in perspective as by the principle-based arguments they muster, and an appreciation of this more emotional aspect of the conflict is critical to give students a well-rounded appreciation of what goes so terribly wrong between them.

If Shackleton demonstrated great sensitivity to his context and shaped his actions to it, how do you grade Antigone and Creon? What was Antigone *not* seeing? What was Creon *not* seeing?

The last set of questions translates these observations into something more tactical. If Ernest Shackleton was an example of an actor deeply in tune with his environment, able clearly and accurately to see the weather, the wave movements, the condition of the boats, and the psychological condition of each member of his crew, Antigone and Creon were, by contrast, frustratingly blind to the most obvious facts of their situation.

What did Antigone *not* see? Polynices in civic terms: as leader of civil war against his city – Polynices as traitor; Polynices in family terms: who wages war against his brother and uncle; Ismene and Haemon – family and future family members, who Antigone might have been able to continue to love and enjoy, were she not so bent on defying Creon. And what did Creon *not* see? Polynices in family terms: as nephew; Antigone in family terms: as niece and future wife of his son; the living polis and their feelings; Haemon and his feelings.

Through these questions you are introducing "seeing" to the students as a metaphor for something far more powerful and useful: the ability to perceive our own situation clearly, unblocked by prejudice, clear of blinding conviction,

67

having overcome a perhaps natural unwillingness to entertain another's point of view.

4 PASSING JUDGMENT (25')

Students are at last ready to pass judgment. Which of these two positions and characters do they find more compelling? Where do they come out in the debate? If forced to choose, which character strikes them as more defensible, which more admirable?

When asked for their judgment, students find that the preceding analysis has made it hard for them to take the kind of single-threaded point of view they may have come in with. They see subtleties that were not evident before, and their judgment is more measured than it would have been if they had started class off with an evaluation of Antigone and Creon. Imprinting this method – describe – analyze – judge – is important for this and future discussions. The class dynamic at this point is one of assertion and challenge. Sometimes the challenge comes from the instructor in the form of the questions; sometimes it comes in open dialogue and disagreement among the students.

This discussion is payback for all of the hard work that precedes it, and you will want to allow students a full field of play – a chance to evaluate from the vantage point of emotion as well as reason. We come to our judgments as a whole self, and students should be validated for giving voice to their full range of reactions.

"I just didn't like her" is now defensible, because it has been tested against and perhaps amplified by the prior discussion. It is not complete as a judgment in itself, but without it students are asked to leave far too much of their selves behind in the experience of this magnificent story and characters. As will become increasingly clear, this marriage of elements – reason and emotion – illustrates the wholeness that is required to handle moral challenges, engage in moral reasoning, and exercise moral leadership.

Now let's evaluate what we've laid out. How do you evaluate each of these positions and principles? Which strikes you as more viable?

Antigone is the natural hero. To some students her consistency is admirable; for others it is her stated reasons for acting – being true to her gods and to her family. Students sometimes connect Antigone's rebellion to battles for civil, political, or human rights; they posit a moral duty to defy unjust laws and liken Antigone to Martin Luther King or to Mahatma Gandhi.

A subset of students find Antigone's airs and unwillingness to compromise irritating and, to some, just dumb. "Why can't she yield?" And where some students see brave, principle-driven action a few see a potential terrorist blinded by her own point of view.

The debate over Antigone's motives is renewed, and her logic is exposed to scrutiny. Some are appalled by the argument: ". . . I could have had another husband/And by him other sons, if one were lost/But, father and mother lost, where would I get/Another brother?"[5]

Antigone's perceived rush to death, while noble to some, seems incomprehensible to others. Students begin to ask, "How can we decide whether any principle is worth dying for – what evil is so great that even a failed challenge to it trumps our will to live?"

If the discussion seems too one-sided, you can break a seeming consensus with probes:

What would happen if everyone took the law into their own hands? Why does Antigone refuse to let Ismene help her? Isn't this moral self-righteousness?

Creon is of course the far less sympathetic character, and students resent not just his rejection of Antigone's logic, but even more his refusal to listen to Haemon, the Elders, and Tiresias until the end. Creon's human failings are many: hypocrisy – claiming a desire for counsel he obviously doesn't value; rampant, blinding disrespect – a stubborn insistence that all others are motivated by greed and a desire for material gain; pride and conviction in the rightness of his own decisions and judgment. This characterization of a ruler may resonate with students with less than fortunate work experience; to me, it is wonderfully contemporary.

To create balance and tension, it is useful to support Creon through the questions you ask.

What are the obligations of the leader of a city that has just come out of a horrible civil war? What is wrong with making an example of a traitor? Why don't we applaud Creon for not letting family relations matter? He is applying the law objectively – isn't that justice?

Some students will defend Creon's actions: "He needs to establish public order, particularly in the aftermath of a civil war;" "He can't give ground to Antigone without losing status as a leader;" "How could he make an exception to a law for a family member?" Other students will sit the debate out – claiming that neither character is particularly positive or admirable.

Your questions provide a way to challenge students' positions, and require them to offer more nuanced and carefully defended versions of their initial arguments. Several of the questions are aimed toward generalization: Is this always right – or wrong? If not, why is it so in this case? The conclusion of this block is a good review of students' judgments and the beginning of disciplined challenge of positions taken, offered up by the instructor and by the members of the class.

5 EXPLORING MORAL ALTERNATIVES (25')

Many students are unsettled by the conclusion from the preceding block. How could two principled people each have sound reasons for action, but still fail spectacularly in the working out of their decisions and actions? The final block builds on this question and explores what alternatives might have existed: how might another Creon and another Antigone have worked their way through this clash of principles?

Creon's and Antigone's positions proved to be irreconcilable in the play, but do they have to be? Besides simply yielding, is there any other option that takes into account both points of view?

By this point in the discussion students have a firm picture of the personalities and characteristic ways of responding of both of the main actors. To free up their imagination, you may need to stress in this first question that students can imagine a different Creon and a different Antigone, ones perhaps more motivated to negotiate and settle their differences.

Given this prompting (and sometimes the opportunity to talk with students they are sitting next to), students are quite creative and come up with several alternatives to the problem of the burial of Polynices. Some suggest a "bury but still condemn" solution, separating out burial as a religious and private act, presumably presided over by Antigone, from a public condemnation of Polynices as traitor, led by Creon. Others suggest an "anywhere but here" solution – allowing Polynices to be buried somewhere outside the city limits of Thebes. Finally, some take a more conceptual approach, suggesting that burial be "reframed" to cast it in terms that do not connote approval by the state. In developing these solutions, students proceed, as in a negotiation, to separate the *interests* of Antigone and Creon from the *positions* they have taken. A satisfactory solution is measured by the degree to which it allows the principal tenets of each character's point of view to be respected.

At this point in the discussion, you may find it helpful to provide a brief summary of the type of moral challenge that has been the focus of discussion – a challenge of *right versus right*, in which each party to a conflict has a strong and defensible moral posture and rationale for action. Students find this reminder helpful, and a good explanation of the difficulty they have had in deciding which of the two characters, and positions, to support.

Students will be pleased with their progress in finding alternative ways to resolve the conflict but quickly point out that the Antigone and Creon we encountered in the play were not the kind of people who were so ready to find common ground. This leads to the last question:

We have seen that moral action is not just driven by principle; it is enabled by personality – by the self. Based on what you've seen here, what personal attributes would allow someone to be good at handling a situation with two "rights"?

I have found it useful to put students into *buzz groups* – small groups of two to three – for several minutes to allow them to answer this last question.

Students create a map – quickly sketched – of at least a portion of their concept of what is required to lead a morally responsible life. Some of the characteristics are positive and aspirational, as in: "Empathic;" "not carried away by your own feelings;" "self-confident enough in your own views that you can listen to and hear out others;" "tolerant of ambiguity and uncertainty;" "patient;" "able to not impose on others an answer that works for you."

At the same time, students worry about how much of the self can exist in moral decision-making, since they may also identify: "Selfless;" "emotionless;" "cold;" "rational." The question that triggers this list is quite specific: **What does it take to handle successfully a situation with two "rights"?** Through it students begin to speculate on some of the personal characteristics that may be useful to cultivate to handle other moral challenges as well.

You will not want to tie the bow too neatly on this last discussion block. The purpose is not for students to feel that they have resolved the conflict in *Antigone*, but, rather, for them to appreciate the depth of analysis that can be brought to it, and that they can, by virtue of imagining alternatives, understand even more clearly how context and situation, our own principles, and the characteristics of the self work together in determining the choices we make.

Analyzing the conflict
- Positions of Antigone and Creon
- Antigone and Creon – as People

Judgment

Moral alternatives

Figure 5.1 Antigone *roadmap*

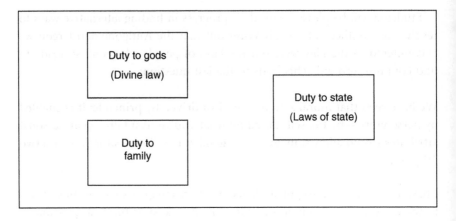

Figure 5.2 Antigone *board plan*

NOTES

1   *Antigone,* in *The Theban Plays,* translated by E. F. Watling, New York and London: Penguin Books, 1947, p. 140.
2   Martha Nussbaum, *Love's Knowledge: Essays on Philosophy and Literature,* New York and Oxford: Oxford University Press, 1990, p. 15.
3   *Bibliotheca Classica* or *A Classical Dictionary,* 3rd edn, by J. Lemprière, DD, London, 1797.
4   George Steiner, *Antigones,* New Haven, Conn.: Yale University Press, 1984, pp. 231–233
5   Sophocles, op. cit., p. 150.

Chapter 6

Blessed Assurance

The challenge of a moral dilemma

ONE VERY OLD WOMAN seemed to peek from every door. Toothless, blue-black, her shy grin looked mischievous, a small head wrapped in the brightest kerchief. At some doorways, her hands might be coated with flour. At others she held a broom or some white man's half-ironed white business shirt. She wore male work boots four sizes too large, the toes curled up like elf shoes. Sometimes she smoked a pipe (this was in the Forties). Her long skirt dragged the floor, pulling along string, dustballs. She asked, "What they want now. You ain't the one from before – you a young one, ain't you?" and she chuckled at me. I smiled and swallowed.[1]

. . .

One month into the job, nobody knew my name. I'd stayed "Assurance." And my clients still looked pretty much alike to me. Maybe it sounds bad but, hey, they *were* alike. People started having names when I deciphered the last collector's rotten handwriting. One morning, it yielded like a busted code. Then the ladies began standing out from one another. Oh, man, I couldn't believe some of the tallies!

"Vesta Lotte Battle, 14 Sunflower Street – commenced payment on policy #1, Mar. 2, 1912, four policies complete, collected to date: $4,360.50."[2]

. . .

My ninth week on the job, all clients permanently broke down into themselves. There was the one missing two fingers, the one who always tried to give me geranium clippings for my mom, the plump one in the bed, the pretty young one in the wicker wheelchair, the old one in her metal wheelchair who wore a cowgirl hat, the one with the wig, the one who told the same three easy riddles each week, the one, the one . . .

> My rounds sure felt easier when people had the decency to stay blended. Now I started worrying over payer and nonpayers too. You know how it is, once a crowd splits into separate faces, nothing can ever mash them back into that first safe shape.[3]

BLESSED ASSURANCE: THEMES AND QUESTIONS

Moral awareness

Blessed Assurance continues the module on Moral Challenge, in which students explore fundamental moral problems and the strategies used to come to terms with them. The discussion of *Endurance* revealed a *right-versus-wrong* problem set in the context of survival: What is morally permissible under survival conditions? Although leaders have answered that question in various ways, using different justifications, for Shackleton the answer was clear: Everyone had a right to be saved; there would be no sacrifice of the few for the many, and his actions were consistent with that belief.

Antigone extended the students' understanding of the shape that moral challenges can take, presenting a conflict in which duty to the gods and to family competed with duty to the state, each being a morally defensible aim. The principal characters were unshakably convinced of their individual positions, and the connection between their beliefs and the actions they took seemed clear and inevitable. The play thus presented to students a *right-versus-right* moral conflict: each side of the conflict has moral merit and can be translated into action that itself can be morally justified.

Blessed Assurance takes a step back from these moments of seeming certainty and allows students to examine a particular instance of **the dawning of moral awareness** and **the struggle with whether and how to translate awareness into action**. A challenge to injustice is at the heart of the story, but beneath it lies an essential moral concept. Before injustice can be perceived as a moral issue, we have both to identify and acknowledge its victim. *Blessed Assurance* allows students to explore this terrain, **the very foundation of morality – our ability to perceive another's humanity.**

Dawning is used to describe the gradual coming to a state of awareness of the other, a nearly invisible process that – in this text at least – looks more like a shadow being pierced than a deliberate or intentional act of cognition. Is the acquisition of moral insight always like this? Probably not, though social psychologists have demonstrated how prevalent even unconscious biases are, and how they affect many aspects of decision-making.[4]

What mechanisms allow bias, conscious or unconscious, to be overcome? *Blessed Assurance* details one example as it traces the evolving relationship between its nineteen-year-old white protagonist, Jerry, in a rural Southern town in America at the end of the 1940s, and Vesta Lotte Battle, one of the African-American clients from whom he collects weekly premiums for funeral insurance. Students follow Jerry's transition from perceiving "one old black woman" to the many individual clients he collects from, and they watch as he allows himself to be moved, some will feel even transformed, by the presence, dignity, and acceptance he finds in Mrs Battle.

A moral dilemma

Blessed Assurance is not just about sentiment, but also about action – the translation of moral sentiment into action. *Antigone* exhibited conflicting duties among protagonists, and Jerry is likewise caught; but, where Antigone and Creon evinced conviction and certainty, Jerry finds doubt and indecision. He is torn between competing claims of duty and loyalty: to his family; to the business he works for; and to his clients. Jerry is thus the first character students encounter to wrestle with a true *moral dilemma:* a type of right versus right conflict consisting of obligations that are impossible to simultaneously satisfy.[5] The story allows students to see that translating moral vision into action is not a straight shot. The youthful Jerry wavers, painfully, between opposing positions.

Jerry initially rebels against the insurance system of Windlass Funerary Eventualities by paying the weekly premiums owed by Mrs Battle and a small group of other non-paying clients who would otherwise lose their policies and their already-paid-for funerals. At the same time, Jerry wants to end his rebellion, a stance that forces him to lie to his boss and takes earnings that he needs to fund his college education and to support his sick parents.

Once Jerry discloses these payments to his boss and stops paying them, he appears to try to right the balance with wildly extravagant gestures: paying to have the body of Mrs Battle's daughter transported from Michigan to be buried; offering his entire premium collection for a week, and his car, as a gift to an African-American church. One perceptive student described Jerry as "undershooting" and "overshooting" his moral obligations – and that disorderly lurching toward moral coherence and consistency may offer a vital lesson: Do not look for an easy path, either in deciding to act, or in determining what moral action consists in.

Future impact of moral decisions

Written in the guise of autobiography, *Blessed Assurance* is largely a retrospective narrative, allowing students to see the long shadow that moral action (or inaction) casts, its ability to influence our lives long after an event is over. **Time is a critical element in moral reasoning (the focus of the second module), which depends on the ability to forecast actions and to assess them, in the present, in light of their potential consequences.** Hindsight is a natural extension of this assessment process in which, instead of guessing what the outcome of an act will be, we know with certainty what we did, which actions led to particular outcomes, and how at some specific point in time we judge the effect we caused. Alan Gurganus explores this process in *Blessed Assurance: A Moral Tale.*

It is not surprising that stories about moral challenge use the device of time to powerful effect. **What we worry about in making moral decisions is not just what we think about them now, but how, in retrospect, we shall think about them in the future.** Students will encounter stories told from a retrospective viewpoint at several points in the course, most notably in the novel *The Remains of the Day*, but also in Joseph Conrad's *The Secret Sharer*, and in the autobiographies of Kay Graham and Ben Bradlee. These stories are modeling a perspective – looking forward to be able to look back – that is central to students' ability to make moral choices in their own lives.

STUDENT ASSIGNMENT

READING: *Blessed Assurance: A Moral Tale,* by Allan Gurganus (from *White People*).

1 How do you assess the business model used by Windlass Funerary Eventualities, Inc., the insurance company Jerry worked for?

2 How would you describe Mrs Battle's character?

3 What is the nature of her and Jerry's relationship?

4 Do you agree with all of the actions Jerry took? Why? Why not?

5 Jerry looks back on his early decisions with some regret. Be prepared to weigh in on this argument, by agreeing, or mounting a defense of the ways in which Jerry might have been changed, for the better, by his actions.

CLASS PLAN OUTLINE: DISCUSSION BLOCKS

1 Introduction: Why Does Jerry Thank Us for Reading His Story? (10′)

2 Assessing the Business Model of Windlass Funerary Eventualities (25′)

3 Assessing Jerry's Job Performance (30′)

4 Understanding Jerry's Relationship with Mrs Battle (20′)

5 Evaluating Jerry the Elder (20′)

CLASS PLAN OVERVIEW

Few, if any, students will be familiar with *Blessed Assurance,* and this novella stretches them individually and as a group. Except for the hardy outdoor types who could identify with the challenge of adventure in *Endurance,* students did not expect to find themselves in the Antarctic, or in ancient Greece. But *Blessed Assurance* – with African-American clients and a young white collection agent all contending with the social, economic, and racial stresses of a small town in the rural South of 1940s America – is close enough to be familiar to some who have handled similar pressures, even if they are of a different time and place.

This close-but-distant relationship to the characters is useful because this class (like the next, on *Things Fall Apart*) requires students to overcome their reluctance to talk about race, a central issue of the story. *Blessed Assurance* is nicely complex as a moral tale. Windlass Funerary Eventualities was founded by an African-American, so class discussion cannot become easily polarized; students recognize that the firm's exploitative business model harms black funeral insurance policyholders, but also its white management and collection agents.

Overcoming a reluctance to broach the topic of race – which is central to the story – depends on how minority students are engaged in the discussion. I have found it helpful to raise questions that require all students to speak from personal experience and to exercise their moral imagination. One such question early in this class plan is **What does this product – a funeral – mean to the people who buy it?** The material in the student textbook bridges the divide, giving students with no or little understanding of American race relations and African-American culture in the post-Second World War period a frame of reference from which to speak, and permission to enter imaginatively into the lives of the clients who pay, week after week, for the right to be buried in a manner of their own choosing. Minority students have often been generous in their answers, sometimes referencing their own experiences or those of their parents and especially grandparents. You will want to give time for these responses to come out, and to allow the follow-up questions that their classmates may ask.

Some students cannot readily identify with the racial conflict at the heart of the story, but for many there is a nearly equal sense of social stigma and shame in being poor; many students see in the young Jerry their own struggles or those of their families to overcome economic hardship. Jerry the elder is a tougher sell, and students frequently have difficulty empathizing with the remorseful fifty-nine-year-old narrator. Mrs Battle, however, reminds many students of encounters with deeply affecting adult figures. Overall, this rich story provides multiple subjects for identification and interpretation, and all students grasp the conflict Jerry faces.

1 INTRODUCTION: WHY IS JERRY THANKING US? (10′)

A way of opening the discussion

We are blessed in this course with powerful material. We've seen the power of the weather, of the gods, of choices made in dramatic circumstances. In this class we move to another kind of power: of choices made in everyday life among people transacting business, and the meaning that one of the participants attempts to construct out of them as he looks back on his life. Let's start, very briefly, at the end of this tale, with Jerry the elder.

Questions driving the discussion are in bold

Why does Jerry thank us for reading his story? Why does he need us to be involved? Why not just judge himself?

Unlike *Endurance* and *Antigone,* which are written in the third person, Jerry narrates *Blessed Assurance* himself, changing perspective from the past, to the present, and back again. The need for summing up, for an accounting, is a principal motivation of Jerry's story, and students do a good job of describing why, at the end, he thanks the reader.

Some students recognize a considerate, well-bred young man who, even in his fifties, continues to be the kind of person for whom please and thank you seem to come naturally. Others reach for more ambitious explanations: "Jerry needs to share his burden – many hands make a light load;" "Jerry needs us because he is looking for redemption." Students sometimes criticize Jerry's account, "This is a selfish confession – he uses us – readers – because he wants to feel better." The most sophisticated students characterize Jerry's storytelling as "a way of reconstructing himself," of creating his own life through the telling of it.

This opening discussion is a form of table-setting: getting some of the themes out in the open before they are discussed in more detail. It also enables instructors to assess how members of the class are viewing Jerry. Students can be critical of him, so these early intimations of sympathy are useful, and can be called upon when it's time to consider Jerry as an adult if the discussion appears to be too one-sided.

2 ASSESSING THE BUSINESS MODEL OF WINDLASS FUNERARY EVENTUALITIES (25')

In this discussion, you ask students to use the reading skills of description and analysis to examine the business of Windlass Funerary Eventualities. As with the prior two classes, you will establish the context of action before allowing students to move to judgment. And, while the ironically named business Jerry worked for may have been typical for its time, some students will remind the class that the exploitation of poor consumers is not unique. (For example, one student described the unsavory practice of selling household security alarm systems to residents of dangerous neighborhoods even as the firm acknowledged that customers would be unable to maintain the stream of payments required for ownership.)

What is being sold here? How do people pay for it?

Without prompting, students will raise the unfairness of Windlass Funerary Eventualities' business model for insurance. Many are outraged by a scheme in which any two-week lapse in premium payments allows the entire amount previously paid to be forfeited to the company. This criticism can be refined by asking: **How different is this from any other good – say, a mortgage, that gets paid for over time, and which is forfeited if the purchaser or borrower can't repay it?** The question forces students to distinguish a common time-based payment scheme from its design and execution in this instance. Students will then focus on the problem of a two-week lapse in payment as excessively stringent for poor consumers, and on the unfairness of forfeiting completely paid-for policies.

Some students defend the funeral insurance business, however. "I take a libertarian view. If customers know the terms of the deal, this gives them a way to pay for something they value and couldn't otherwise afford." Others acknowledge the benefits of such an approach, but suggest "there are some businesses you just wouldn't want to be in." Many are highly critical: "Just because a deal is legal and disclosed, does not make it moral," and, "It's horrible to take advantage of death." Some students find the discussion of the business model of Windlass Funerary enlightening. "I knew I didn't like it, but I didn't know why!"

What does this product mean to the people who buy it?

The next question digs beneath student reactions to press on the nature of the product – a funeral – and what it means to the people who buy it. The question invites a more personal analysis, and African-American students can at times be seen to look among themselves as if silently asking, "OK, who among us is going to help out here?"

Patient instructors can be rewarded by enriching comments about the vital role of religion and the church in African-American communities. One student observed that paying for a funeral is "a way to control the manner by which we leave this world, even if we can't control what happens to us while we're in it." Another contended that the insurance company's clients understood the deal, but as children of slaves (highly likely in 1940s America) funerals had a particular meaning, representing "a better life after the sorrows of this one."

Students are often careful to state that they are speaking for themselves, as well as (or possibly instead of) a group. A particularly good discussion is one in which minority students provide insight without laying claim to exclusive knowledge, allowing all students to exercise their moral imagination based on their reading of the story, their own life experience, and background information provided in the student textbook.

This discussion helps many students answer the question of motivation: **Why would people this poor sacrifice so much for their own funerals?** Until this question is answered, it is hard for students to empathize with the problem Jerry faces as he begins the task of collecting, week by week, from the residents of Baby Africa, as the African-American part of Jerry's town is called.

This business was started by an African-American entrepreneur. Does that make it better? Worse?

If students haven't already raised this point, you can deepen the discussion of racial tensions by asking students to consider that Windlass Funerary Eventualities was started by an African-American entrepreneur.[6] How does this affect their analysis? Some students are offended: "The exploitation is worse because it's a black entrepreneur." Others observe that the firm is not just preying on poor blacks, but by using young white collectors like Jerry, the business is even more exploitative than it appears to be initially.

3 WAS JERRY GOOD AT HIS JOB? (30′)

The discussion of the business model of Windlass Funerary Eventualities leads naturally to an assessment of Jerry's performance as a collection agent. This debate is a crucial part of the class, forcing students to come to grips with the conflicting ways Jerry's performance could be evaluated. From which perspective should we make this assessment? The business? The clients? Jerrys?

What role do people like Jerry play in this product?

The first question extends students' understanding of the business Jerry worked for by imagining what good performance as a collection agent might consist of. Students recognize that some of Jerry's qualities fit this job very well. They point out that his desire to please, his courtesy, even his shyness make him the kind of person who clients would not be unhappy to see, and who might make the weekly search for the 50-cent insurance premium a less grueling ordeal. Others paint a darker picture. The ideal candidate would be "a machine," someone who is "heartless," "immovable," "uncaring," more motivated by pay than by the benefit he provides to clients.

Was Jerry good at his job?

Probes for "No" position

What wasn't he good at? What are you basing your assessment on?

Students who take a *No* position – usually a majority – conclude that Jerry was not particularly good at collecting money. Worse, he didn't follow the orders or advice of his boss, Sam, and allowed himself to become too involved with Mrs Battle, losing perspective on his duty to Windlass to collect from each policyholder. You can probe these students, **How did Jerry decide which** non-payers to help? They then extend their criticism to point out Jerry's inconsistencies – indulging some clients but not others, with no apparent criteria to guide his decisions. Students can be pressed to defend their position by reminding them that Sam observed, **He turned in the fewest non-payers of any young collection agent: isn't that good from the company's point of view?**

Probes for "Yes" position

What was he good at? What are you basing your assessment on?

Students who assert *Yes*, Jerry was good at his job, describe him as conscientious, compassionate, someone who extended himself: "He was friendly, kept at it, and was nice to people like Mrs Battle."

Did Jerry improve at his job? In what ways?

Some students observe that Jerry gave the role definition of collector a personal interpretation, that, wittingly or not, some of his own self was inserted into the job, making it more pleasant, if not for Jerry, then for his clients. The fundamental question in this assessment (which would obtain for anyone serving as a collection agent) was how Jerry handled non-paying clients.

Jerry blew the whistle on non-paying clients – that's good – yes?

Students taking the *Yes* position point out that Jerry finally did disclose the list of non-paying clients to his boss, and that the amounts that Jerry covered, while a drain on his personal resources, were not large.

Did you approve of Jerry's paying for Mrs Battle and the others?

The discussion leads to a debate about how students judge Jerry's actions, and, in particular, whether they approve of his paying some of his clients' premiums. Some supporters offer the view that "At least Jerry tried; he didn't just avoid the situation," and he deserves credit for that. Others disagree; in their view Jerry was primarily (even if not exclusively) motivated by the pay he earned. Some students conclude that it is hard to judge: Jerry was "just a kid with more responsibility than he should have had at his age."

Most of you were highly critical of this business. Why should we care if Jerry pays the premiums in such a crooked venture?

You can press the debate further by asking students why we should care about Jerry's paying insurance premiums for a few (nine) policyholders, given their harsh assessment of how Windlass Funerary Eventualities does business. Further, Jerry's actions can be seen as a victimless crime – the premiums are paid, clients are off the hook, and no one (except him) is harmed. Some students agree, asserting that it is hard to argue that the company is being hurt, since it is receiving the premiums anyway. Others object, pointing out that Jerry has created a way of doing business that cannot be sustained except through the good graces of young collection agents, hardly a promising proposition.

Why did Jerry start breaking the rules?

Students will recount the gradual process by which Jerry became aware of the humanity of his clients – the transition from seeing "one composite old black woman" to the recognition of the individual identities of each one. You can deepen the discussion by asking students to articulate the moral or ethical principle that seems to be motivating Jerry: **What changes when we see people as individuals instead of as anonymous members of a group?** Some students assert that morality is based on our ability to acknowledge the humanity of another; that is the start of a moral or ethical relationship with them.

4 UNDERSTANDING JERRY'S RELATIONSHIP WITH MRS BATTLE (20′)

Several factors conspire to change Jerry's perspective on his African-American clients, but chief among them is his relationship with one client, Vesta Lotte Battle. It is of course possible to consider the humanity of others in the abstract, but what is it about a single person that becomes so compelling that it can change the way we think? This melding of the emotional with the rational or cognitive is an ongoing theme in the course, an important grounding for students in the foundation for moral sentiment, decision-making, and action.

What allowed Mrs Battle to influence Jerry so strongly?

The block starts by inviting students to describe how Mrs Battle is able to exercise so much influence over Jerry, a straightforward question that is none the less not easy to answer. How do you describe how one person influences another? How do you know? Physical acts are easiest for students to detail. They describe how Mrs Battle reaches out to Jerry in their first important encounter, ensuring that he gets the help he needs to change the tire on his car (something he did not know how to do). Tea with Mrs Battle becomes a feature of the weekly collection regime, an event Jerry treasures, saved as an end-of-day reward for collecting from the rest of his clients. By the end of their weekly meetings, Jerry uses his own money to bring Mrs Battle's daughter home to be buried, and, after, writes a check for $200 as a donation to a local African-American church. How did these changes occur?

Mrs Battle's extraordinary skill at mending broken china, identified by a sign of a tea-pot with the label "Can Fix," is a metaphor some students use to describe the ways she helps Jerry: Mrs Battle "broke down the barriers between them;" she allowed Jerry "a space in which to define himself;" the dignity she gave to him, he returned to her; "she took the parts of him and made him whole."

The discussion can be extended by asking: **Is this all just embedded in their relationship? Is Mrs Battle compelling on her own? What is the nature of her appeal?** Some attributes of Mrs Battle are easy for students to identify: her dignity, her composure, her honesty, her role as caretaker. Others are evident but harder to understand: How is it, for example, that she becomes a magnet for other people's affection and trust? One answer seems to lie in her individuality and self-sufficiency. People feel safe with someone who is so consistent, so defined; because she makes choices for herself, she can be counted on.

Some of you see Mrs Battle in benign, almost loving terms. Did anyone see her differently?

Amidst the admiration and praise, you will want to create an opening for students who disagree, by asking whether anyone saw Mrs Battle's appeal in different terms. This usually unleashes a number of comments from students who found Mrs Battle manipulative: even as she takes care of other people, she gets them to take care of her. How else to describe why Jerry pays her insurance premiums, and brings her daughter home for burial? The two seem to derive very different satisfactions out of their relationship. Mrs Battle's help to Jerry is largely existential – it helps him begin to define himself. Jerry's help to her is largely instrumental – he helps her, so self-sufficient, in ways that she cannot help herself.

Was the influence of Mrs Battle on Jerry a good impact? Bad impact?

Students are usually split in their assessment of Mrs Battle's influence. Some argue that Jerry becomes a better person, someone who can see, who is more open, who has gained a whole new perspective. Others focus on negative aspects. Jerry "appears to have lost control;" his decisions are "erratic." Rather than having gained a new perspective, he seems to have lost his way and his sense of proportion. "Why should he – such a poor boy – use his own money to pay the weekly premium for non-paying clients?" Even harder to imagine: Why use his own money to bring Mrs Battle's daughter home to be buried, money that he and his family need?

If this relationship is so meaningful to Jerry, why does he include Mrs Battle on the list of non-payers he turns in to his boss, Sam? Even more confusing: if this relationship is so meaningful to Jerry, why does he say he *slept so well* after he turns the list in to Sam?

The discussion is closed by a series of questions that purposefully take the flow in a new direction. These are difficult questions to answer; they require students to empathize with the conflict Jerry faced. It is easy to romanticize Jerry's relationship with Mrs Battle and lose sight of the pressures that forced him to take a job as collection agent: his need to pay for his college education and to support his parents; the limited prospects for employment for a poor boy with no connections. In examining Jerry's actions, students confront an example of a true moral dilemma: Jerry is unable to fulfill conflicting moral commitments to his employer, to Mrs Battle and other non-payers who are caught in an unfair system, to his family, and to himself.

Many students are sympathetic; one observed that "Jerry did more than I might have done under similar circumstances." Others are pragmatic: Jerry's actions were "not sustainable;" in their view it was better for him, the company, and even (some will argue) for the black policyholders if the status of their policies is brought to light.

But these answers don't get to the psychological stresses of the conflict Jerry was living with, and other students will press on. "It's reassuring to give in, even to an uncomfortable position, rather than live with uncertainty and the need to decide each time whether or not to cover the weekly premium for a non-paying policyholder."

> What did Jerry do after he turned in the list of names? Why did he do those things?

The final questions in this block move the action forward, since the story of Jerry the younger does not end with his handing the list of names over to Sam. After this, Jerry avoids Mrs Battle's house, but continues collecting premiums for a few more weeks. During that time his behavior appears to become increasingly erratic. By accident, he comes upon the burial service for Pearl, Mrs Battle's daughter, and is able to talk with Mrs Battle one last time. Later, he discovers that Mrs Battle has died and, apparently in response, he goes to a funeral at a black church for a woman he doesn't know. Overwhelmed by a host of emotions, Jerry makes an offering to the church of the entire amount of his weekly premiums – all the nickels and dimes he has collected – as well as his premium book, and even the keys to his car. When the church's pastor returns the car keys, book, and money to him, he writes a check for $200.00 to pay for a college scholarship for children of the church.

Students are asked to detail these surprising events and to offer their explanations for what Jerry is doing and why he is doing it. Students describe Jerry as in a "damned if you do and damned if you don't situation," in which he is torn between conflicting desires: to help the blacks in Baby Africa, to support his parents, and to pay for his college education – his own way out of a poverty not that different from the African-Americans he collects from. Students acknowledge the inconsistency of his actions, and begin to see these as a logical response, if a torn and divided one, to the situation he finds himself in.

5 EVALUATING JERRY THE ELDER (20′)

Many students come to the course with belief in the "sleep test" as a measure of the moral or ethical rightness of a decision. Recent brain studies show that moral problems stimulate both our emotions and our reasoning powers,[7] so it is not surprising that we feel relief (and sleep well) at the resolution of a problem that causes us emotional distress (such as lying to a boss, or using our own money to cover others' debts, as Jerry did).

At the same time, many moral challenges assume the shape of a moral dilemma – a conflict between opposing principles, commitments, and beliefs, in which a decision favoring one position inevitably means subordinating or even abandoning or repudiating the other. In these situations, as Jerry finds, our early ability to sleep soundly may very well be followed by a period – in his case forty years! – in which the other shoe drops, the one representing the choice we couldn't or didn't make. Our sleeping and waking remain disturbed for the necessary reason that we *could not* satisfy the opposing choices we were faced with.

The last discussion brings students face-to-face with this situation, and asks them to make sense of how Jerry's early decisions affected the person he became, and whether they, like him, end up condemning him for his actions of forty years ago.

As you know, Jerry judges himself harshly in retrospect for the decisions he made. He saw Mrs Battle for the last time at the funeral for her daughter Pearl, whose body Jerry paid to have transported back from Michigan. Jerry recounts Mrs Battle saying to him: "Fact is, been missing you more than we miss it, Assurance. You steadily helped me to find my Pearl, to get her back on here. Don't go fretting none, child, you tried. – You gone be fine. I'm gone be fine."[8] If Mrs Battle can forgive Jerry, why can't he forgive himself?

The first question is meant to re-open the empathy students expressed at the beginning of class, and they will revisit the difficulty of the choice Jerry had to make and the regret that he still feels about it. They ask each other, "Who can give forgiveness – is it only ourselves?" "Does forgiveness from others matter – and how much?" Some students are empathetic: "It's worse *because* she forgave him!" To these students, Mrs Battle's forgiveness – another sign, they believe, of her moral greatness – shows Jerry's betrayal as all the more undeserved, and they understand why it might make his already severe guilt even more painful.

What do we know about what Jerry has done since age nineteen?

Few students respond positively to Jerry the elder, the narrator of the story. It is hard for them to identify with the fifty-nine-year-old near-retiree, and they cut him little, if any, slack. For these reasons, it is useful to ground this discussion in a little context-setting. Students will recall Jerry's accomplishments in the forty years that have elapsed since his stint at Windlass Funerary Eventualities. Jerry didn't just complete college, he went on to obtain a law degree and established a successful small-town legal practice. He achieved financial success by inventing a mechanical device useful to owners of Laundromats (stores with coin-operated washers and dryers). He married "up" to a woman from the part of town he always envied, joined a country club, built an expensive summer home, and fathered two daughters, each successful in her own right.

Jerry says this episode continues to haunt him. In your view, how was Jerry changed by what happened?

A few students observe that Jerry seems changed, at least in part, by his encounter with Mrs Battle and the conflict with Windlass Funerary Eventualities. Jerry opens his own chain of Laundromats to black patrons, even in the racially charged Virginia/Carolina region of the US South, and he volunteers as a consultant in a local brown-lung class-action suit[9] against the cotton mill his parents worked in. But other students protest, noting that Jerry's transformation was hardly complete. Some point out the irony of Jerry making his fortune on Laundromats, another nickel-and-dime operation that provides an essential service to the poor. Others point out the discomfort he feels over the relationship of one of his daughters with an African-American man.

What do you think? Is Jerry too hard on himself? Not hard enough?

You will want to press students to bring together the competing strands of Jerry's life to a final assessment: **Is Jerry too hard on himself? Not hard enough?** Some students support his decisions. "[As a young man] he had three decisions to make: whether to take the job at Windlass; whether to turn in the names of the non-payers; and whether to put Mrs Battle's name on the list. Each one of these decisions are morally defensible – he has no reason to feel bad about what he did." Others feel quite sorry for Jerry: "He'd give anything he had to sleep well for just one night."

But many (often, most) students push back. Jerry could have done even more with his life, given the substantial financial resources he amassed. They criticize his expensive summer home (called "Jerry's Taj Mahal" by his wife), and wonder why, if he felt such regard for Mrs Battle, he should have negative reactions to his daughter living with an African-American man. Other students have difficulty accepting the realistically complex picture of Jerry that emerges: sympathetic to blacks but concerned about the relationship of his daughter with one; guilty about early acts yet willing to make his fortune on a business that serves the poor. These students judge Jerry as fundamentally unchanged, and give little or no credit for later decisions that stem, arguably, from Jerry's early experiences and choices.

How would you characterize the nature of the moral challenge Jerry faced?

When empathy seems in short supply, you can turn to the board, on which the poles of Jerry's choices are laid out, and ask students to characterize the type of moral challenge Jerry faced. Students will usually respond by building on the right-versus-right conflict they encountered in *Antigone*. How, they may ask, is this different?

Usually a member of the class will observe that in *Antigone* the conflict between two rights was between two individuals, each of whom represented one of the "right" positions. Further, while Antigone and Creon were not able to reconcile duty to the gods, duty to family, and duty to the state, students explored in their discussion alternative scenarios that would have allowed all of these duties to be brought into alignment. That Antigone and Creon could not bring about this alignment was characteristic of them, not of their conflict.

Jerry, by contrast, carried the entire conflict inside him, and they will describe the conflict as a "damned if you do, damned if you don't," or "between a rock and a hard place" kind, in which no decision can be made which satisfies the requirements of the conflicting positions. You can offer up the label of a *moral dilemma* as one way to describe a conflict between mutually exclusive moral choices.

Using Jerry as an example, how do people seem to behave in the face of a moral dilemma?

Students return to earlier descriptions of Jerry's vacillating and erratic decisions – trying first to satisfy the needs of Mrs Battle and other non-payers, and then to meet the needs of his parents, his duty to his boss Sam, and his own desire for a college education. And they will return, as well, to his regret that he couldn't do it all.

Some philosophers talk about a *moral residue* that is left behind when we are forced to subordinate one set of moral goals or claims for another. Attitudes of sorrow, regret, and even repentance are to be expected when well-intentioned individuals, who want to live morally responsible lives, are forced to choose between moral goods. The last discussion is meant to expose students to this phenomenon, to help them become more realistic about the emotional toll that moral decisions can take, particularly in situations of moral challenge that take the form of a moral dilemma. The discussion also is meant to remind students of their earlier description of moral choosing as a clumsy, human endeavor, in which perfect certainty, like perfect comfort, is probably not a realistic goal.

Why thanked by Jerry?

Business model of Windlass Funerary Eventualities, Inc.

Jerry the Younger

Jerry the Elder

Figure 6.1 Blessed Assurance *roadmap*

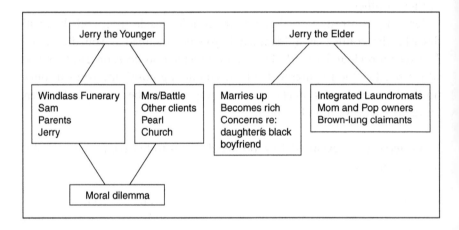

Figure 6.2 Blessed Assurance *board plan*

NOTES

1   A. Gurganus, "Blessed Assurance: A Moral Tale," in *White People*, New York: Vintage Contemporaries, 1990, p. 197.
2   Ibid., p. 200.
3   Ibid., pp. 210–211.
4   See the special issue of *Social Justice Research*, 2004, vol. 17, no. 2, for a literature/field review and new findings in the study, by social psychologists, of "ordinary unethical behavior" resulting from unconscious and therefore largely uncontrolled bias.
5   A moral dilemma is a situation in which "an agent believes that, on moral grounds, he or she is obligated to perform two (or more) mutually exclusive actions. In a moral dilemma of this form, one or more moral norms obligate an agent to do *x* and one or more moral norms obligate the agent to do *y*, but the agent cannot do both in the same circumstance." T. L. Beauchamp and J. F. Childress,

Principles of Biomedical Ethics, Oxford and New York: Oxford University Press, 2001, p. 10.

6   A highly likely occurrence, as detailed in the background in the student textbook.
7   See, for example, Joshua D. Greene, R. Brian Somerville, Leigh E. Nystrom, John M. Darley, and Jonathan D. Cohen, "An fMRI Investigation of Emotional Engagement in Moral Judgment," *Science*, 2000, vol. 293, 2105–2108.
8   Gurganus, op. cit., p. 230.
9   Class-action lawsuit: A lawsuit in which the court authorizes a single person or small group of people to represent the interests of a large group. Bryan A. Garner (ed.), *Black's Law Dictionary,* 8th edn, St. Paul, Minn.: Thompson West, 2004, p. 267.

Chapter 7

Things Fall Apart
The challenge of new principles

OKONKWO WAS CLEARLY cut out for great things. He was still young but had won fame as the greatest wrestler in the nine villages. He was a wealthy farmer and had two barns full of yams, and had just married his third wife. To crown it all he had taken two titles and had shown incredible prowess in two inter-tribal wars. And so although Okonkwo was still young, he was already one of the greatest men of his time. Age was respected among his people, but achievement was revered. As the elders said, if a child washed his hands he could eat with kings. Okonkwo had clearly washed his hands and so he ate with kings and elders.[1]

. . .

As the palm wine was drunk one of the oldest members of the *umunna* rose to thank Okonkwo:

"If I say that we did not expect such a big feast I will be suggesting that we did not know how openhanded our son, Okonkwo, is. We all know him, and we expected a big feast. But it turned out to be even bigger than we expected. Thank you. May all you took out return again tenfold. It is good in these days when the younger generation consider themselves wiser than their sires to see a man doing things in the grand, old way . . . You may ask why I am saying all this. I say it because I fear for the younger generation, for you people." He waved his arm where most of the young men sat. "As for me, I have only a short while to live, and so have Uchendu and Unachukukwu and Emefo. But I fear for you young people because you do not understand how strong is the bond of kinship. You do not know what it is to speak with one voice. And what is the result? An abominable religion has settled among you. A man can now leave his father and his brothers. He can curse the gods of his fathers and his ancestors, like a hunter's dog that suddenly goes mad and turns on its master. I fear for you; I fear for the clan." He turned again to Okonkwo and said: "Thank you for calling us together."[2]

THINGS FALL APART: THEMES AND QUESTIONS

The challenge of new principles

Things Fall Apart closes the module on Moral Challenge by posing a funda-mental question: **What happens to moral beliefs when they are challenged by a set of new and different principles?** Can beliefs and value systems become obsolete? Are all value systems an artifact of their time and place, or do universally valid ethical principles exist? These questions are central to Chinua Achebe's novel about the conflict between the Umofia, an Ibo clan of Nigeria, and Christian missionaries and governing officials who arrive as part of the expansion of English colonial interests at the turn of the twentieth century. In the prior three stories, the general context stayed largely the same for the duration of the action, but here we have a story about a context shift, a dramatic change in circumstances that affects the very nature of beliefs and principles that are used to guide action.

Culture, beliefs, and choice

The story is focused on Okonkwo, an ambitious and flawed "great man" whose personal struggles allow students to take a detailed look at an attempt to hold on to established values in the midst of enormous changes.

Some of the practices of the Umofia are abhorrent to a modern sensibility, raising the question of **how culturally and historically bounded our beliefs might be at any time.** But the book also lays out the dangers of taking too simple a view of such a system of beliefs – on what it requires of adherents, and how much room there is within it for individual choice.

Relatives and fellow tribesmen question Okonkwo's interpretations of what the clan's belief system demands. These challenges represent important qualifications to the concept of a value system, suggesting that **a system of beliefs requires interpretation in individual situations,** and that **there exists room for nuanced reasoning and limit setting on personal action within its boundaries.**

The particular stamp Okonkwo puts on the clan's religion is a result of his own personal history, and, as in *Blessed Assurance,* the novel allows students to examine **the interplay between history, the self, and belief.** Our principles come from somewhere, and while Okonkwo's guiding beliefs are founded on the clan's traditions it is clear that he shapes these principles for action in ways that will allow him to repudiate the values and life of his father. Okonkwo's character reprises the intransigence and single-minded thinking that dominated the principal actors in *Antigone,* again raising the question of whether one can hold strongly to values and still be flexible.

93

Beliefs in changing times

The challenges to Umofia values and practices are more than personal and intra-tribal, and the story gradually evolves into a clash of beliefs between the clan and the Christian missionaries. Here students confront some of the hardest questions faced by individuals looking to lead a morally responsible life: **Do universal ethical principles exist?** And **How might I know whether my own beliefs and principles have such universal validity?**

Achebe is even-handed in describing the conflict in beliefs that underscores the story, building sympathy for the clan and its way of life even as clan members challenge practices such as letting twins, who are believed to be evil, die at birth. These challenges take the form of increasingly overt action as the missionaries and imported government gain in strength. At the same time, the dark side of colonialism and missionary principles and behavior are depicted, leaving students with a nuanced view of rights and wrongs on both sides, of **moral complexity.**

Strategies for action

The story also continues the exploration of strategies for action, for moral behavior and choice, and raises the question: **How are the proponents of beliefs expected to navigate a changing terrain?** Three different strategies are shown: Okonkwo's steadfast loyalty to the clan's way of life, leading to suicide when that way of life appears to be lost; the actions of his friend Oberieka, a "thinking man" who attempts to reason his way through the challenges; and the response of Okonkwo's son Nwoye, whose profound uneasiness with some of the clan's practices leads him to join the missionaries. Choices are also presented in the two missionaries who feature in the story, between Mr Brown's reasonableness, curiosity, and attempt to meet the tribe on its own terms, and Mr Smith's muscular, divisive, and confrontational tactics. Each of these strategies exacts costs on the actor, and none of them produces fully satisfactory results.

Finally, the story raises disturbing, equilibrium-shaking questions: **How would *we* know if we are the Umofia – if it is our beliefs and values that should be questioned?** and **How might we want to be treated if we were?** Achebe does not attempt to resolve the question of beliefs in changing times, but rather lays out the options for students, who will certainly face similar challenges in their own lives.

STUDENT ASSIGNMENT

READING: *Things Fall Apart*, by Chinua Achebe.

1 How would you describe the evolution of Okonkwo's character through the story?

2 How do you assess his actions?

3 How would you describe the evolution of Umofia's culture?

4 What can we learn from this story?

5 What kind of moral challenge is this?

CLASS PLAN OUTLINE: DISCUSSION BLOCKS

1 Why Did Okonkwo Choose to Die? (30')

2 Examining Alternative Strategies for Action (20')

3 What Are We to Learn from This Story? (35')

4 What Kind of Moral Challenge Is This? (20')

CLASS PLAN OVERVIEW

Each of the classes in the module on Moral Challenge requires students to move beyond their immediate context and historical time. Of the four texts, *Things Fall Apart* requires the most extensive use of moral imagination, even for students from Africa, I have frequently had in class.

Students are curious about the norms for discussing a book in which a young boy is killed to settle a tribal conflict, twins are exposed to die after birth, and a steady, heavy-handed misogynist viewpoint affects many, but not all, family and social relations. These practices make the debate in *Blessed Assurance* about a young white man's collecting insurance premiums from poor black policyholders look comparatively uncontroversial. Concerns about discussing race are compounded by worries about weighing in on another culture's beliefs and practices; students wonder what kind of permission they have to proceed.

The pedagogical sequencing of describe/analyze/judge bears full fruit in this class. The question sequence requires increasingly detailed description and analysis of the behavior, intent, and principles of the characters, giving students time to digest and understand the actions of the Umofia clan and the missionaries and English authorities.

Student judgments are consequently more measured and thoughtful. At the same time, the class plan reinforces the view that, in the end, moral judgment of the characters is not just tolerated but required. Achebe has written a story in which it is difficult to approve fully of any of the main actors. There is blame to be found for all, and the sparce prose and lean descriptions make it easy to find room for personal judgment.

Since the story's core theme is a clash between cultures, practices, and beliefs, the one student reaction you may be required to address is an attempt to bar discussion of the clan's practices on the grounds that only people from that culture can judge it. This view, once offered by a Nigerian student, had a predictably chilling effect on class discussion.

I have found three responses possible. First, is to ask the class to respond to the premise that only members of a culture or group can criticize its practices and beliefs. *What would be the consequences of such an assumption? Is it viable in a world of differing beliefs?*

Second, is to extend this line of questioning to the course itself. *What would be the implications, for this class and its learning, of accepting such a view?* This question might first be put to the student who raises the initial objection, requiring a defense of the position, and hopefully helping him or her understand the closing off of class learning that would come from accepting that position. Other students could then be engaged, allowing a broader debate on the merits of allowing differing judgments to be expressed.

A third option is to address the issue directly yourself, laying out ground rules for the discussion in your introduction, during class as the situation requires, or clarifying your own viewpoint in summary remarks.

I prefer to allow the subject to come up organically as part of the class discussion, but, depending on how you read your group, you may choose to take a preemptive approach and address the question at the beginning of class.

INTRODUCTION

A way of opening the discussion

Things Fall Apart raises a question for us as a group: Is it appropriate to be critical of various practices engaged in by Okonkwo and the Umofia? There is a serious debate between a universal view of ethics – which posits standards that can be applied to actions across time and space, and moral relativism – the view that we cannot judge moral systems that arise from a different context from our own. We shall not resolve this debate for all time, but we need a point of view in this course on what subjects are and are not off limits for discussion.

I suggest we apply a commonsense guideline of the kind you would expect to find in a course dedicated to an exploration of moral leadership. That guideline would say that all of the characters, actions, belief systems, and ethics we find in our readings are well within the boundaries of our discussions.

I appreciate the sensitivity you have shown, and your evident desire to be respectful of each other. And I expect that our discussions will continue to reflect a sincere effort to put ourselves into the context of the characters we encounter – truly to understand the world they inhabit and the values they subscribe to.

But I believe that the path to moral leadership lies in the ability to think, talk about, and debate complex and even troubling issues. So let's move forward and take the same approach in class that we shall hopefully take when we leave here, and learn to put these kinds of issues on the table for reasoned analysis and debate.

How do you pronounce those names?

You will want to begin class by asking students to practice saying out loud the names of the principal characters and groups from *Things Fall Apart*. One of the main lessons of the *Blessed Assurance* class is that a moral relationship begins by acknowledging the humanity of another. At a minimum, this recognition is demonstrated through the use of someone else's real or proper name. (The antithesis is also true – recall the use of numbers to identify individuals in prisons and in concentration camps, and other unfortunately common methods of dehumanizing others by calling them by names other than the ones they would use for themselves.)

I write the characters' names on the board before class, and explain that we want to avoid dodgy references ("I can't really say his name"). Without great seriousness, I ask students to pronounce the names together. The following phonetic guide is somewhat accurate based on guidance offered by Nigerian students and those who have spent time in the country. The purpose of this exercise is comfort and a willingness to use the Ibo names, regardless of the actual pronunciation offered by the student.

Okonkwo = Ookungwo
Nwoye = Nooya
Obierika = Oberreeka
Ikememfuna = Eekaymayfoona
Umofia = Oomofwa.

1 WHY DID OKONKWO CHOOSE TO DIE? (30′)

The *Blessed Assurance* class sets the table for *Things Fall Apart* by allowing students to attain some measure of comfort in discussing the issue of race. The first block in this class goes even further, allowing the group to approach the subject matter of *Things Fall Apart* with sympathy. The question **"Why did Okonkwo choose to die?"** asks students to find value in the Ibo clan's way of life, even if just for Okonkwo; by so doing, they begin to appreciate the depth of commitment that can be formed to a set of beliefs and practices very different from their own.

While the dominant experience may be distance and discomfort, some students find the act of engaging with the culture of Umofia to be an experience of development and growth. I have had several report the care with which they looked up every new word in the glossary of Ibo words and phrases provided by Achebe; these students view the novel as an opportunity to push their own appreciation for different ways of living.

Questions driving the discussion are in bold

In the previous classes we spent a fair amount of time trying to understand why the principal characters behaved the way they did. Let's get right to the culminating act of this story: Why do you think Okonkwo chose to die?

There are many reasons why Okonkwo may have decided to commit suicide, and students do a good job of exploring and articulating their interpretation of his motives and possible goals. They note the accumulation of humiliation over time, beginning with Okonkwo's return from exile when he finds that few, if any, of the Umofia care about his status and family accomplishments as they once did; to his son's defection from the tribe to join the missionaries; to degrading encounters with representatives of the colonial authority, who beat and starve Okonkwo and other clan leaders.

Okonkwo was willing to be exiled for seven years in punishment for inadvertently killing a fellow clansman. Why would such a dutiful follower of the clan's way of life be willing to break the prohibition against suicide?

"He recognizes that he is unable to adapt – he can't live in this new world," "He decides not to live in this new world." Given the brutal and locked-in character of Okonkwo, many students are surprisingly empathetic, holding the view that everything that gave Okonkwo's life meaning no longer mattered.

As one student put it, "No one cared whether Okonkwo's father had been weak, emotional, and a debtor, so Okonkwo's lifelong efforts to shape himself in opposition to his father were now unimportant and a waste." Another attributed noble motives to Okonkwo, "He died defending the tribe, taking the punishment on himself so they wouldn't be punished [for killing a colonial messenger – which Okonkwo had done]."

Is it possible Okonkwo felt he wouldn't be seen as breaking a prohibition? How flexibly do members of the clan interpret their duties?

Students will readily distinguish the practices of Umofia from those that are unique to Okonkwo, stemming from his history, personal characteristics, and life goals. Popularly referred to as "Roaring Flame," Okonkwo puts a particular stamp on his actions, looking always to be the most violent, the strongest, and the most assertive bearer of clan values and practices. In his personal life Okonkwo has a nearly ungovernable temper, which causes him to break clan rules inadvertently and at times to act with a careless disregard for the priority others hold for sacred moments and practices.

It is particularly useful to ask students how restrictive or flexible the clan's belief system is. In one of the central acts of the story, Okonkwo is advised by the clan's oldest member, a well-respected, fearless leader and warrior, to "not bear a hand" in the killing of Ikemefuna, the boy taken from another clan to settle a conflict and who Okonkwo had raised for three years, on the grounds that "that boy calls you his father."[3] This injunction is later repeated by Okonkwo's friend Obierika, who tells Okonkwo, "But if the Oracle said that my son should be killed I would neither dispute it nor be the one to do it."[4] The advice introduces an important concept: individual choice and personal responsibility are still expected within a well-specified set of communal beliefs, and distinctions can be made between what is obligatory and what is permissible.

Is Okonkwo making a statement? If so, what is this statement about?

Many students believe that Okonkwo's suicide was intentional – a deliberated act, and several ascribe to him a desire to have his death convey a message to the clan. They describe this message in various ways: "To show the clan what has fallen apart;" "to show that a great man can no longer live under the conditions the clan has accepted." Others disagree, noting Okonkwo's inability to control his temper, and describe his act as nothing more than a lashing out, similar to many such actions detailed in the novel.

Did Okonkwo change during the course of the story? If so, how?

You can ask students to decide whether Okonkwo changed during the course of the story – whether his suicide was the logical conclusion of a change process, or something more random. Some students point to Okonkwo's treatment of his two sons as evidence of change: early in the story he insists on participating in the murder of his fostered son, Ikemefuna, despite the arguments from fellow tribesmen cited above, while later, near the end of the novel, he listens to those who persuade him to stop his furious attacks on Nwoye, stimulated by the boy's attraction to the missionaries. Some students also claim that Okonkwo changed himself to adapt to the tribe's requirements: "He *made himself* participate in the killing of Ikemefuna; he *made himself* go into exile" – these were acts of will, not of blind obedience.

We've spent some time describing and analyzing this act now for assessment. How do you judge what Okonkwo did?

Students express a wide range of judgments of Okonkwo's suicide: "If the goal was change, it wasn't very effective;" "it seemed to be a waste;" "it was in violation of the clan's beliefs and therefore wrong;" "it was a rash and angry act, of a piece with many other actions by Okonkwo;" it was "selfish and cowardly, leaving Okonkwo's family and friends to contend with the consequences."

Did Okonkwo have to act as he did? How much of a choice do you believe he had?

Many students see Okonkwo's suicide as purely volitional – something that could have easily been avoided by someone of a different temperament, history, and view of himself. But others counter that the many changes in the context of the clan, and in particular the subordinated status that its members now play in their own land, made the suicide all but inevitable, particularly for someone as proud and tradition-bound as Okonkwo. Okonkwo had tried to rally the clan against the colonial authorities, but failed, and at that point "he had no choice – no other action was possible since he wasn't supported by the clan."

2 EXAMINING ALTERNATIVE STRATEGIES FOR ACTION (20′)

Many students convince themselves and others that Okonkwo *had to* commit suicide, that anyone in his position would be forced to do so, owing to the lack of options he faced. This leads, naturally, to a discussion of strategies adopted by other members of the Umofia clan in response to the coming of the missionaries and colonial authorities.

If Okonkwo's suicide was so inevitable, why didn't his friend Obierika kill himself?

Students readily recognize that Obierika is depicted in *Things Fall Apart* as "a man who thought about things," someone who is in many ways a foil to the volatile Okonkwo. Even among matters of clan practices and beliefs, Obierika is capable of nuanced reasoning as demonstrated in the example cited earlier.[5] Students see Obierika as a realist who tries to adapt to the new conditions of the clan, or, at least, as someone who chooses his battles. A man of moderate temperament, he is not driven to extreme acts as Okonkwo was, and suicide was, of all acts, an abomination to the Umofia.

Many students are attracted to the mild and reasonable Obierika; one student described him as "ahead of his time, questioning the ways of the tribe even before the missionaries came," and they defend his actions as "thoughtful" and "more pragmatic" than those of Okonkwo. Others challenge his stance, describing Obierika as "cowardly for not killing himself," as someone who "caved in" and who deserves blame. His actions are most strongly challenged on the basis of utility, since his inaction and accommodations are no more successful in helping the clan than Okonkwo's aggression and suicide; some students argue that Obierika's (and others') willingness to give in to the missionaries and to the colonial powers doomed the clan.

There is a third choice, the one taken by Okonkwo's son Nwoye who, responding to the same circumstances as Okonkwo and Obierika, joins the missionaries. What do you make of Nwoye's decision? Why did he do what he did?

Nwoye is harder for the students to identify with. They understand that he is driven by questions he could not satisfactorily answer about the most violent of the clan's practices; at the same time, they don't know quite what to make of his choice to join the missionaries. Missionary-educated himself, Achebe uses the character of Nwoye to depict the yearning that some of the Ibo felt for a new system of beliefs, and even though Nwoye's defection from the clan reflects students' negative judgment of many Umofia beliefs and practices, there is none the less a whiff of disapproval among them. "Was he simply too weak to participate in a struggle against the missionaries?" Repudiating the clan seems disloyal and hard to justify, even in the face of practices that Achebe surely intends the reader to disapprove of.

Students' inability immediately to praise Nwoye's defection is testimony to the fairness and clarity of Achebe's description of life among the Ibo clan – the way that it is described as not just exotic or an anachronism, but as having beauty, community, understandable values, and coherence.

3 WHAT ARE WE TO LEARN FROM THIS STORY? (35′)

The preceding discussions lay the groundwork for this discussion, in which students are invited to consider various lessons that can be taken from *Things Fall Apart*. The discussion builds out from Okonkwo and the Umofia clan, to the missionaries, to more general lessons prompted by the novel.

Achebe presents us with three choices: Okonkwo's suicide; Obierika's accommodation; and Nwoye's joining the missionaries. What is Achebe trying to tell us? What are we to learn from this story about choices and moral action in the midst of change?

You can focus this discussion by laying out on the board the three choices that Achebe presents in the text: Okonkwo/Resist; Obierika/Accommodate; Nwoye/Join.

Are any of these choices presented as better than the other?

Students grapple with an uncomfortable truth: nearly all conceivable reactions to the coming of the missionaries and colonial authorities are described, yet none appears to be fully satisfactory, either to the character or in terms of the consequences it produces.

Okonkwo and Nwoye appear to have followed their conscience, yet one has done so by violating a rule of conduct and turning himself into an outcast, beyond even the normal rites of burial, while the other has found peace by turning his back on all he knew before. And the middle stance, accommodation, appears no better – even a "thinking man" cannot find a way out of this situation.

The powerlessness of the Umofia in the face of superior colonial force, technology, and will to dominate is dismaying, and students struggle to find a metric – some yardstick to use to evaluate these three courses of action. Are they all really failures? What does success look like in a confrontation with another set of beliefs and governing principles?

How should we add the two missionaries into this schema? There seems to be two pairings: Okonkwo with Mr Smith and Obierika with Mr Brown.

These pairings aren't as we would expect, black with black, and white with white. What are we to take from this – what is Achebe conveying with these unusual combinations?

It is useful to separate the power imbalance inherent in any colonial struggle from the clash of principles, ideals, and ways of life between the Ibo and the British. The ability of one group forcibly to subdue the other is not in itself demonstration of a superior philosophy, or culture, or guiding beliefs. For our purposes, the heart of the story is the view from the inside – the question of whether one should ever allow one's own principles to be subjected to inquiry and change.

In this regard, you will want to broaden the discussion by asking students to add the two missionaries into the schema of choice and action. Thoughtful students readily see that there are two pairings: Okonkwo and Mr Smith – unyielding, uncompromising, confrontive, who see the world as battle; and Obierika and Mr Brown – thinking men who are curious about "the other," and who look for ways to let competing worldviews coexist.

This unusual pairing of opposites, black with white rather than black with black and white with white, appears to signal that these are characteristic approaches that can be taken, not culture-specific, but person-specific. Achebe thus opens the door to choice, showing that even in extreme circumstances when adherents of differing views face each other (or, perhaps, most importantly in these situations) rival paths lay before us, one path is of tolerance, coexistence, and voluntary change; the other is its opposite: intolerance, uniformity, and forcible conversion.

Of course you knew I'd ask this: What fell apart?

The discussion then moves to the broader question of "What fell apart?" Students usually refer to the quote from the W. B. Yeats poem "The Second Coming" that serves as the epigraph to *Things Fall Apart*:

> Turning and turning in the widening gyre
> The falcon cannot hear the falconer;
> Things fall apart; the centre cannot hold;
> Mere anarchy is loosed upon the world.

Students answer the question of what fell apart by describing the loss of a way of life, and inability, for some, to change.

Are we supposed to approve of the Umofia clan and its culture? Is the message that wife beating, exposing twins, killing individual children is OK? Or is this a culture that deserved to pass on?

This in turn allows students to be asked what stance they believe Achebe wants us to take to this passing of a culture. One American student who had spent time in Nigeria asserted, "Achebe does not want us to judge this culture, he wants us to understand it. His goal was to help Africa understand what had happened to her." Others interpret the message as a kind of "yes, but," in which the Umofia way of life would be seen as inevitably and rightly bowing to what the students perceive as historical and cultural progress, but where there would none the less be a sense of sadness and loss at a way of life that has passed.

Are we supposed to approve of the missionaries or condemn them?

You can challenge this somewhat comforting conclusion by asking students whether Achebe similarly meant for us to approve of – or condemn – the missionaries. Here many students become uncomfortable, recognizing the role the missionaries played in the conversion, forcible as well as voluntary, of the Ibo. One asked, "Does anyone really have the right to try to change the views of another?" Other students explore the tactics, "What might be permissible, even if this were OK to do?"

So what general lessons do you take from this story?

"Usually strong beliefs are a good thing, but here it appears they are not. I'm confused: is strength willingness to allow others to hold to their beliefs, or keeping to my own?"

"My people were dominated by the Turks for centuries and shouldn't have been. You do need to resist, or you'll just be run over."

"We actually need both of these approaches in organizations: thinking – for strategy, like Obierika, and acting – for execution, like Okonkwo."

"We all have some of Okonkwo and Oberieka in us. I'm most worried about my own rigidity – the rules I follow without questioning, without deciding if that is what I want to do."

4 WHAT KIND OF MORAL CHALLENGE IS THIS? (20')

This discussion provides students with practice in identifying and characterizing a type of moral challenge – a necessary preface, as they have seen, to thinking about how the challenge should be addressed. Despite the fact that the challenge is clearly labeled in the student textbook as "the challenge of new principles," students do not feel particularly bound by that description (this is a good thing) and enjoy developing their own perspective on the type of moral challenge that is laid out in *Things Fall Apart*. The final questions, in which you ask students to explore the challenge as if they were the Umofia, and not the colonial powers, are the most important part of the class.

So what kind of moral challenge is this?

Some students defend the characterization of the challenge as a challenge of new ideas, "values and things I hadn't thought about before." Others build on that idea, describing the challenge in institutional terms as "the problem that emerges when there is no mechanism in place for two sides to resolve their conflict – no common framework or way to bridge the gap between them." Some students dispute the description of two sides as too simple, "This is a conflict between two cultures – each of which has great variety within them."

Other students describe the challenge as a conflict of right versus wrong: "The way the missionaries came in was wrong; they were wrong to impose their views." Not surprisingly, students reference current events: "This reminds me of the US and Iraq – who is to say if the democratic principles we are imposing on them are right or not? We won't know for 100 years." And others see the challenge as raising a fundamental question: "Do universal ethical principles exist?"

There are other interpretations, and the variety is healthy for the class, showing a willingness on the part of students to build skills in characterizing types of moral challenge and in learning how to describe, and defend, their perspective to others.

How would we ever know if *we* are the Umofia – if it is our values and beliefs that should be challenged? And how would we want to be treated if we were?

As a transition to this last set of powerful questions, you can observe that, while many descriptions can apply to the situation in *Things Fall Apart*, it can be seen as describing a challenge to the very foundation of beliefs and principles of a group, a challenge to their view of what a moral life should be based on. You can then ask the students to divide into small buzz groups to prepare answers to the two questions: **How would we ever know if we are the Umofia? How would we want to be treated if we were?**

One student responded, "It's always helpful to think of oneself as the Umofia, but (unlike Okonkwo) you need to be open to different ideas and perspectives." Others extend this idea, advising listening to the dispossessed and to other outsiders for the perspective they can offer on what is wrong, or should be questioned, in a given society. Another student suggested looking for underlying ethical *principles* or *values* that groups have in common, rather than focusing on *practices* that may differ.

In this discussion, students are asked to consider the purpose and process of a morally responsible life. Few believe that it is possible to not judge, since that would imply that all principles and behavior are morally acceptable, and students don't believe that. But students recognize that the need to judge brings other obligations – the need for tolerance, for respect, and for finding ways to bridge seemingly incompatible ways of thinking, believing, and acting.

And, if students can see themselves as members of the Umofia and not as the outside force, the question is squarely put on the table that it may be *our views* that require change, that it is *we* who might need to be open to engagement. That is a tougher conclusion to accept; and even, while they acknowledge the usefulness of the question, many students are made uncomfortable by the loss of certainty and tolerance for ambiguity that such a stance requires.

How can we know if the values we use for moral decisions are sound, and if the process we use for reasoning through moral challenges is a good one? These questions are taken up in the next module, on Moral Reasoning.

Why did Okonkwo commit suicide?

Alternative strategies for action

What are we to learn from this story?

What kind of moral challenge is this?

Figure 7.1 Things Fall Apart *roadmap*

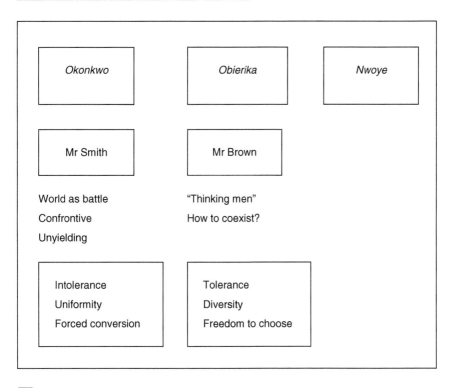

Figure 7.2 *Things Fall Apart board plan*

NOTES

1   Chinua Achebe, *Things Fall Apart*, New York: Anchor Books, 1994, p. 8.
2   Ibid., pp. 166–167.
3   Ibid., p. 57.
4   Ibid., p. 67.
5   "If the Oracle said that my son should be killed I would neither dispute it nor be the one to do it."

Moral Reasoning Class Plans

Moral Reasoning Module Map: Themes and Learning Points

Central theme	Text and setting	Storyline	Learning points
Reasoning from moral theory	*Trifles*, by Susan Glaspell Early twentieth-century rural America "Moral Theories," from *Principles of Biomedical Ethics*, Tom L. Beauchamp and James F. Childress	Two friends must decide whether to help a farm wife accused of murdering her husband	Moral analysis Mounting a morally defended argument The danger of unconscious assumptions
Reasoning from personal perspective	*The Sweet Hereafter*, by Russell Banks Contemporary America	Four individuals respond in the aftermath of a school bus accident	One event – many viewpoints Moral logic versus legal logic Emotion in moral reasoning
Reasoning from a moral code	*The Remains of the Day*, by Kazuo Ishiguro Britain between world wars	A butler reckons with the consequences of a life in service to a British lord	The limits of agency Benefits and drawbacks of fixed beliefs Balancing professional and personal commitments
Reasoning from multiple moralities	*A Man for All Seasons*, by Robert Bolt Sixteenth-century England	Sir Thomas More looks for a way to reconcile duty to King, religion, family, and self	Making good on multiple obligations Capacity for complexity and tolerance for ambiguity Constitutive commitments

Chapter 8

Trifles

Reasoning from moral theory

COUNTY ATTORNEY: And what did Mrs. Wright do when she knew that you had gone for the coroner?

HALE: She moved from that chair to this one over here (*pointing to a small chair in the corner*) and just sat there with her hands held together and looking down. I got a feeling that I ought to make some conversation, so I said I had come in to see if John wanted to put in a telephone, and at that she started to laugh, and then she stopped and looked at me – scared. (*The* COUNTY ATTORNEY, *who has had his notebook out, makes a note*) I dunno, maybe it wasn't scared. I wouldn't like to say it was. Soon Harry got back, and then Dr. Lloyd came, and you, Mr. Peters, and so I guess that's all I know that you don't.

COUNTY ATTORNEY: (*Looking around*) I guess we'll go upstairs first – and then out to the barn and around there. (*To the* SHERIFF) You're convinced that there was nothing important here – nothing that would point to any motive.

SHERIFF: Nothing here but kitchen things.

(*The* COUNTY ATTORNEY, *after again looking around the kitchen, opens the door of a cupboard closet. He gets up on a chair and looks on a shelf. Pulls his hand away, sticky.*)

COUNTY ATTORNEY: Here's a nice mess.

(*The women draw nearer.*)

MRS. PETERS: (*To the other woman*) Oh, her fruit; it did freeze. (*To the* LAWYER) She worried about that when it turned so cold. She said the fire'd go out and her jars would break.

SHERIFF: Well, can you beat the woman! Held for murder and worryin' about her preserves.

COUNTY ATTORNEY: I guess before we're through she may have something more serious than preserves to worry about.

HALE: Well, women are used to worrying over trifles.[1]

TRIFLES: THEMES AND QUESTIONS

Moral challenges require moral reasoning

The *Trifles* class introduces the module on **Moral Reasoning**. By this point in the course students have begun to acquire some facility in recognizing and debating the nature of moral challenges and the strategies that are chosen to come to terms with them. The deeper they go in this endeavor, however, the clearer it becomes that these challenges are, in fact, quite complex.

Simply having principles to rely on does not help Antigone and Creon, since they each start from a different moral conviction and neither set of underlying beliefs – on the surface at least – is demonstrably wrong. In *Blessed Assurance* students see that we sometimes find ourselves in situations in which we operate under conflicting moral imperatives, imperatives that it is impossible to satisfy in the same act. Okonkwo's predicament may be the most troubling of all, since it introduces the possibility that new principles might arise that call into question the values and practices we have been following, perhaps for generations or more, and that our own beliefs might legitimately be challenged.

These are hard problems, without easy answers, and students are responsive to the focus of this new module, in which we explore how we make decisions about moral problems and whether there are methods or tools to help us systematically think them through. The *Trifles* class is an introduction to this topic, and is structured to accomplish two related goals.

How we reason

To attain substantive skill in moral reasoning, we first have to become aware of *how we reason*, that is, how we take in data about the world around us, and draw conclusions from what we see, understand, and believe. The first goal for this class is to provide a forum for reflection, a situation in which students' reasoning processes are laid bare for examination, so they can think about *how* they think.

How to reason morally

The second goal is to provide students with an opportunity to experience what it feels like to reason from a particular point of view – to mount an argument that is based on a specific moral perspective. When we reason morally, we apply moral criteria to the search for morally defensible actions, or to the evaluation of actions already taken. It is not just any kind of argumentation, but a particular kind; this class is designed to give students first-hand experience with making arguments that are defended by moral rationales.

The role of assumptions in moral decision-making

The literary text for this class is only eleven pages long, the equivocal play *Trifles* by Susan Glaspell. By its very brevity, *Trifles* will enable students to analyze the ways in which their own assumptions shape the judgments they form. Like the characters in the play, students piece bits of fact together and weave theories about the motives and actions of the characters. This intermingling of fact and assumption is untangled in class, giving students a concrete example of **the dangers of unconscious and unexamined assumptions in moral decision-making.**

Four moral theories

Accompanying the play is a reading, roughly forty pages long, which describes four moral theories. The assignment for students is either to justify or critique the actions of the play's two female protagonists, using one of the four moral theories in the reading to make their case. The class is described to students as **an exercise in moral reasoning, an opportunity to apply a moral theory systematically to a question of moral action.** The assignment requires students to use a single framework consistently for resolving a moral problem. Most students are unused to the discipline of arguing from a particular moral point of view, and the exercise is an important learning event, helping to build **first-hand familiarity with the act of moral reasoning,** what it feels like and sounds like to both the person making the argument and the person receiving it.

The reading comes from a text on practical moral reasoning, *Principles of Biomedical Ethics*, which is written for practitioners in the fields of medical care, biomedical research, and healthcare management. The descriptions students read were developed to help practitioners make decisions in situations involving biomedical problems with moral or ethical stakes.

How should I decide what is right to do?

The four moral theories each answer the question: **"How should I decide what is right to do?"** and students see "right" translated into different modes of reasoning or categories of analysis and justification. Within the broad general question, the theories differ in the specific questions they pose: **Will my action produce morally good *consequences*?** (Utilitarianism, or consequence-based theory). **Does my action allow me to fulfill basic *duties or obligations*?** (Kantianism or obligation-based theory). **Do I need to consider the *rights* of people my decision affects?** (Liberal individualism or rights-based theory). **How does my decision affect the interests of the *community* of which I am part?** (Communitarianism or community-based theory).

113

The reading is clear yet doesn't over-simplify the concepts; students without any background in moral philosophy experience no evident difficulty in grasping the essential points of the different theories. In fact, for many there is a sense of relief to see concepts they have previously thought about in general terms more specifically defined. No prior knowledge of the moral philosophies is required to participate in the class, or to teach it successfully.

The value of multiple moral perspectives

Somewhat to their amazement, the application of the theories in class allows students to understand that **plausible arguments can be made from a variety of** *different moral* **perspectives.** They see the strengths and limitations of each of the moral theories, since some prove to be more relevant to the situation in *Trifles* than others; each theory is also tested by how easy or hard it is to use to persuade others of one's own point of view. The exercise thus introduces students to **the value of systematic and disciplined thinking in moral reasoning,** and also to the perspective that **it is helpful to use multiple categories for moral inquiry and analysis,** since each theory sheds a different light on the actions taken by the play's actors.

STUDENT ASSIGNMENT

READINGS: *Trifles,* by Susan Glaspell. Student Textbook: Excerpts from Chapter 8, "Moral Theories," from *Principles of Biomedical Ethics,* by Tom L. Beauchamp and James F. Childress.

1   The four moral theories in the reading represent fundamental categories for moral reflection and decision-making. Be prepared to summarize each of them briefly.

2   Do you approve or disapprove of the actions taken by the two women in *Trifles*? Using just one of the four moral theories, make a case for either justifying or criticizing what they did. Be prepared to defend your case in class.

CLASS PLAN OUTLINE: DISCUSSION BLOCKS

1   Review of the Four Moral Theories (30′)

2   Application of Theories to *Trifles* (35′)

3   Separating Facts from Assumptions (30′)

4   Reflections on Moral Reasoning (10′)

CLASS PLAN OVERVIEW

This class is one of the most enjoyable of the course to teach. It is conducted as an exercise, and students are even given name cards as they enter class to identify the position that they will take on the actions of the two characters – Mrs Peters and Mrs Hale – and the moral framework they will use for their argument (for example, "Obligation – Critique" or "Consequences – Justify"). This change in pace is welcome, even as students are somewhat flustered by the need actually to choose one or another of the theories to work from, ("You mean I really have to choose just one?").

Students grasp many of the basic points of the four moral theories, but I have none the less found it helpful to begin the class by asking them to summarize their understanding of each of the theories. This allows me to use the members of the class (and myself, if necessary) to clarify any points of confusion, and to make sure that the playing field is relatively level for the discussion of student positions that follows.

Student arguments – justifications or critiques of the main characters' actions – are often well reasoned, and sometimes highly imaginative. There is usually a good-faith effort to stay within the framework of a given moral theory as the student understands it; and, if students start to wander, their classmates quickly speak up (or can be encouraged to do so), asking how the case being made fits within the theory the student says she is basing her argument on.

The *Trifles* play is short and deceptively simple, and it is just plain fun to see students confounded by the final discussion which asks them to identify what they know of the facts of the situation. What students discover is that each of them has made a series of assumptions from these facts, a narrative created to justify their judgments. More surprisingly, they find that their classmates have made other, different assumptions, and hence have arrived

115

at a very different assessment of whether Mrs Peters' and Mrs Hale's actions were justifiable or not. These rather straightforward insights come to them with all of the force of a ten-pound ball, since the students believe (as all of us do) that they are simply exercising common sense and ordinary powers of deduction and judgment. The class is in this sense an excellent introduction to moral reasoning, which students now see as not as obvious as it at first appeared, and as a capability well worth acquiring.

PRIOR WEEK'S INTRODUCTION TO THE *TRIFLES* CLASS

Because the assignment for the *Trifles* class is different in kind from other classes in "The Moral Leader," I find it helpful to give students an advance orientation to the class goals, materials, and method. This can be done either at the beginning or the end of the class on *Things Fall Apart* that precedes it.

A way to introduce students to the *Trifles* class and assignment

The moral challenges we have been looking at are tough, without easy answers, so it's not surprising that we turn in the next module of the course to examine how we make decisions about moral problems, and whether there are any methods or tools to help us systematically think them through.

Next week's assignment is designed as an exercise in moral reasoning, an opportunity to apply a moral theory systematically to a question of moral action. As such, it is a chance to practice what we'll be looking at in this module, to practice moral reasoning.

You'll study an eleven-page play and then a reading, which I'll describe in a moment, on four moral theories. Your assignment: Either to justify or critique what two women (Mrs Hale and Mrs Peters) did, using One of the four moral theories in the reading to make your case.

The reading comes from a terrific book, Principles of Biomedical Ethics, *which was written for practitioners in the fields of medical care, biomedical research, and health care management. The descriptions you will read were put together to help practitioners make decisions in real situations involving problems with moral stakes. These four theories can be thought of as ethical schools or modes of reasoning. Each is independent, and each grew up as a way of thinking through – and deciding about – moral questions and dilemmas.*

How should I decide what is right to do? Do I consider the consequences of my action? Whether it allows me to fulfill basic duties or obligations? Do I need to consider the rights of people my decision affects? How does my decision affect the interests of the community of which I am part?

Some of you may be familiar with the material covered here, but prior exposure is by no means required. The reading will help us share a common base of understanding of these different modes of reasoning. You'll see a specific example from the medical realm that adds a concrete, realistic dimension to the descriptions of the moral theories.

INTRODUCTION TO *TRIFLES* CLASS

As students enter class, invite them to take one of the prepared labels that represent the position that they will be taking in the discussion of Mrs Hale and Mrs Peters' actions that follows the initial review of the four moral theories. I have found color-coded labels work best (see Table 8.1) since they allow me (and the students) to scan the room and immediately identify which position the student will be arguing from. Needing to choose a *single* position surprises many students, and some will change their label as the class unfolds.

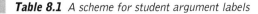

Table 8.1 *A scheme for student argument labels*

Yellow label = Consequences – justify	Yellow label = Consequences – critique
Pink label = Obligation – justify	Pink Label = Obligation – critique
Green label = Rights – justify	Green Label = Rights – critique
Blue label = Community – justify	Blue Label = Community – critique

A way of opening the discussion

This week's class begins our module on Moral Reasoning. In the last module we certainly saw the need for this kind of capability. Creon and Antigone refused to engage each other on the basis of rational discourse. Jerry seemed to be unclear about how to think about the dilemma he found himself facing. And Okonkwo seemed, at least until the end, and possibly through it, to substitute action for thought and discourse.

Today's class is foundation building for us, an exercise of sorts – stylized learning. The goal is not to force you to choose a point of view and stick to it for ever, but to get used to working within one moral reasoning framework systematically. The purpose is to enhance your skill and give you tools to persuade, to listen to others, and to help others clarify their point of view.

1 REVIEW OF THE FOUR MORAL THEORIES (30′)

I have conducted the *Trifles* class without this review and found that it suffers from a lack of precision: the theories start to blend together, and students lose their way. I was delighted to have found the description of the moral theories in *Principles of Biomedical Ethics*, both for the explication of the theories through a realistic moral problem that engages student interest,[2] and for the even-handed description that includes each theory's strengths and weaknesses.

Questions driving the discussion are in bold

Let's start with a brief review of the four moral theories – or categories of moral reflection and judgment – that were outlined in the reading. For each one: What matters – what is the core idea? How is "moral" defined? What is the basic approach to resolving moral problems?

Your role in this section of the class (and this class in general) is not to present yourself as an expert on moral philosophy (although some of you may be just that) but to help students get to the heart of the theories, each of which is well described in the assigned text. The important point is not nuances within each theory, but how they differ from each other and what fundamental set of concerns each theory addresses. See Table 8.2 for a brief review of the four theories corresponding to the questions posed to students.

You may find it helpful to consider the theories as *categories for moral reflection*, each of which points to a different fundamental question, set of principles, and perspective about what is most important in judging an act's moral rightness or wrongness.

One of the most practical approaches to help students understand the theories, described earlier, is to consider them in light of the specific questions they set out to answer. Will my action produce morally good *consequences?* (Utilitarianism, or consequence-based theory). Does my action allow me to fulfill basic *duties or obligations?* (Kantianism or obligation-based theory). Do I need to consider the *rights* of people who my decision affects? (Liberal individualism or rights-based theory). How does my decision affect the interests of the *community* of which I am part? (Communitarianism or community-based theory).

Students will be able to summarize the most important points of each of these theories, and it is helpful to give each theory enough time for the major concepts it is based on to be surfaced. The theories also prompt reflection, and students raise interesting questions. One student wondered, for example,

Table 8.2 Overview of moral theories

	Core idea	Definition of 'moral'	Approach to solving moral problems
Utilitarianism: consequence-based theory	Actions are right or wrong according to the balance of their good and bad consequences[1]	"Utility" should be the major principle in ethics, meaning that actions may be considered right or wrong according to the balance of value and disvalue – value being measured in total happiness or pleasure – they bring	The right act in any circumstance is the one that produces the best overall result, as determined from an impersonal perspective that gives equal weight to the interests of each affected party[2]
Kantianism: obligation-based theory	The moral worth of an individual's action depends exclusively on the rule of obligation (or "maxim") on which the person acts[3]	"I ought never to act except in such a way that I can also will that my maxim become universal law"[4] "One must treat every person as an end and never as a means only"[5]	One must act for the sake of obligation – to intend what is morally required[6]
Liberal individualism: rights-based theory	To have a right is to be in a position to determine, by one's choices, what others should do, or need not do[7]	Positive right: the right to receive a good or service Negative right: the right to be free from some action by others[8]	Individuals and groups have rights – justified claims that individuals can make upon other individuals or upon society[9]
Communitarianism: community-based theory	Everything fundamental in ethics derives from communal values, the common good, social goals, traditional practices, and cooperative virtues[10]	An action's moral value can be judged based on its positive or negative effects on society's well-being as a whole	Much of what a person ought to do is determined by the social roles assigned to or acquired by this person as a member of the community[11]

1 Tom L. Beauchamp and James F. Childress, *Principles of Biomedical Ethics*, Oxford and New York: Oxford University Press, 2001, p. 340; 2 Ibid., pp. 340–341; 3 Ibid., p. 349; 4 Ibid., p. 350; 5 Ibid., pp. 350–351; 6 Ibid., p. 350; 7 Ibid., p. 357; 8 Ibid., p. 358; 9 Ibid., p. 357; 10 Ibid., p. 362; 11 Ibid., p. 364.

how Communitarianism takes into account the fact that a community's values and principles may change (a reference, at least in part, to *Things Fall Apart*). Such questions are an indicator of student engagement and, even if they can't be fully explored, allow the theories to assume a more vivid, lived reality in the class.

Of the four theories, utilitarianism can at times prove problematic, since students trained in economics immediately translate utilities into the preferences of individual actors (sometimes even attempting to quantify these utilities in their analysis as they would in an economics course). While not wrong, it is important to help students understand the philosophical underpinnings of the theory – its emphasis on consequences as a basis on which to judge the morality of an action, and the balancing of benefits and harms for a greater good. Students often make these corrections themselves; and, if they do not, I have found it possible to offer this interpretation of the theory by asking students to describe it in terms that are closer to the description they found in the reading.

2 APPLICATION OF THEORIES TO *TRIFLES* (35′)

The theories are principally used in this class as a means to an end, a way to help students learn how to apply systematic reasoning to a moral problem. Moral reasoning is not just the ability to mount an argument to defend a case, but a controlled approach to justification from a specific point of view:

> *Justification* has several meanings in English, some specific to disciplines. In law, for example, justification is a showing in court that one has a sufficient reason for one's claim or for what one has been called to answer. In ethical discourse, the objective is to establish one's case by presenting sufficient grounds for it. A mere listing of reasons will not suffice, because those reasons may not support the conclusion. Not all reasons are good reasons, and not all good reasons are sufficient for justification. We therefore need to distinguish a reason's *relevance* to a moral judgment from its final *adequacy* for that judgment; we also need to distinguish an *attempted* justification from a successful *justification*.
>
> For example, chemical companies in the United States at one time took the presence of toxic chemicals in a work environment to be a legally and morally sound reason to exclude women of childbearing age from a hazardous workplace, but the US Supreme Court overturned these policies on the ground that they are discriminatory. The dangers to health and life presented by hazardous chemicals

may constitute a *good* reason for excluding employees from a workplace, but this reason may not be a *sufficient* reason for a ban that impacts women alone. Even a worthy attempt at justification may not succeed, because a successful justification requires a sufficient reason.[3]

If students have not as yet committed themselves to a position, it is time to ask them to do so and take a label to identify the point of view they will be arguing. The review of moral theories often clarifies student understanding (that is its purpose, after all), so it is helpful to allow students to exchange labels they may have taken at the start of the class for ones that represent positions they now wish to argue.

Let's apply these theories now as we discuss *Trifles*. Your assignment was to choose one of these theories and apply it – systematically – either to justify or criticize what Mrs Hale and Mrs Peters did.

As a transition, you may want to restate the purpose of the theory review, in part to alleviate student concerns that you have suddenly transformed the study of literary works about moral leadership into an introductory philosophy course: *I thought it was important to get a common definition of these theories before we applied them to the judgment of what Mrs Peters and Mrs Hale did. Let's get to the core issue now and hear the arguments that you constructed using these theories.*

The clearest path through this discussion is to entertain arguments for each theory separately – starting with student justifications of Mrs Peters and Mrs Hale's actions, and then moving to criticisms of their actions from the standpoint of the same moral theory. There is usually a good distribution of the eight different positions that could be taken, although critiques of the two women often dominate justifications or defenses of their action, and rights-based arguments (either justifications or critiques) typically are appealed to the least.

Let's start with justifications of the actions of Mrs Hale and Mrs Peters based on consequence-based theory; we'll then move to the critiques based on consequence-based reasoning.

In the discussion, you will call on students who have identified themselves as prepared to make an argument from the standpoint of the moral theory under consideration. The questions that follow (which you may or may not need) are constructed as challenges to each of the student positions to allow you (and, hopefully, the class) to sharpen student thinking and the presentation of each argument. The questions are listed in the order that seems to work best in covering the theoretical positions.

Utilitarianism, or consequence-based theory

Probes for justifications

Which consequences do you believe justified the women's actions? Impact on Mrs Wright? The two women? Their marriages? The community? Did you have to weigh consequences, that is, to decide that some were worth more than others? How did you do that? How certain are you that the consequences you anticipate will happen? Why are you so sure?

Probes for critiques

Even if the women's assumptions are right and Mrs Wright did kill her husband, how likely is it really that she will ever kill again? Don't you believe that a miscarriage of justice is about to occur – the men seem to have a strong conviction that Mrs Wright is guilty.

Utilitarianism starts the discussion because it usually has the most adherents; to many students it is also the most familiar and pragmatic justification. Interestingly, many students have not thought of a defense of an action on the basis of its consequences as a *moral* argument, so it is particularly helpful to dig into which consequences the students choose to focus on, helping them to understand that consequences are never neutral, and that there are a host of possible consequences to consider from any action. The debate about whether utility should be considered from the standpoint of individual actors or the good of an entire group or community may surface, and throughout this discussion there are frequent journeys back up to the theory level, as student arguments raise more questions about the general thrust of each theory and how it should be applied.

Kantianism, or obligation-based theory

Probes for justifications

Did you see Mrs Hale and Mrs Peters operating out of a sense of duty? How would you characterize that duty? What is it based on? How do you compare that obligation to others they have – to their husbands, or to the law that Mrs Peters is "married to" [Mrs Peters is the Sheriff's wife]? Why, in your view, does their duty to Mrs Wright dominate these other obligations?

Probes for critiques

The intent of Mrs Hale and Mrs Peters may very well have been to circumvent the law, but what should they do if they believe the law won't be administered fairly?

Questions of Mrs Peters and Mrs Hale's duties are nicely complex. Students struggle with how the women should weigh their duty to Mrs Wright, their neighbor who the two women fear is being wrongly accused (or, if not wrongly accused, wrongly prosecuted) for the death of her husband, against their citizen duties to the laws of the state, and even Mrs Peters' duties to uphold the law as the wife of the Sheriff.

Liberal individualism, or rights-based theory

Probes for justifications

Whose rights did you see Mrs Hale and Mrs Peters protecting? How sure are you that those rights would be violated? What other rights might be placed in jeopardy by the women's support of Mrs Wright?

Probes for critiques

But Mr Wright is dead now. We can't bring him back! Why are you so sure that Mrs Wright will be treated fairly?

Rights-based arguments begin sometimes with questions about whether or not Mrs Wright was abused by her husband and what right she had to a life without abuse. Students struggle with time – how should they account for the rights of Mr Wright, who is dead? And how are they to compare these now violated rights against the right of Mrs Wright to a fair investigation and trial?

Communitarianism, or community-based theory

Probes for justification

Which community did you focus on in your justification? The town? The Wright family? The community of women? (Is there such a thing?) How did you decide which community to focus on?

Probes for critiques

If it ever came to light that Mrs Hale and Mrs Peters hid evidence, belief in the community's respect for law would be compromised. But how likely is this really? Why do you think their actions will be found out? Why isn't the "community of women" an institution with the same weight and import as the town community?

Communitarian arguments are often the most imaginative. Students understand the implications of what it means to take the law into one's own hands, but some none the less argue for actions that promote the community of women, whose hardships and concerns are ignored or denigrated by the male characters throughout the play. The dead bird, hidden by Mrs Hale and that might constitute evidence against Mrs Wright, is one such "trifle," and some suggest that the men more or less get what they have coming to them by ignoring the importance of domestic values and contributions.

3 SEPARATING FACTS FROM ASSUMPTIONS (30′)

Mrs Wright's guilt or innocence is at the heart of the previous discussion – did she really kill her husband? This is of course a factual question, so it makes sense to turn from student debates and arguments to the more elementary issue of what we can learn, from the play, about the facts of the situation.

We have lots of plausible moral positions. How should we decide among them? Let's start with something pretty fundamental. I assume that all of this discussion is based on a similar appreciation of the facts. After all, we have only an eleven-page play. What facts can we be sure of? Let's list them.

Students enjoy this discussion, even (or perhaps because) they find their own reasoning being challenged. The list of facts is enlightening (if at times quite funny) to put on the board: Mr Wright – dead; Mrs Wright – alive and in jail; a bird cage with a broken door and a hinge pulled apart; one dead canary with its neck wrung [found by the two women in Mrs Wright's sewing box and put by Mrs Hale in her pocket at the end of the play]; a messy kitchen; erratic stitching in Mrs Wright's quilt [that Mrs Hale rips out before the men see it]; Mrs Wright acting strangely [according to Mr Hale]; what Mrs Wright asked for in prison [her apron, her shawl]; what Mrs Wright worried about in prison [the fire in the kitchen going out and her preserved jams]; the fact that Mrs Wright used to sing in the choir.

Challenges to what is factually known initially come from the instructor, but students quickly perceive the thrust of the discussion and begin to challenge each other when assumptions are presented as fact, (for example, "Mr Wright tore the door of the bird cage off its hinges and killed the canary" prompts a "We don't know that!" response).

What assumptions did you make?

What do you think Mrs Hale and Mrs Peters actually did? Hid evidence? Protected Mrs Wright? Took a stand? Broke the law? What are you basing your belief on?

What did you assume would happen to Mrs Wright? What is that based on?

What did you assume about the dead bird? How did it get killed? What do you think the bird meant – to Mrs Wright? To Mr Wright? What is that based on?

How did you understand Mrs Wright's behavior when Mr Hale visited the house? How did you understand the messy kitchen? The erratic stitching in the quilt? The requests Mrs Wright made from jail? What did you assume her behavior meant? What is that based on?

Students' assumptions are probed more fully through the questions provided; even without them, they are quite willing to describe the ways in which they put the facts together to tell the story of Mrs Wright, Mr Wright, and what transpired in the house that led to Mr Wright's murder. The assumptions about Mrs Wright's actions depend critically upon her motive, and many students construct (perhaps rightly, perhaps wrongly – we are not meant to know for sure) a history of domestic abuse that is used to justify Mrs Wright's murder of her husband. This view, in turn, is challenged as students try to

125

articulate what would, or would not, constitute sufficient abuse to justify murder.

We've heard the arguments, and examined the facts. How should we decide?

The final question asks students to consider again the actions of Mrs Peters and Mrs Hale and to revisit, if they wish, the argument they made earlier in the class. You may want to ask students to break into two-to-three person buzz groups for several minutes to review the case, as they now understand it, providing them with time to incorporate the prior discussions into their final judgment.

As students describe the assumptions they made about the likelihood of Mrs Wright ever committing murder again, the possibility that she would receive a fair trial, and other concerns related to the defense or criticism of the actions that the two women took, they become quite clear about the relationship between their assumptions and the judgments they made. "If we had started with the facts we would have taken a totally different path and the things we said would not have made any sense;" "These arguments are just a house of cards." Students are also struck by the different assumptions that classmates brought to the play: "I had thought Mrs Wright snapped – went crazy – but after the discussion I saw other assumptions about her actions as more plausible."

They also are far more aware of the process that has been followed: "We often do things in the order we did them here: judge and then make assumptions about the facts in light of our judgment. Our process really should be the other way around: examine facts then make assumptions about them in order to make a moral judgment." Others agree, asserting the need to develop an unbiased interpretation of the facts. Anticipating the class that will follow, students observe that it is important to see facts from the perspective of multiple parties, "a better process than thinking them through on your own."

4 REFLECTIONS ON MORAL REASONING (10′)

The last minutes of the class are used to help students generalize from the prior discussion and consider what they have learned about moral reasoning in this first class of the module.

What lessons do you take out of this first exercise in moral reasoning?

Students are usually quite ready to reflect on their experience in this class, and what they now think about the exercise of moral reasoning.

Some representative comments: "I looked for a theory to justify my position." "What we assume leads us to different theories to use; should it work like this? Aren't we predisposing our outcome if we do this?" "Knowing all four theories makes decision-making more complex, but it's a good exercise to go through." "Each moral theory leads you to look at some facts, or see the situation through a certain lens, but how do you decide which one to use?" "The theories really are different – the theories are better or worse for different kinds of problems."

One student described the goal as a good-faith effort to apply a moral theory correctly, to use it in a systematic way and not to bend the principles on which the theory is based to support a preferred evaluation or conclusion.

Students are also interested in the broader questions the play raises about the nature of law and the relationship between law and justice. Students may talk about the role of law as the cornerstone of society and civilization and stress obedience to the law as crucial to the sustainability of the state. Other students take a more nuanced view, distinguishing between the goal of the law – to promote justice – and its actual practice ("Sometimes laws don't really create justice"). This topic will be explored extensively in the next class on *The Sweet Hereafter*, and in the final class of this module on Sir Thomas More, *A Man for All Seasons*.

The *Trifles* discussion is a powerful learning experience that raises as many questions as it answers about moral reasoning. Students will pursue these questions, building on the energy of this class, in the next three classes of this module.

Review of moral theories
– Main ideas
– How is "moral" defined?
– Approach to moral decision-making

Making your case

Reviewing the play

Lessons about moral reasoning

Figure 8.1 Trifles *roadmap*

Review of moral theories			
Utilitarianism	*Kantianism*	*Liberal individualism*	*Communitarianism*
Consequence-based theory	Obligation-based theory	Rights-based theory	Community-based theory

Figure 8.2 Trifles *board plan (1)*

Trifles – Facts vs. Assumptions	
Fact	*Assumption*

Figure 8.3 Trifles *board plan (2)*

NOTES

1   Susan Glaspell, *Trifles*, in *Plays by Susan Glaspell*, Cambridge: Cambridge University Press, 1987, pp. 37–38.

2   A father, confronted with the choice of whether to donate a kidney to his daughter, asks a doctor to declare him medically unfit for the procedure. The father could donate the kidney without significant risk if he so chose, and the doctor's decision – how he should respond to the father's request – is explored through an application of each of the four moral theories. The text demonstrates the different ways in which each of the theories explicates and provides a path for resolution of the doctor's moral problem.

3   Tom L. Beauchamp and James F. Childress, *Principles of Biomedical Ethics*, Oxford and New York: Oxford University Press, 2001, p. 385.

Chapter 9

The Sweet Hereafter
Reasoning from personal perspective

Mitchell Stephens, Esquire, the lawyer
"They do that, work the bottom line; I've seen it play out over and over again, until you start to wonder about the human species. They're like clever monkeys, that's all. They calculate ahead of time what it will cost them to assure safety versus what they're likely to be forced to settle for damages when the missing bolt sends the bus over a cliff, and they simply choose the cheaper option. And it's up to people like me to make it cheaper to build the bus with the extra bolt, or add the extra yard of guardrail, or drain the quarry . . . That's the only way you can ensure moral responsibility in this society. Make it cheaper."[1]

Dolores, the bus driver, translating for Abbott, her husband
"What Abbott said was: The true jury of a person's peers is the people of her town. Only they, the people who have known her all her life, and not twelve strangers, can decide her guilt or innocence. And if Dolores – meaning me, of course – if she has committed a crime, then it's a crime against them, not the state, so they are the ones who must decide her punishment too. What Abbott is saying, Mr Stephens, is forget the lawsuit. That's what he's saying."[2]

Nichole, a survivor
"It just wasn't right – to be alive, to have had what people assured you was a close call, and then go out and hire a lawyer; it wasn't right. And even if you were the mother and father of one of the kids who had died, like the Ottos or the Walkers, what good would it do to hire a lawyer? . . . [T]o be the mother and father of one of the kids who had survived the accident, even a kid like me, who would spend the rest of her life a cripple, and then to sue – I didn't understand that at all, and I really knew it wasn't right. Not if I was, like they said, truly lucky."[3]

129

> *Dolores, reflecting on Billy, eyewitness and father of two children killed*
> "I didn't know what to think of how Billy had changed since the accident. He scared me; but mostly he made me sad. He had been a noble man; and now he was ruined. The accident had ruined a lot of lives. Or, to be exact, it had busted apart the structures on which those lives had depended – depended, I guess, to a greater degree than we had originally believed. A town needs its children for a lot more than it thinks."[4]

THE SWEET HEREAFTER: THEMES AND QUESTIONS

One event – many viewpoints

The Sweet Hereafter builds on the foundation of *Trifles* by taking moral reasoning beyond a simple four-wall setting and largely opaque cast of characters to an entire community of voluble, self-aware narrators. The story is of a horrific school bus accident that kills more than a dozen children one morning and leaves another crippled – this in a tiny town called Sam Dent; a devastating, unforgettable loss.

At one level, the central focus of the novel is whether the cause of the accident, and what or who is responsible for it, should be prosecuted. Ultimately, the story reveals that no legal case will be tried. At another level, the story uses the device of exploring the memories and thoughts of four characters involved in the accident: Dolores, the bus driver; Billy, a possible witness to the crash – but also someone whose two children died in it; Mitchell Stephens, the lawyer who arrives ready to make the case for community action; and Nichole, a survivor, crippled, and whose life and actions vis-à-vis the potential lawsuit take surprising turns. These four voices provide a narrative of the accident and its aftermath as well as individual, complex responses.

The device of multiple narrators requires students to move from interpreting events, decisions, and rationales for action from the slight conversations and quick, nearly silent acts of *Trifles*, to deciphering what is true and believable from events described, words spoken, and rationales freely provided. *The Sweet Hereafter* thus introduces to students **the multiplicity of perspectives that accompany any event and the actions that surround it.**

The theme of **one event – many viewpoints** emerges in the backstories, history, and relationships described by the narrators, all lenses through which the accident and subsequent actions are interpreted and acted upon. **Facts are not as much fact as individual assertions,** translated through the characters' own histories, needs, and motivations. In the *Trifles* class students experienced the plasticity of facts, weaving assumptions into storylines that would enable them to defend their criticism or support of Mrs Hale and Mrs Smith. This additional exposure to the likely differences that individuals will bring to their perception of any event gives students **a realistic view of how the development of a fact-base, critical to moral reasoning, needs to include a method for confronting and testing differences in perspective.**

Moral theories in use

Students will also find **strands of the moral philosophies** they read about and used in the *Trifles* class. But where the *Trifles* exercise showed what it is like to reason consciously from the standpoint of consequences, or duty, or rights, or community, here **students see these moral approaches and rationales as nearly unconscious reference points**, appealed to by characters but without the label of a particular moral philosophy. The four quotes that began this chapter provide a flavor for the way that moral principles show up in the realistic dialogues and interior monologues of the novel, and this picture of moral reasons appealed to shows students **how hard they may have to listen to themselves and to others to find the basis on which moral arguments are being made.**

Moral reasoning and the law

Moral principles are woven seamlessly with other positions and perspectives, and two additional perspectives are central to the text. The first is that of the law. *The Sweet Hereafter* allows students **to continue their search for ways to discriminate between what is legal and what is moral.** This search began, of course, in *Antigone,* in the students' evaluation of Creon's edict against the burial of Polynices. It featured as well in the assessment of the practices, decisions, and judgments of both the Umofia clan and the colonial administrators in *Things Fall Apart,* and in the morally troublesome prosecution of Mrs Wright in *Trifles.*

In *The Sweet Hereafter* students **explore how legal reasoning is different from moral reasoning, and the ways in which a legal approach to a problem is, and is not, helpful.** Legal concepts of responsibility, justice, fairness, and retribution derive from moral or ethical roots, but they have taken on specific meanings in the US case-law system, encoded in regulation and precedent, and enacted through the courts and legal processes. Residents of Sam Dent must decide how to determine accountability and apportion blame for the accident, how to handle compensation if any should be required, how to reconcile individuals to loss, and even how to heal a grieving community.

131

The law is tested for its ability to accomplish these moral objectives, as well as for its ability to resolve more narrow questions of whether legal liability and compensation from economically viable parties should be sought, and whether these actions will have any deterrent effect in Sam Dent or other communities.

The US legal system is on display in *The Sweet Hereafter,* and its rationale and moral effectiveness are frequently challenged both by American students and by students familiar with other legal paradigms.

Moral reasoning and emotion

The Sweet Hereafter is particularly powerful in prompting students to examine the ways in which emotion is woven into the experience of, and reaction to, moral problems – the ways in which emotion plays into moral reasoning. This is tricky territory, and students see a full range of emotions having a full range of impacts, from driving individuals to clearly ill-considered actions, to inspiring them to help others. While sometimes justifying the view that our emotions run contrary to reason and logic, at other times the characters' emotions are a useful lens, an essential window into the full truth of a situation, one that allows appropriate plans and responses to be formed.[5] These plans coexist with moral foundations for behavior in a complex and sometimes uncomfortable way; in fact, the central action of the plot sits on a lie, but one that some students will defend as necessary to resolving the conflicts that the accident has introduced into the community.

The Sweet Hereafter challenges the view of moral reasoning as essentially cognitive and purely rational, and the view of moral reasoning that emerges is a blend of emotion, law, personal interests, and morally justified actions. Perhaps the quintessential story of mixed motives, *The Sweet Hereafter* forces students to see the role of these decisions and actions in the life of each of the characters and the ways in which their reasoning combines many elements. The question students are left with is whether a more systematic approach to moral problems might lead to happier consequences. That question is taken up in the following class on the novel *The Remains of the Day.*

STUDENT ASSIGNMENT

READING: *The Sweet Hereafter,* by Russell Banks.

1   Do you think the community of Sam Dent benefited from not pursuing the lawsuit? Why or why not?

2   How would you explain the choices and actions taken by Dolores, Billy, Nichole, and Stephens?

3   You will find evidence of the moral theories discussed in the *Trifles* class in the rationales provided by the four characters. Be prepared to discuss examples you have identified of reasoning based on consequences, duty, rights, or community.

CLASS PLAN OUTLINE: DISCUSSION BLOCKS

1   Were You Satisfied With the Outcome of This Story? (20')

2   Was the Town Better Off without the Lawsuit? (30')

3   How Was the Lawsuit Avoided? (35')

4   Constructing a Different Ending to the Story (20')

CLASS PLAN OVERVIEW

I was initially quite leery of this book. Enthusiastic as I was about the value of a story told from the standpoint of multiple narrators for the module on moral reasoning, I wondered: four narrators – each one of whom must be empathized with, understood, and (eventually) judged. Would the students be able to keep track of the comings and goings of the narration or would they end up in a muddle?

Having been told of the plot, I also asked how eager I was to impose such sorrow on myself, much less, on my students. *The Sweet Hereafter* is arguably one of the most emotionally charged books in the course. Beyond the school bus accident, sad enough on its own, the plot also features realistic and raw details in the personal histories of the characters: an extra-marital affair; drug use and addiction; sexual abuse in a family setting. But *The Sweet Hereafter* plays a vital role in the course, pushing students beyond a potentially narrow definition of moral reasoning to one that must encompass the trials and even tragedies of everyday life, and the mix of motives and reasons that drive ordinary people in making their (moral) decisions.

The class plan is designed to channel – and succeeds in channeling – the complexity of the multiple narrators, and the intensity of students' emotional reactions, into a series of discussions that allow students to come to terms with the rationales and moral reasoning of the characters and to examine and to share their feelings for and judgments of them.

The plan begins by canvassing students for their reactions to the somewhat surprising end of the story,[6] then moves back in time to examine whether they agree or disagree with the town's decision to reject the lawsuit, then further back to their assessment and judgment of the rationales provided by the four main characters for their actions. The plan ends by inviting students to exercise their moral imagination and, if they wish, to craft a new ending to the story, bringing their emotional involvement with it full circle, and providing a provisional sense of closure.

While true for all of the class plans, it is particularly useful in this class to stay flexible about the order of the discussion blocks. For example, the logic of a particular group of students may lead them to move naturally from the initial block, which focuses on their reactions to the end of the story, to an attempt to fashion new and potentially more satisfying endings (described below as the last discussion block). Each of the discussions will build students' understanding of how moral reasoning works in what they recognize as a real-world setting, and the emotional pull of the story allows them to understand how deeply emotions are entwined in moral decision-making and judgment.

As the instructor, it will be important for you to display the same accepting attitude toward the characters' actions and student comments as in the stories that featured race as a central tension. Students are alert – and resistant – to moralizing; they will find their own equilibrium for how to talk about the characters' sexual misconduct and illicit drug use if given a neutral and supportive climate for discussion and debate. I have worked hard to maintain an objective stance and have never been asked about my own reactions to the events in the story or to the actions of the characters.

If I were asked for my personal opinions, I would point out the dilemma inherent in any judgment I could offer. Since some students will have expressed disapproval of the characters while others are supportive of at least some of their actions, I would describe how I would inadvertently split the class into two groups: those who would feel that I approved of their reactions and those who would feel I didn't. Because I want all students to feel comfortable in class, it would be unworkable (and inconsistent) for me to appear to be making judgments about the content of student comments or their reactions to characters and events in the novel.

INTRODUCTION

A way of opening the discussion

Today's class on The Sweet Hereafter *will build on the foundation we set in our last class. Our goal will be to see how a set of characters reasons their way through a terrible situation that affects all of them. In last week's class we had to infer moral reasoning from the outside in. Working back from the actions of the characters and their very brief exchanges, it was up to us to ascribe motivation and intent – and to speculate on the likely consequences from a small but significant moment of choice.*

In today's class we move inside. We can look at how four people attempted to deal with the terrible event that affected them (and others, of course) personally. We have characters who think out loud about the nature of the situations they find themselves in. We have an opportunity to explore their reasoning, and the context surrounding their choices. And, unlike last week, we have a chance not just to speculate, but to see the impact of their decisions on others.

We'll try to understand how different assumptions about the facts of the situation play a role in the decisions that the characters make. We'll also want to analyze the moral justifications, or rationale, that the characters offer for their actions.

As we do this, we can look for strands of the moral theories that we worked with in the last class. To what degree do we see characters making choices based on potential consequences? Are they motivated by duty and, if so, duty to whom or for what? Are any character's rights at stake, and do we see evidence of a rights-based justification for action? Finally, to what extent are we seeing communitarian or community-based justifications for action? As we look, we'll also want to identify the other reasoning processes and motivations that seem to determine the choices and actions of Nichole, Billy, Stephens, and Dolores.

1 WERE YOU SATISFIED WITH THE OUTCOME OF THIS STORY? (20′)

The opening question is a terrific way to move students into discussion, allowing them to get a handle on the book as a whole and to vent, a little, their feelings about the ending. You will find it helpful to give students as much as seven or eight minutes in small two- or three-person buzz groups to collect their thoughts on this multi-layered and complex story. Their small group discussions are very lively; and, after they've had a chance to talk, you may want to cold call or solicit one or more groups to discuss their reactions before opening up the discussion for general participation. Do not expect consensus from the groups; the report-outs will be more in the nature of individual reactions and a description of the ways in which the group either did, or did not, agree.

Questions driving the discussion are in bold

Were you satisfied with the outcome of this story?

The opening question allows students to range broadly over the entire story, and they touch on nearly all of the issues that will be discussed in more detail as the class proceeds: whether or not the town is better off for having avoided the lawsuit; whether anyone is guilty or whether the crash was just an accident; their judgment of Nichole's lie (that Dolores was speeding as she drove the bus), and Billy's silence about it.

Probes for "Yes" position

In what ways did you find the outcome satisfying? Was justice served? For whom? Who has benefited by what happened here?

Some students who claim satisfaction with the end of the story focus on individual town members who benefited from the fact that the lawsuit was not pursued, such as Billy or Nichole (see the discussion below for reasons why this might be the case). Others follow a communitarian logic, describing Sam Dent and towns like it as "a way of life worth preserving;" they describe how the demolition derby[7] shows the entire town coming to closure, with Dolores re-integrated back into the social fabric of the community. There are also psychological interpretations: Dolores needed to feel guilty because she was, in fact, responsible for the accident, even if she was not speeding as Nichole claimed.

Probes for "No" position

Why didn't you find the outcome satisfying? What was missing? Where did you see harm?

Other students are not so sanguine, and the *not satisfied* contingent has some vocal advocates. Dolores speaks of feeling "absolutely alone,"[8] adding, "And even if we weren't dead, in an important way which no longer puzzled or frightened me and which I therefore no longer resisted, we were as good as dead."[9] These are tough feelings for students to absorb, and several will keep coming back to the puzzle of why Dolores felt so alone – and glad to be alone – and to the implications of Dolores' apparent satisfaction for how they should judge Nichole's lie and Billy Ansel's acceptance of it. A few students may be critical of the actions of the main characters, observing that their drug use and other failings showed that they were "faulty before" and that at the end of the novel many of the characters "seem to have nothing left to live for." Finally, many students argue that it is not fair for Dolores to shoulder the burden of guilt for the entire community. The sandpit had not been drained for years, and the guardrail that should have protected the school bus failed – surely these suggest that more parties were at fault than Dolores.

2 WAS THE TOWN BETTER OR WORSE OFF WITHOUT THE LAWSUIT? (30′)

The next question follows naturally from the opening discussion. The *Trifles* class showed how important it is to define the *scope of moral analysis*, and you may find it helpful to list the various levels at which the moral questions and challenges of *The Sweet Hereafter* could be analyzed (see Table 9.1).

Table 9.1 The Sweet Hereafter: *levels of analysis*

Redesigning school buses and highways so accidents don't happen again
The town
Affected families
Dolores / Nichole / Stephen / Billy

This discussion focuses on the town level of analysis; students are guided through the question flow to analyze the legal case for a lawsuit and the impact it might have had on the community.

No legal background is necessary to lead this discussion, but it may be helpful to recall that the case could take two forms: a possible criminal case of negligence, as well as a civil case, both potentially directed at a variety of entities: Dolores Driscoll, the school bus driver; the town of Sam Dent, which hired Dolores to transport children to school, and which, along with the state of New York, might have been responsible for draining the sandpit and providing safe guardrails above it. Other possible defendants include the manufacturers of the school bus and of the guardrails. The novel focuses on the civil case, through which financial retribution would be sought from parties deemed responsible and liable for the harm inflicted – the death of the children, and the crippling of the student Nichole Burnell.

In general, more students are against the lawsuit than for it, so it may be necessary to probe or reinforce the rationale for it. Arguments in this discussion are frequently intense, as students struggle over the difference between responsibility and liability, and the ways in which societies can – or even whether they should – demand financial compensation for the value of a human life.

Was the town better or worse off without the lawsuit? What impact would the suit have had on the community?

Prompted by this question, students are more or less even-handed in their assessment of the suit and they lay out some of its more obvious advantages. A positive judgment would have punished guilty parties, such as negligent town or state officials responsible for road safety and repair. It would provide financial compensation to the families of children who had died and support for Nichole Burnell's costs of medical care. A trial would in all likelihood clear Dolores Driscoll of the false charge of speeding, since Billy Ansel would presumably be unwilling to perjure himself, saving Dolores' reputation and restoring the confidence of town members in the judgment of the school board that had hired her. By having the guardrail fixed and the sandpit drained, future problems may well have been avoided for the town of Sam Dent. Finally, some students point out that a suit might have a deterrent effect on other communities, publicizing the issue of school bus safety and demonstrating the financial consequences of negligent actions.

Students opposed to the lawsuit marshal many arguments. Some see it as inconsistent with communitarian theories of morality, believing it would lead to less, rather than more, town cohesion. They picture a town torn apart by differential payments as families receive varying amounts of compensation for their harm or loss, a perverse system in which "haves" and "have nots" would be created through the mechanism of some children's death or maiming.

Other students are offended by the concept of "monetizing" the dead children through financial compensation, even though such suits are common in the United States. They ask if the parents would later suffer guilt for having appeared to reduce the value of their child's life to financial terms. Students point out the evident fact that compensation will not bring the children back from the dead, and find it hard to believe that the money would help any parent deal successfully with his or her loss.

Let's step back: What is the legal case here?

Asking students to describe the legal case for the lawsuit deepens the discussion. There are two possible legal cases to be made. The first puts responsibility and liability on the town of Sam Dent as negligent in not having drained the sandpit, and in not having provided guardrails that were sufficiently strong to withstand a crash of a vehicle as large as a school bus. This case, pursued by the lawyer Mitchell Stephens, would ensure that the "deep pockets" of the town of Sam Dent would be used to compensate victims' families. A second case, either linked to the first or alternative to it, would directly charge Dolores Driscoll, the school bus driver, with responsibility and liability for the accident.

Do you agree that liability [for damages] exists in this situation? Who is liable – and why?

Some students argue that liability for the crash exists, but as a group they usually don't agree on who should be held liable. Some claim that town officials are responsible for public safety, and should have taken care of safety hazards on a known school bus route. Others find Dolores at fault for the accident, since she was driving the bus, caused it to swerve (to avoid hitting an animal she thought she saw crossing the road) and crashed it down the embankment into the sandpit.

A second group of students does not accept that liability exists in the situation at all. They argue that accidents happen and that Dolores should not be held liable for her actions, even if they had horrible consequences. Members of this group also argue that the town of Sam Dent, poor and dependent on the tourist trade, has many other priorities – and that the crash was a low-probability event that town officials could not have been expected to foresee.

Is the law in this case an instrument for justice? Is it the *best* instrument for justice for Sam Dent?

By this point in the discussion, students are experiencing – and probing – the complex relationship between the law and justice. A legal case against the town of Sam Dent offers the highest possibility for financial compensation for victims' families, but to many that case doesn't seem fair, since Dolores did, in fact, crash the school bus.

Students familiar with other legal systems may challenge why US law links responsibility and financial accountability so tightly – surely it is possible to find Dolores and the town responsible for the accident without holding either party accountable for compensating victims' families. And they argue that other legal systems focus more on what one student described as the "majesty of the law" than on financial reward and punishment. In these systems, the purpose of a trial is justice – the telling of the story, and making a judgment about it, "cloaked in the dignity of the law, and the community it represents."

3 HOW WAS THE LAWSUIT AVOIDED? (35′)

Despite the arguments for and against the lawsuit, students know that it was not pursued, and the next discussion asks students to explore how the lawsuit was avoided. While the prior discussion focused on the town level of analysis, in this discussion we move to the level of individual actors. Why did Nichole lie about Dolores speeding? Why did Billy Ansel, who was following Dolores in his car, not challenge the lie? Why was the lawyer Mitchell Stephens so intent on pursuing the lawsuit in the first place? And how does Dolores cope with Nichole's lie and the consequences of the accident she herself caused?

The lawsuit unraveled because of a lie – a matter of no small importance in the study of moral reasoning – and students are asked to consider the circumstances under which lying might be defensible, and, more generally, how the personal histories, emotional engagements, and motives of the characters influence the decisions they make. In their assignment students are asked to find examples of the moral theories discussed with the *Trifles* play; this discussion provides an opportunity to extend learning from the prior class by seeing how these complex characters use moral theories in their rationales. You probably will not have time to discuss all of the characters, or at least not all in comparable depth. Be prepared to follow student energy and interest – the characters *they* want to focus on – in managing the scope of this discussion.

How was the lawsuit avoided?

The question "How was the lawsuit avoided?" prompts students to start the discussion with Nichole.

What did Nichole do?

Ask someone to describe Nichole's action, so all students are clear on exactly what she has done: During a legal deposition, Nichole lies, claiming that

Dolores was speeding while driving the school bus. This lie undermines the lawsuit against the town by focusing on Dolores' recklessness as the cause of the accident, rather than on the town's negligence. Like the other characters in *The Sweet Herafter*, Nichole offers her own rationale for her actions. As in other discussions, it is important for students to focus on the character's *own* explanation, before asking them to offer their independent analysis and evaluation of it.

What rationale does Nichole offer for her actions? What principles does she say – to herself – she is upholding?

A few students describe and defend Nichole's lie, as she does, as an act of justice. This principle is detached from its legal context and asserted as a *moral principle*, i.e., "fair, equitable, and appropriate treatment in light of what is due or owed to persons."[10] Nichole claims not to understand why, if she is "lucky" to be alive, her parents should receive any compensation for the accident. Why is this needed?

Nichole also defends the lie because it helps Billy Ansel. She had frequently babysat for Billy's children and is moved by his grief following their death in the accident. Billy had argued with Nichole's parents to drop their support of the lawsuit. As the only known witness to Dolores' driving besides the children on the bus, the suit would require Billy to testify and to relive the accident, perhaps many times, as a lawsuit or a number of suits were pursued, and Nichole appears sympathetic to Billy's desire for a private sorrow.

Finally, Nichole claims, in easy-to-recognize communitarian terms, that the lawsuit is destroying Sam Dent, pitting victims' families supporting the suit against those opposed to it, and, in general, tearing the fabric of the town even more than the accident has done already.

What other motives was she acting on?

While substantial, few students accept these explanations as complete, and many are highly critical of Nichole's lie, seeing in it motives quite separate from the pursuit of justice, or a sympathetic handling of victims of the accident and the town.

Nichole's personal story, described in the novel, is a sad (and dismaying) history of sexual abuse, perpetrated by her father. Most students attribute Nichole's primary motive as a desire (and even need) for control and revenge, which, they claim, drives her to lie and to thwart her parents' pursuit of the financial rewards of the lawsuit.

Students debate whether Nichole's lie is justified, taking sides for and against Nichole's right to exact her own justice from her father. This justice comes at a price – and those opposing her action ask why it is fair for Dolores to suffer the burden of presumed guilt for the accident in the eyes of the town. The fact that Nichole – at least initially – seems to not understand how Dolores will be regarded once word of her supposed speeding gets out, does little to satisfy those who are critical of Nichole. At the same time, Nichole inspires some supporters, who argue that she had a right to a life without abuse, and, as a fourteen-year-old child, that she should hardly receive the same blame as an adult like Billy Ansel, who, knowing better, did nothing to contradict her story.

If Nichole's was the first lie, Billy's was the second. What rationale does he offer for his actions?

Students are more sympathetic to Billy, drawn in the novel as a fallen hero, and their judgment of his acquiescence in Nichole's lie is far less harsh than their criticism of Nichole. But even here students debate, asking whether Billy's need for privacy should trump Dolores' – and the town's – right to the truth. Billy's standing is compromised in some students' eyes by an affair he is conducting with the wife of a good friend. This, and his drinking, makes even this kindhearted character difficult for students fully to support. But Billy is seen to redeem himself, at least in part, at the end of the novel, when he discloses Nichole's lie, and the town's acceptance of it, to Dolores and her husband.

How does Dolores fare in all of this? What is her rationale for action?

Students describe Dolores as driven by duty. She claims always to act on the side of the angels, and the accident is caused when she swerves the bus to avoid hitting an animal she thought she saw on the road. Others agree, reflecting on Dolores' attendance at the funerals of the children who died in the crash – an obviously painful tribute in the face of certain censure by those present.

Do you agree with Abbott (Dolores' husband) that her community should judge Dolores? Is that what happened here?

Billy's disclosure prompts the final actions of the story, in which Dolores appears to come to her own peace with the town's judgment. Dolores' acceptance of emotional isolation from the town allows some students to claim that the chain of lies and belief is "worth it" and justified. Some students make the additional claim that, regardless of whether or not she was speeding, Dolores felt guilty and wanted to be punished. To these students, avoiding the lawsuit by claiming Dolores was at fault was "a questionable means but a moral end." Others argue against this, noting that fault had been shifted from the town to one person: Why, they ask, is that better?

What do you make of Stephens and the rationales he offers for his actions?

Mitchell Stephens, the lawyer, is complexly drawn, and here, too, is a personal story – in his case, of a drug-addicted daughter – which seems to drive and motivate his forceful pursuit of the case.

All of these characters appear to be acting for emotional reasons far more than out of what we might think of as moral reasoning. What should we do with that – what role do emotions play in moral reasoning?

This question prompts a very nice discussion, in which students pursue alternative theories. Some argue that it is important to take emotions out of moral decisions in order to be objective: "It's because of emotion that we have something objective like a court and laws to use to resolve disputes. The legal process provides people with a place to go with their feelings while letting others, who can be objective, decide." Others agree, describing the purpose of moral theories as providing a way to move beyond emotion to reason – a more reliable basis on which to make important decisions.

Other students take the opposite view, maintaining that at heart all moral theories are grounded in emotion. "Emotion is the starting point of community, of duty, of why we care about consequences." "If I see injustice, or harm, it's the emotion I respond to first." Students also argue that the powerful emotions of Nichole and Stephens gave them energy and the confidence to go ahead in the face of long odds and strong countervailing forces.

A particularly pragmatic and intuitive student observed: "This is an academic discussion. Emotions are involved! The important question is what kind of emotions are they? Anger? Compassion? Which emotions are engaged matters!"

4 CONSTRUCTING A DIFFERENT END TO THE STORY (20′)

The final discussion asks students to engage in an exercise that enables them to explore the feelings of dissatisfaction prompted by the messy plotline and ambiguous ending of *The Sweet Hereafter*. The novel amply demonstrates the complexity that seems to accompany real people as they go about their daily lives. Would a neater ending feel more satisfying? More importantly, was a different approach to moral reasoning possible, one that would have enabled the characters to handle better the challenge the accident presented to the town and to themselves?

We started this class with a discussion of how dissatisfied many of you were with the way *The Sweet Hereafter* ended. Let's explore this question of moral method a little further. Imagine that you could roll the tape back to the time before Nichole acts. Can you construct a different ending to this story? The situation is as we know it: the accident has occurred, children have died, Nichole is in a wheelchair, we're in a grieving town. I don't want us to imagine a different Nichole, or a different Billy, but the same characters we know from the book. Think for a few minutes – just to yourself: Could someone else have acted on behalf of the town and its people? You can even imagine a new character, if you have to, but is there some other process that could have taken place?

Even though it is not in the assignment, students appear to have thought about this question, and there are many different interpretations of what a better moral method might have looked like, and the events it would have caused.

Some students aim to redress the harm done to Nichole by her father without involving Dolores, suggesting, for example, that during her deposition, Nichole reveals the details of her abuse, causing her father to be tried, found guilty, and sent to jail. Other students focus on proving Dolores' innocence, either through a criminal trial, in which she is found not guilty of reckless driving, or through the introduction of characters such as an FBI agent, who investigates the accident and elicits supporting testimony from Billy Ansel of Dolores' innocence.

Many students stress the importance of bringing the town together, and students often suggest a town meeting in which "people can confront each other, yell at Dolores, and vent their feelings." One student presented a "five point plan" covering nearly all of these events: Nichole's father is found out and sent to jail; Nichole apologizes to Dolores for lying about her; the town goes forward with the lawsuit which Stephens wins on behalf of the families of the victims; many, including Billy, give their financial windfall to the town, to support Nichole's medical expenses, and even to Dolores.

But, as these cheerier endings (and more morally sound methods) are outlined, other students push back. Some find the story's ambiguous ending insufficient. These students want to make the contrast between who benefits and who is harmed by events even sharper, suggesting, for example, that Dolores be sent to jail for reckless driving as a result of Nichole's lie and Billy's acceptance of it.

Finally, other students conclude that "as a reader," they don't want another ending. "I don't want this tied into a neat bow; what is satisfying is the way that everyone just has to go on."

By the end of the class, students will have plumbed some, but certainly not all, of the rationales that appeared to motivate the characters in *The Sweet Hereafter*. They see moral theories as intuitive, appealed to without conscious reference to underlying or original sources, but necessary to express moral reasons for action. They have a far more complex view of moral decision-making, one that appears to need to make room for personal history and context, and for the weaving of emotions into decision processes and justifications. But they are also left with a question – does moral decision-making always have to be so messy? Wouldn't it be better if people knew how they thought about their own moral views before events require them to make a decision? That question – what it looks like to reason from a moral code – is explored in the next class, on *The Remains of the Day*.

Satisfaction with story's ending?

The lawsuit

How the lawsuit was avoided

Moral method: alternatives

Figure 9.1 The Sweet Hereafter *roadmap*

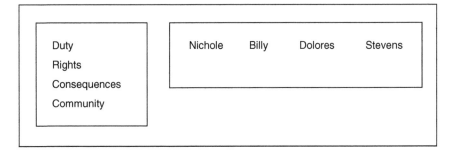

Figure 9.2 The Sweet Hereafter *board plan*

NOTES

1 Russell Banks, *The Sweet Hereafter*, New York: HarperPerennial, 1991, p. 91.
2 Ibid., p. 151.
3 Ibid., p. 171.
4 Ibid., pp. 235–236.
5 See Antonio R. Damasio, *Descartes' Error: Emotion, Reason and the Human Brain*, New York: G. P. Putnam, 1994, p. xiii, for example: "At their best, feelings point us in the proper direction, take us to the appropriate place in a decision-making space, where we may put the instruments of logic to good use."
6 At the novel's end, the school bus driver who caused the accident is simultaneously welcomed back into the grieving town *and* decides, paradoxically, that she no longer feels part of it.
7 A demolition derby is a spectacle in which derelict cars – old and without value – are engaged in a battle for survival. The car of the school bus driver, Dolores, is first the object of attack by all others, but as her car prevails and finally wins, outlasting all the others, it is cheered by town members, who appear to be welcoming Dolores back into the Sam Dent community.
8 Ibid., p. 254.
9 Ibid., p. 254.
10 Tom L. Beauchamp and James F. Childress, *Principles of Biomedical Ethics*, Oxford and New York: Oxford University Press, 2001, p. 226.

Chapter 10

The Remains of the Day
Reasoning from a moral code

IT IS MY IMPRESSION THAT OUR generation was the first to recognize something which had passed the notice of all earlier generations: namely that the great decisions of the world are not, in fact, arrived at simply in the public chambers . . . Rather, debates are conducted, and crucial decisions arrived at, in the privacy and calm of the great houses of this country. What occurs under the public gaze with so much pomp and ceremony is often the conclusion, or mere ratification, of what has taken place over weeks or months within the walls of such houses. To us, then, the world was a wheel, revolving with these great houses at the hub, their mighty decisions emanating out to all else, rich and poor, who revolved around them. It was the aspiration of all those of us with professional ambition to work our way as close to this hub as we were each of us capable. For we were, as I say, an idealistic generation for whom the question was not simply one of how well one practiced one's skills, but *to what end* one did so; each of us harboured the desire to make our own small contribution to the creation of a better world, and saw that, as professionals, the surest means of doing so would be to serve the great gentlemen of our times in whose hands civilization had been entrusted.[1]

. . .

"I've been doing a great deal of thinking, Stevens. A great deal of thinking. And I've reached my conclusion. We cannot have Jews on the staff here at Darlington Hall."

"Sir?"

"It's for the good of this house, Stevens. In the interests of the guests we have staying here. I've looked into this carefully, Stevens, and I'm letting you know my conclusion."

"Very well, sir."

"Tell me, Stevens, we have a few on the staff at the moment, don't we? Jews, I mean?"

"I believe two of the present staff members would fall into that category, sir."

"Ah." His lordship paused for a moment, staring out of this window. "Of course, you'll have to let them go."

"I beg your pardon, sir?"

"It's regrettable, Stevens, but we have no choice. There's the safety and well-being of my guests to consider. Let me assure you, I've looked into this matter and thought it through thoroughly. It's in all our best interests."[2]

THE REMAINS OF THE DAY: THEMES AND QUESTIONS

An agent's duties[3]

Kazuo Ishiguro explained his decision to write a book on the experience of Stevens, a butler, in an interview: "I chose the figure [of a butler] deliberately, because that's what I think most of us are. We're just butlers. It is something I feel about myself and many of my peers . . . If you acquired certain abilities, your duty was to put them toward something useful. But for most of us the best we can hope for is to use our rather small skills in serving people and organizations that really do matter."[4]

Whether his decisions and actions "really do matter" is the question that Stevens attempts to answer, and that students must eventually decide. In this third class on moral reasoning, *The Remains of the Day* presents students with their **first example of a protagonist who has a clearly thought out moral philosophy, which not only provides guidance for decisions**, but *also purpose – moral purpose – to life.* Through the novel, Stevens lays out a comprehensive worldview that links his professional life to a larger, and (to him) moral purpose. The novel is narrated by its protagonist as a retrospective view, an accounting of choices made over the course of a lifetime.

Stevens served as butler to Lord Darlington in Britain in the period between the first and second world wars. This period marks a transition between well-intentioned amateurs, upper-class gentlemen like Darlington, who attempted to ease the perceived injustice to Germany stemming from the Treaty of Versailles, and diplomats and other foreign-policy professionals who rejected the influence on Britain's foreign relations of citizens outside government.

However, the beginning and ending of the book reveal that Stevens must adapt to different circumstances in the post-war period. His new master, an

American living in England, is far less formal than Lord Darlington, with a very different notion of what the role of butler constitutes. This change in assumptions is a major challenge for Stevens, who is about 70, and is the trigger for his reflections.

A moral code

The class and learning centers on **the role of agent** and **the manner in which duties to a principal can conflict with other obligations and commitments.** The process of judgment comes in two forms. Students first assess how clearly they believe *Stevens* understands the forces and decisions he recalls having had importance to his life, and whether the rationales he provides make sense in light of his beliefs and aspirations. Students also do *their own accounting,* their own toting up of gains and losses, as they attempt to come to terms with **what it means to have a primary life mission,** and **whether the related worldview, system of beliefs, and reasoning have led to sound and defensible decisions.**

This judgment is particularly useful in light of many students' belief in the existence and efficacy of an essentially *fixed* moral code. Students are asked to compare Stevens' beliefs to their own definition of such a code, **to understand what a moral code might consist in.** This, in turn, leads them to reflect on effective moral reasoning and **the extent to which fixed systems help or hinder the act of reasoning through individual situations.**

The absence of emotion

The theme of emotion in decision-making, so central to the discussion in *The Sweet Hereafter*, also returns. Students find that **if the presence of emotion in moral reasoning is problematic, so, too, is its absence.** Stevens seems unable to give proper weight to his relationship to his father (also a butler), or to Miss Kenyon, Darlington Hall's housekeeper, with whom he might have been able to build a more personal connection. This is a concern to students, who understand, even if Stevens doesn't, that subordinating all relationships to his responsibilities to Lord Darlington has left Stevens adrift, without criteria to use to make decisions in other areas of his life, particularly when these areas intrude upon his role and duties as butler.

The joys of a professional life

Stevens' world is not without its own satisfactions, however, and students also can see in him the **motivating role that a central passion or mission can give,** and **the ways in which it leads to self-improvement to meet ideals of**

149

professional conduct. In the end, these benefits must be compared to what many perceive to be Stevens' losses, and students are left to wonder whether, and how, multiple commitments and obligations can be reasoned through and pursued. This question is explored in the final text of the moral reasoning module, the story of Sir Thomas More in the play *A Man for All Seasons*.

STUDENT ASSIGNMENT

READING: *The Remains of the Day*, by Kazuo Ishiguro.

In an article in the *LA Times* in 1989, Kazuo Ishiguro said: "I chose the figure [of a butler] deliberately, because that's what I think most of us are. We're just butlers. It is something I feel about myself and many of my peers ... If you acquired certain abilities, your duty was to put them toward something useful. But for most of us the best we can hope for is to use our rather small skills in serving people and organizations that really do matter."

1 How does Stevens think about *butlering*?

2 How would you characterize his relationship with Lord Darlington?

3 What lesson does this story suggest to you about moral reasoning – and, in particular, about the challenges of agents?

CLASS PLAN OUTLINE: DISCUSSION BLOCKS

1 Connecting to Stevens (25′)

2 What Is Stevens' Definition of a "Great Butler?" (15′)

3 Stevens' View of His Own Performance (20′)

4 Our Evaluation of Stevens (30′)

5 Does Stevens Have – and Use – a Moral Code? (15′)

CLASS PLAN OVERVIEW

The Remains of the Day depicts a world that few students are familiar with, and the world is as complete in its own way, with its own spoken rhythms and assumptions, as Achebe's *Things Fall Apart*. And, just as it was necessary to devote considerable time to understanding Okonkwo and the beliefs that he was acting on before judging, it is essential for students to try to understand and even to empathize with Stevens before they assess how successfully he has applied moral reasoning to the situations he confronted as Lord Darlington's butler. This is no easy task, since students feel separated from Stevens by nearly as many characteristics as can be counted: age; socio-economic class; professional aspiration; value placed on family; perspective on democracy and the inherent equality of people.

The class plan has been designed to bridge this gap. The opening block asks students to reflect on their own experiences with the agent role, before they are asked to unpack and analyze Stevens' definition of a "great butler." This discussion, and those that follow, helps students reflect on a philosophy of agency, critical not just to their understanding of the story but, even more, to their understanding of work roles (since all but a small proportion of us work for someone else – *our* principal).

Even as Stevens represents an exotic figure to the students, he is also, to many, alarmingly real. Whether they admit it or not, students are worried that they, too, will face Stevens-like conflicts between their professional and personal selves. They are dismayed and even angry at Stevens' unquestioning yielding to authority. You may therefore find it necessary to encourage students to discuss some of their feelings about Stevens well before the evaluation or judgment discussion near the end of the class.

One sign to look for is a discussion that appears to be *immovable*: students, normally voluble, fall silent, and are unable to answer even basic questions, such as those about Stevens' definition of butlering. I have handled such moments with a straightforward inquiry, such as **"I don't know about you, but to me this discussion appears to be stuck. Are we? What do you think?"** Asked in one of my recent classes, this question unleashed a torrent of reactions as students described their feelings about Stevens and the way he handled his responsibilities; we were then able to move into the discussion with greater depth and more personal connection to the story than usual.

1 CONNECTING TO STEVENS (25′)

The opening discussion is designed to prepare students for their analysis of Stevens' decisions and actions by reminding them of how common the agent role is, and how familiar they are with the dynamics of subordinate–superior relationships – even if they've never encountered a butler in their lives. By posing the question in positive terms – *What do excellent agents do?* – students are required to examine the benefits of such roles, and the behaviors of agents are examined in a friendly, admiring, and at times grateful manner. These positive assessments will stand in contrast to the negative judgments of Stevens that follow in later discussions, and particularly observant students may pick up on the discrepancy in perspectives, and point it out to the class.

Since this is a question students were not expecting, you will probably want to ask them first to answer the question in pairs before opening it up to the group.

A way of opening the discussion

Today we shall examine moral reasoning in the context of a role we all have and will play – the role of agent to a principal, or subordinate to a superior. All of the texts we've studied have asked us to engage with people who are more – or less – like ourselves. Today's novel presents a particular challenge, as we think about the role of a butler in a great house in England.

We want to get into the mindset of someone who serves as a butler; a possible analog that you may have direct experience with is the role of administrative or personal assistant. Some of you may have had PAs you have supervised; others may have served as one.

Questions driving the discussion are in bold

So think about a person in this role (or the subordinate in any superior–subordinate relationship you are familiar with) and answer these questions:

How does a really excellent PA or administrative assistant operate? What do they do? What distinguishes them from someone who is only adequate, or not good at their job?

Depending on the age and professional experience of students, they will discuss these roles from the vantage point of either the person who served as an assistant, or someone who supervised one. Valuable attributes of the subordinate emerge quickly and include thinking "ten steps ahead" of all of the things that could go wrong in a situation; being "unflappable – no matter what happens;" the person who "has my interests at heart – loyal to me and to what will help me." More sophisticated students may observe that there is not just one profile of excellence: principal–agent relationships are tight, even symbiotic, and depend very much on the particular supervisor and her needs, as well as on the unique capabilities of the subordinate.

Prompted by the character of Stevens, students frequently debate the merits and liabilities of an assistant or agent who pushes back – questioning the decisions or actions of the superior in a situation. How much questioning is desirable is an open issue, with some students advising that assistants need to "pick their shots," and others trying to stipulate an amount of questioning that is useful: "More 3 percent of the time than 90 percent."

Other students display concern; too close, themselves, to the assistant role, they wonder whether a superior really wants a very capable subordinate. What distinguishes that person from the supervisor, they ask; a question of relevance to them, and one that will resonate in the discussions that follow.

2 STEVENS' DEFINITION OF A "GREAT BUTLER" (15′)

Having described contemporary examples, you then ask students to consider the definition that Stevens elaborates on, through the novel, of a "great butler." Stevens has made the pursuit of greatness as a butler his life's work, so this definition establishes a basis *he would agree with* to use in evaluating his decisions and actions.

Stevens casts *butlering* in grand and explicitly moral terms. It is vital for students to ascertain how – and why – he can take such a view of what many regard as a limited and demeaning livelihood. Stevens recounts his long and sometimes heated discussions with other butlers about the profession of butlering. Along with Stevens' own reflections, these conversations present students with an intriguing and surprising example of the joys of professional commitment and the search for excellence in a professional domain.

Students slip naturally from *description* of Stevens' definition of butlering to their *assessment* of it as an occupation and a role. These reactions push students more deeply into the debate about what it means to be a great butler, and lay out opposing positions about the role Stevens aspires to.

Stevens is consumed by a question: "What is a 'great butler'?" How does he answer it?

Ishiguro masterfully depicts the era between the First and Second World Wars, the particulars of how a great house like Darlington Hall would be run, and, especially, the highly structured world of butlering, complete with its own professional societies, leading practitioners, and communications vehicles such as *A Quarterly for the Gentleman's Gentleman.*

Stevens' answer to the question "What is a great butler?" is represented as being from a letter to the *Quarterly* from the Hayes Society, a professional organization (self-)charged with setting standards for butlers: "'the most crucial criterion is that the applicant be possessed of a dignity in keeping with his position'."[5]

Why is dignity such a central characteristic? What does Stevens mean by dignity? How is it demonstrated?

The theme of dignity is woven through the novel, and students easily recall – and relate – the stories that Stevens tells of butlers who displayed "a dignity in keeping with his position." For example, there is the butler who dispatched (i.e. shot and killed) a tiger foolish enough to venture into a dining room in India immediately before a formal dinner. The butler's report of the incident to his master was much admired by Stevens' father, Stevens, and his butler friends: "Dinner will be served at the usual time and I am pleased to say there will be no discernible traces left of the recent occurrence by that time."[6]

For Stevens, butlering was a generational calling, and his father features in many of his stories as an embodiment of professional excellence. Stevens elaborates on these incidents, declaring, "The great butlers are great by virtue of their ability to inhabit their professional role and inhabit it to the utmost; they will not be shaken out by external events, however surprising, alarming or vexing."[7] Dignity thus allows a butler to master himself and to fulfill the many responsibilities of his role no matter how great the challenge or how disturbing the provocation.

How did Stevens define a "distinguished household"? Why was attachment to it a part of the definition of a great butler?

As illustrated in the opening quote, a butler is great not just by virtue of his own standards and performance, but also by the greatness of the "distinguished household" to which he is attached. Greatness to the idealistic Stevens and to his generation of butlers was *moral greatness*. In his reflections on butlering Stevens observes, "professional prestige lay most significantly in the moral worth of one's employer."[8]

Students recall Stevens' image of the world as a wheel with the hub represented by the great houses of England, home to the great men "in whose hands civilization had been entrusted."[9] This is the setting in which Stevens has placed his ambitions, and through which he hopes to realize his professional ideals. Stevens' definition of butlering is a cosmology that establishes the world as an ordered place, and shows the role, and relative relationship, of people within it. Not just a personal philosophy, then, but one that is based on a perception of how the world works and how it can be made to work well.

Student views on butlering

Students are divided on their reaction to all of this. Some cannot accept the description of butlering as a noble profession, at the extreme calling Stevens a "slave" and criticizing his father for raising him to be one. Stevens is described as having no sense of his own humanity and is harshly criticized for "giving up all family feeling for his job," and of having "no difference between Stevens the man and Stevens the butler. His definition of self *was* his role" – a failing to students (even if consistent with the definition of butlering as Stevens lays it out).

Other students advise the group to take into account the context of the times and the setting: "Britain has a long tradition of service, and the times were far more hierarchical than today." They urge each other to try to understand what it would mean to be a butler "back then," and to understand what the role might have entailed.

Some students see Stevens and his role in far more positive terms. They point to his evolving definition of butlering, which stretches through major sections of the book, and admire the "raised bar" that Stevens accepts in each new challenge. "That's why he can be so positive: he can always get better at butlering, and clear the next hurdle." Others accept the importance of the choice of master and strongly defend the worldview Stevens has constructed: "I identify with him and this role. Isn't what he says what we all want? To serve a good cause, and to work for a good person?"

In Stevens' view, what are the consequences of good butlering?

The final question asks students to think beyond the definition of butlering to the impact it can have. The answer: "Great men" will be able to order the world as it should be because *their* world has been ordered by the butlers (and others) who serve them. Stevens' grandiose descriptions of the impact of butlering appear, at times, to be validated in the novel. Stories are related of the salutary impact of impeccable household silver (the polish of forks, knives, and spoons is a hallmark of a great house's butler) – offering a pleasant distraction at a tense moment between adversaries; or the positive effect of a butler's patient attention to the painful blisters of an important guest. This leads some students to agree with Stevens, at least in part, and to conclude that the consequence of good butlering is that the world is a better place because of what butlers do. In the main, however, students are skeptical. How much of this has to do with the role, and how much with Stevens' interpretation of it, will be explored in the remaining discussions.

155

3 STEVENS' ASSESSMENT OF HIS OWN PERFORMANCE (20′)

The long set-up lays the groundwork for intimations through the novel, faint at first, but increasingly clear as the story unfolds, of the ambiguous moral standing of Lord Darlington, the great man to whom Stevens devoted his life. The relationship between the two is explored in the two following blocks. In the first, more general discussion, students are asked to describe how satisfied they believe *Stevens* is, overall, with his life and how well he has lived up to his espoused philosophy. The second block will provide *students* with an opportunity to come to their own judgment of how well Stevens has done; that discussion will be conducted at far greater depth, asking students to evaluate Stevens based on specific examples.

Stevens' story is told as a retrospective narrative, and in this analysis students must follow his at times tortured logic and the events – and reflections on them – that shape his self-evaluation. In making sense of the account, students must wend their way through Stevens' internal narrative as it shifts through the novel, suggestions of contrary opinions on his part, reflections made in passing that he seems not to notice, and the students' own sense of a disparity between Stevens' espoused beliefs and what his evaluation *should have been* using his philosophy and worldview as the frame of reference.

The novel begins with Stevens being offered a road trip by his current master, and while on this trip he appears finally to be far enough away from Darlington Hall to pursue a summing up of his life.

This has been a very good analysis of Stevens' definition of a great butler. How does Stevens see himself performing in this role?

Stevens offers compelling statements of satisfaction with the performance of his duties, and some students observe that according to his own criteria he's done very well. The first half of the novel culminates in Stevens' description of a pivotal 1923 conference.[10] Stevens reports that this conference was

> . . . a turning point in my professional development . . . if you consider the pressures contingent on me that night, you may not think I delude myself unduly if I go so far as to suggest that I did perhaps display, in the face of everything, at least in some modest degree a "dignity" worthy of someone like Mr Marshall – or come to that, my father. Indeed, why should I deny it? For all its sad associations, whenever I recall that evening today, I find I do so with a large sense of triumph.[11]

The "sad associations" Stevens refers to focus on the death of his father, by that time a lower-level servant at Darlington Hall. Stevens is evidently quite satisfied with how he handled the conflict in duties presented by his father's failing health and the conference. The next discussion will allow students to describe whether they, too, have a sense of "triumph" for what he was able to achieve.

How does Stevens see his relationship to Lord Darlington? In *his* view, what allows a butler–employer relationship to work?

You can deepen the analysis by asking the students to turn next to the question of Stevens' assessment of his relationship to Lord Darlington, and in particular what Stevens believes has allowed the butler–employer relationship between them to work so well.

There are several incidents in which Stevens is tested, and nearly all of these appear to be tests of loyalty. Indeed, Stevens describes the relationship in these terms: "For it is, in practice, simply not possible to adopt . . . a critical attitude towards an employer and at the same time provide good service . . . a butler who is forever attempting to formulate his own 'strong opinions' on his employer's affairs is bound to lack one quality essential in all good professionals: namely, loyalty."[12]

Loyalty is colored by the class-conscious view of the world that Stevens displays, which directs his loyalty to "great gentlemen in whose hands the destiny of civilization truly lies."[13] At the end, much seems to depend on whether the object of Stevens' loyalty was worthy of his professional dedication and years of service.

When he looks back on his butlering days with Lord Darlington, on balance, how does Stevens feel?

As his road trip proceeds, Stevens encounters others who are highly critical of Lord Darlington and his actions. Gradually, the details emerge of a general judgment that Lord Darlington and his cohort of well-meaning amateur diplomats were inadvertent enablers of Hitler's Germany, now condemned widely for their actions. So, while some students see in Stevens a realization of professional standards of conduct, others call him, even by his own lights, a failure. They return to Stevens' definition of what makes a butler great – the quality of the person he works for. As he becomes convinced (and admits to himself) that Darlington's life was "a sad waste"[14] Stevens has no choice, they argue, but to consider his own life a waste as well.

Somewhat surprisingly, some students contest this view, arguing that what matters to Stevens is how well he's done *in his role*, not who he does it for.

By this time several students will have pointed out a particular quality of Stevens' mental process: his ability to rationalize his decisions and actions, and to deny to himself inconsistencies of logic that are evident to the reader. As one student put it, "In the beginning, I thought he believed what he said about the role, but the more the book went on, the clearer it was that he was hiding from himself all he'd given up to *be* the role." Stevens' rationalizations raise an important question about the relationship between people's roles and their ability to engage in moral reasoning: are these rationalizations particular to Stevens, or is there some larger force at work – something in the *role* of agent that leads to self-censorship and denial? The next discussion will allow students to explore their answers.

4 OUR EVALUATION OF STEVENS (30')

This discussion asks students to lay out their own assessment of Stevens and to defend it through reference to particular incidents. Three of these are especially powerful: (1) Stevens' handling of Lord Darlington's request that he fire two Jewish maids who worked at Darlington Hall (see second opening quote); (2) Stevens' actions in regard to the death of his father which took place during the 1923 conference at Darlington Hall; (3) Stevens' personal relationship to Miss Kenton, housekeeper of Darlington Hall.

You may not have time to dig into each of these in equal detail, and the class takes on a different tone depending on which challenge is discussed. The first and second are most evident as *moral challenges* (see below), while the third reflects more of the tension between professional and personal lives. I have found most students will focus on the first two, but the third is never completely out of sight, since it represents a deep concern over the tradeoffs between work and family/self students believe they will have to negotiate.

How do you evaluate Stevens as a butler?

The discussion begins with an open-ended question, and a debate rapidly mounts between opposing assessments. The first position, a critical one, focuses on Stevens and what students believe he gives up in being a butler: emotion; meaningful connections to anyone other than Lord Darlington; the lonely life ("lifestyle") of a butler. Students arguing this position will usually throw their assessment of Lord Darlington into the critique: naïve; misguided; an unwitting tool of the Germans.

Other students focus on Stevens and what they believe he has gained through his life as butler. They argue that, even if Lord Darlington was not the great man Stevens believed he was, Stevens could not have known that at the time. Stevens was true to his professional ideals. Throughout his life, he took on new challenges and received satisfaction from mastering new skills as the requirements of being a butler changed.

For example, as Stevens' career is nearing a close, his new American master, used to more democratic relationships with household staff, expressed (through his own behavior) a preference that Stevens' "banter" with him (i.e. exchange pleasantries and jokes). Stevens takes the requirement to banter seriously, reading light novels and listening to radio programs for examples to learn from, rehearsing bantering in private and attempting it in public, often mystifying those he jokes with. Some students find Stevens' attempts admirable, another example of professional dedication; to others, he is pathetic, an anachronism unsuited to the modern world.

Everyone seems to have a good defense of their point of view, but why do you believe as you do – why judge Stevens as you do?

Thoughtful students respond that their view depends on how they view the role. If the role of butler is judged positively, Stevens is judged positively. If it is viewed negatively, Stevens, too, is criticized.

How well did Stevens handle the moral challenges he faced? For example, how well did he handle the situation with the Jewish maids?

Throughout the majority of the narrative, Lord Darlington is involved with individuals who are sympathetic to German interests; and, while it would later appear that he was not anti-Semitic himself Darlington was concerned that the presence of Jewish maids in his home would offend guests whose support he was cultivating on behalf of the German government.

Darlington's request to Stevens to fire the two maids poses a moral challenge, and you can reinforce concepts introduced earlier by asking students to characterize the type of moral challenge they believe the request represents.

Thinking back to the first part of the course and to the readings for the *Trifles* class, what type of moral challenge is this?

Be prepared for some confusion, as students wend their way through a variety of arguments. While possibly dismaying to the instructor ("Why is this so hard? Didn't they learn *anything*?"), this question is an excellent opportunity for students to exercise moral reasoning, and to practice the art (it is not a science) of characterizing a moral challenge.

159

To some students, Darlington's request is a clear-cut example of a right - versus-wrong conflict. It is wrong to discriminate on the basis of religion; Stevens should have known (or did know) that it was wrong; and he should not have yielded to Lord Darlington's request.

Other students cast the challenge as a moral dilemma – a conflict between two rights, with "right" defined as opposing duties. One is Stevens' duty – as agent – to pursue the interests of Lord Darlington, his principal; with this duty as his compelling rationale, he should fire the maids. The second, opposing duty is Stevens' duty to defend the Jewish maids against discrimination based on their religion. Since he cannot fulfill at the same time his duty to the maids and to Lord Darlington, Stevens thus faces a true moral dilemma.

It is easy to see how the students can use different moral logics to characterize Stevens' challenge. The purpose of pursuing greater precision is not philosophical hair-splitting, but to help students think through the *practical implications* of how a moral challenge should be responded to. In a right-versus-wrong challenge, the actor must simply (although it is rarely "simply") ascertain what is wrong to do, and refrain from doing it. A right-versus-right conflict implies a more negotiated solution. If there is right on both sides, then perhaps some way of accommodating both positions is required.

Should Stevens have attempted to negotiate with Lord Darlington on the maids' behalf? Could he have?

What would constitute a reasonable expectation for Stevens as he faces Lord Darlington's request? Those quick to condemn Stevens point to his later attempts with Miss Kenton to claim that he had objected to Darlington's request. Stevens' recollection is wrong, and Miss Kenton consistently refuses to allow him to rewrite history. One student argued that in this recollection Stevens was revealing his true feelings, even if he did not act on them at the time. In short, he knew the decision was wrong, wrongly carried it out, and deserves to be condemned for what he did.

Other students push hard at the question of what Stevens could have been expected to do, even in the face of a right-versus-wrong conflict. Historically minded students will ask the class to consider the times: the decision about the Jewish maids may not have been seen as obviously wrong in 1932, given the prevalence of anti-Semitism at the time. Other students will argue that the requirements of loyalty as an agent – and even more as a butler – require that Stevens execute Darlington's request. There is "no way" he could have objected and remained consistent to his own view of his duties. Firing the maids would have been a small sacrifice to make if it advanced Lord Darlington's goals.

How well did Stevens handle the 1923 conference and his father's death?

The analysis and critique of Stevens' relationship to his father moves the focus from a conflict involving a more distant "other" – the Jewish maids in the household – to an individual to whom, by nearly any account, Stevens would be seen as having a specific moral duty.

As the 1923 conference is reaching its peak, Stevens rejects the advice of Miss Kenton, who urges him to visit his father who is dying in the servants' quarters at Darlington Hall. In this situation, as with that of the Jewish maids, Stevens allows his duty to Lord Darlington to trump other responsibilities, and most students are highly critical, finding it hard to fathom how he could not have left the events, even for a moment, to see his father. A few students disagree, and instead support Stevens' view that his father, a renowned butler in his day, would have approved of the decision he made to stay at the conference, despite the obvious pull of family attachment and obligation.

How about Stevens' relationship to Miss Kenton?

While Stevens looks back on the 1923 conference with satisfaction, calling it a "triumph" of professionalism of which his father would have been proud, he harbors no such feelings by the novel's end for the possibility that may have existed for him to have a more personal relationship, perhaps even marriage, to Miss Kenton.

Recalling one of many times when he chose not to respond to Miss Kenton and her problems, he admits, "There was surely nothing to indicate at the time that such evidently small incidents would render whole dreams forever irredeemable,"[15] and near the novel's end, as Miss Kenton (now married) refers with regret to the life that they might have had together, he adds: "why should I not admit it? – at that moment, my heart was breaking."[16]

Separate from his professional role, how do you feel about Stevens as a person? Was there any progression here? How did the nature of his reflections change as the book went on?

If *The Sweet Hereafter* showed characters compelled in many ways by emotions they barely controlled, Stevens presents the opposite view, showing students what life would look like without what most would regard as natural emotions. The kinds of decisions made by someone like Stevens, cut off from his feelings, appear to be at least as flawed, if not more flawed, than those made by people whose reasoning includes strong elements of emotion and connection to others. Moreover, Stevens' emotional vacuum appears to be a consequence of dedication to life as a butler, and his inability to express his feelings or respond to those of others, is mirrored in the strained and painful dialogue between him and his father, Miss Kenton, and even Lord Darlington.

Students respond with strong emotions of their own to Stevens. "I found this a really hard book to read. I felt so sorry for Stevens, but he also made me *so mad*." "I hated him. I'm German and he embodied the German mentality – a robot who never questioned anything." "The book hit me like a bullet between the eyes. This book could have been about me. It really makes me think about where to draw the line and how to make the tradeoffs – a real cautionary tale." "We have to make these tradeoffs all the time." "Yes, and what matters is what you do as you are working them out. Do you see them as tradeoffs? Do you try to do anything to ameliorate them?"

5 DOES STEVENS HAVE – AND USE – A MORAL CODE? (15')

Stevens' reflections on butlering can be used to push students to define what they mean by the concept of a *moral code* and to explore the possible limitations, as well as benefits, of a highly specified code of beliefs. The debate that ensues is much more interesting than this description would suggest, and presents an important opportunity for students to wrestle with how they think moral reasoning works.

Some might describe Stevens' definition of the role and duties of a great butler as a moral code. Do you see it that way? Why or why not?

There are three possible positions to take on whether or not Stevens has, and uses, a moral code, and students argue all three.

Stevens followed a moral code

Some students answer in the affirmative: Stevens has a moral code, expressed as duty to his master. Students may compare Stevens' code to that of the military, using the analogy, for example, to defend his refusal to question Lord Darlington's request to fire the two Jewish maids. Other students argue that Stevens followed a moral code because his duty was to someone who he believed was involved in morally worthwhile work. This is true, they argue, even if Darlington's attempts to intervene on behalf of the Germans would later be regarded as a profound moral error. Students may also observe, as one did, that others are unfairly applying their own moral beliefs to Stevens.

"Because we disagree with his priorities, we don't call it a moral code, but it definitely is one, just not one we like."

Students who take the position that Stevens has a moral code can be pressed to describe whether they agree with all of the decisions that his code led to. **Can a moral code lead to immoral decisions (as in, for example, the situation of the Jewish maids) and still be regarded as a moral code? Of what use is a moral code if it leads to such outcomes?**

Stevens' code is amoral – neither moral nor immoral

Others take a middle position, suggesting that Stevens has a code, but it is an *amoral* professional code, and hence outside the realm of a moral code as commonly understood. These students can also be probed. Stevens described his pursuit of being a great butler in explicitly moral terms, grounding the vocation in attributes such as loyalty to another's interests, and in moral choices: a great butler works for a master who is worthy because of the master's moral standing and actions. **In what ways is this an amoral code and set of commitments?**

Stevens doesn't use his code in moral *reasoning*

Finally, some students answer in the negative, but for reasons that are somewhat different from what one would expect. Stevens does not have a moral code, because a moral code is used to *reason with* in coming to a moral decision. To these students, Stevens demonstrates no attempt at moral reasoning, reflexively yielding, instead, all decisions to the primacy of his commitment to Lord Darlington. So Stevens' definition of the obligations of a butler is not a moral code because of the actions he takes with this code, rather than based on its elements or composition.

Do the elements of a moral code matter at all, or is the value of a code based only on its application?

In responding to this question, it becomes clear that, through the preceding readings and discussions, students have become wary of circumventing the reasoning process through the automatic application of a code of beliefs, even of a moral code. Students describe wanting to have a set of beliefs that can be "like a code" but applied *with reasoning* in concrete circumstances. As one student put it, "A moral code is general, but moral reasoning is what you do with your code in particular circumstances." This implies that the code must be in some respects flexible, and it is this inflexibility that they saw was so harmful to Stevens.

But at this point it is still not clear to students what flexibility in relation to moral reasoning would look like. This theme will be picked up in the following class, which also provides students with the hope that it is possible to live up to multiple moral obligations, and not just to one, as Stevens had done.

The role of the agent

Stevens' definition: a great butler

Stevens' assessment: his performance

Our assessment: Stevens' performance

A moral code?

Figure 10.1 The Remains of the Day *roadmap*

Lord Darlington		Jewish maids
	Stevens	Stevens' father
Mr Farraday (American master)		Miss Kenton

Figure 10.2 The Remains of the Day *board plan*

NOTES

1 Kazuo Ishiguro, *The Remains of the Day*, New York: Vintage International, 1988, pp. 115–116.
2 Ibid., pp. 146–147.
3 It is common to cast the relationship between employer and employee, or supervisor and subordinate, as a relationship between a principal and his agent, as in the following definition from a US legal text for accountants: "Agency is a relationship between two parties, a *principal* and his *agent*. In this relationship there is an agreement that one party, the agent, will act to perform work or services as the representative of and under the control of the other, the principal. More simply put, the agent is someone who represents another person, called

a principal. The agency relationship is *consensual*. That is, it is created by the mutual agreement or assent of the parties . . . Four elements must be present to create an agency relationship. First, there must be a manifestation by the principal that the agent will act for the principal. Second, the agent must agree to act for the principal. Third, the agent must be subject to the principal's direction and control. As will be seen later, control is crucial and distinguishes agency from other relationships similar in appearance. And finally, the parties must be legally competent to be principal and agent." Sidney M. Wolf, *The Accountant's Guide to Corporation, Partnership, and Agency Law,* New York, Westport, London: Quorum Books, 1989, p. 183.

4 Patricia Highsmith, "Reminiscences of a Gentleman's Gentleman," Interview of Kazuo Ishiguro, *LA Times*, October 1, 1989, p. 3.
5 Ishiguro, op. cit., p. 33.
6 Ibid., p. 36.
7 Ibid., p. 43.
8 Ibid., p. 114.
9 Ibid., p. 116.
10 The 1923 conference was hosted by Lord Darlington to gain support for reducing the debt imposed on Germany in the Treaty of Versailles following the First World War.
11 Ibid., p. 110.
12 Ibid., p. 200.
13 Ibid., p. 199.
14 Ibid., p. 201.
15 Ibid., p. 179.
16 Ibid., p. 239.

Chapter 11

A Man for All Seasons
Reasoning from multiple moralities

ROPER: Arrest him.

ALICE: Yes!

MORE: For what?

ALICE: He's dangerous!

ROPER: For libel; he's a spy.

ALICE: He is! Arrest him!

MARGARET: Father, that man's bad.

MORE: There is no law against that.

ROPER: There is! God's law!

MORE: Then God can arrest him.

ROPER: Sophistication upon sophistication!

MORE: No, sheer simplicity. The law, Roper, the law. I know what's legal not what's right. And I'll stick to what's legal.[1]

. . .

MORE: The Apostolic Succession of the Pope is — . . . Why it's a theory, yes; you can't see it; can't touch it; it's a theory . . . But what matters to me is not whether it's true or not but that I believe it to be true, or rather, not that I *believe* it, but that *I* believe it . . .[2]

. . .

MORE: . . . My lord, when I was practicing the law, the manner was to ask the prisoner before pronouncing sentence, if he had anything to say.

NORFOLK: . . . Have you anything to say?

MORE: Yes . . . To avoid this I have taken every path my winding wits would find. Now that the Court has determined to condemn me, God knoweth how, I will discharge my mind . . . concerning my indictment and the King's title. The indictment is grounded in an

Act of Parliament which is directly repugnant to the Law of God. The King in Parliament cannot bestow the Supremacy of the Church because it is a Spiritual Supremacy! And more to this the immunity of the Church is promised both in Magna Carta and the King's own Coronation Oath!

CROMWELL: Now we plainly see that you are malicious!

MORE: Not so, Master Secretary! . . . I am the King's true subject, and pray for him and all the realm . . . I do none harm, I say none harm, I think none harm. And if this be not enough to keep a man alive, in good faith I long not to live . . . I have, since I came to prison, been several times in such a case that I thought to die within the hour, and I thank Our Lord I was never sorry for it, but rather sorry when it passed. And therfore, my poor body is at the King's pleasure. Would God my death might do him some good. . . . Nevertheless, it is not for the Supremacy that you have sought my blood – but because I would not bend to the marriage![3]

A MAN FOR ALL SEASONS: THEMES AND QUESTIONS

A man of conscience

A Man for All Seasons is the concluding text in the module on Moral Reasoning. Thomas More is by far the most compelling character students encounter in this module and, for many, in the entire course. They see More as a true man of conscience, **an answer to their own questions about whether it is possible, especially in the real world, to stand on principle.** The theme of standing on principle has been plumbed since *Antigone* and runs through nearly every text the students read. But the depiction of More is a far cry from the willful, unthinking, nearly fanatical protagonists seen in several earlier works. Analyzing how, and why, he is different will help students evolve their understanding of moral reasoning and how it ideally can work.

Reasoning from multiple moralities

The play deepens themes that have surfaced in prior classes. The moral theories introduced in *Trifles* as abstract categories for reflection and choice are transformed here into deeply felt modes of thinking. More's commitment to both the laws of man *and* the law (as he sees it) of the Church and of God shows **that it is not just possible, but *expected,* that each of us will form attachments to, and base our reasoning on, different moral foundations.**

This **multi-faceted view of morality** stands in contrast to the single-minded focus of the butler Stevens in *The Remains of the Day*. Students' understanding of a moral code is stretched nearly beyond recognition into a **flexible structure that accommodates a variety of moral perspectives.** Each of these perspectives or moral reasoning processes relates to a specific set of problems and decisions; each constitutes its own moral domain.

A capacity for complexity

What allows Thomas More to do what other characters cannot? **How can he be so mentally agile and firmly rooted to a *variety* of moral beliefs?** If there is any distinguishing characteristic of More apart from his conscience, it is his complexity. The students consider his many dimensions: loyal yet stubbornly individualistic; a man of the Church and a man of the law; worldly and naïve; a loving father and husband but one who was none the less willing to die for his beliefs.

More illustrates **what it looks like to be skilled at moral reasoning.** Students find that it requires **a capacity for complexity** – the ability to hold multiple perspectives in view at the same time, and **a tolerance of ambiguity** – the ability to work through problems for which there may not be readily apparent solutions. These capabilities are immensely valuable to people, like More, who engage with the world, helping them to manage apparently irreconcilable tensions, and to think comprehensively and in a nuanced way about the situations and choices they face.

Making good on multiple obligations

More not only recognized his many obligations – his capacity for complexity aided in that – **but he actually struggled to make good on all of them.** Students will initially over-simplify Thomas More's story, taking his eventual public stand against the 1534 Act of Supremacy[4] as *the* defining act of his life, which of course, in a manner, it was. But much is gained from an examination of the ways in which More tried, with diligence and over several years, to make good on his multiple obligations.

For a moral individual, More used tactics that anticipate the following week's class on Machiavelli's classic, *The Prince*. He flatters Henry VIII; ducks issues with his family; uses every loophole in the law; and stops writing – all in the interest of balancing his duty to his beliefs, his love for his family, and his duty to his King. So **students learn from More what the struggle to make good on multiple commitments looks like.** This is no simple task, to aim for good consequences across multiple fronts; **it requires talent, dedication, intelligence, and a feel for tactics that students usually would not have predicted.**

This struggle can also be seen as a struggle *not to have to choose*, a belief that living a full life entails making commitments to multiple parties, for *different moral reasons*. Under ordinary circumstances, it is expected that one should be able to fulfill obligations and aspirations that cut across and encompass many relationships and a variety of moral beliefs.

Constitutive commitments

But at the end More is forced to choose, to place one of these obligations above the others. And in his final choice the play illustrates what some refer to as a *constitutive commitment*. **These are values and beliefs that are so strongly felt, so deeply engrained, that they truly become constitutive of the individual: they define who he or she is.** Students learn that some people have a hierarchy within their commitments and duties, a set that they feel they must hold to above all others.

Yet More's defense of his position, quoted above, shows students that **even constitutive commitments can and must be explained.** They are not simply articles of faith, even though they may rest on it. More reminds his interlocutors that the immunity of the Church is promised both in Magna Carta and in Henry's coronation oath. He shows, to the last, a commitment to faith *and* to law and reason, and it is the unreasonableness of the prosecution against him,[5] as well as his final courageous stand, that the students respond to.

The play serves as a moving and memorable culmination of the students' exploration of moral reasoning. It also serves as a bridge to the final module of the course, which focuses, at last, on moral leadership.

STUDENT ASSIGNMENT

READING: *A Man for All Seasons,* by Robert Bolt.

VIEWING: *A Man for All Seasons,* 1966, directed by Fred Zinnemann.

1   What was Thomas More willing to die for?

2   How did he reconcile that decision with his obligations as a husband and father? As a subject of Henry VIII? Do you agree with his reasoning? Why or why not?

CLASS PLAN OUTLINE: DISCUSSION BLOCKS

1   Understanding the Conflict (20′)

2   Analysis of More's Position (15′)

3   Analysis of More's Approach to the Conflict (15′)

4   Judgment of More's Decisions and Actions (35′)

5   Reflections (20′)

CLASS PLAN OVERVIEW

A film *and* a play

A Man for All Seasons is the only text in the course which students are required to see as a film, as well as to read. In fact, students may find it preferable to see the movie first, to immerse themselves in the historical context in which the conflict between Thomas More and Henry VIII is situated. From hard-won experience, I have learned that it is necessary to reinforce (several times) that students are expected to read the play as well as view the film. Robert Bolt's play features memorable passages that students will want to use to defend their arguments, which is the rationale for both viewing and reading.

The screenplay for the 1966 film was adapted by Bolt. Directed by Fred Zinnemann, it won nearly every Oscar possible in 1967: best picture, best director, best actor (for Paul Scofield, whose More is legendary among students of acting), best cinematography, best costume design, and best writing – screenplay based on materials from another source. It won top awards as well from the New York Film Critics Circle Awards, the British BAFTA Awards, and the Moscow International Film Festival, among others.

The film fills in important visual cues that those unfamiliar with the events of the More–Henry conflict can miss in reading the play. It is important to see the eminence of More, his comfortable, even lavish lifestyle, and his close relationship to Henry, for students to appreciate that this is no other-worldly religious martyr, but a secular player of skill and prominence. The follow-up reading of the play allows students to refine their initial judgment of More, his situation, and the actions and choices he made. More's speeches are marvelous – and reading them after viewing the film gives students a chance to locate their favorite passages for further discussion in class.

The plan

Like most of the rest of Europe, sixteenth-century England was in a state of flux. Fundamental questions were being raised about the nature and scope of religious authority as well as the relationship between secular (or at least monarchic) and religious power. The class plan opens with a block in which students are asked to make sense of this conflict. This discussion deepens the remaining analysis of More by laying out how much was at stake, and how central these issues were for Henry, More, the Pope, England, and the rest of Europe. While students who have studied the Reformation and English history enrich these discussions, the main tensions in the conflict are clearly laid out in the play and the movie, supplemented by the play's introduction and background material in the textbook; students readily extrapolate from what is known to speculate on the scope and potential impact of the conflict.

The class plan then focuses on More, his approach to the conflict, actions, and reasoning, and student judgments of all of these. While the blocks are laid out in a sequence that has worked quite well, the flow is variable. It begins with More's position on the conflict, but some groups find it easiest to focus first on what More actually did – his approach, decisions, and actions, before they attempt to understand how and why he was able to take the positions he did. It is useful to be prepared to follow the students in guiding the flow of discussion.

Unlike many of the previous classes in which strategies are employed to help build student empathy for sometimes unsympathetic protagonists, many students are inspired by More. This is of course a benefit, and discussion flows easily; this is a character students like to talk about. But the view of More is not fully positive: to some students, he surfaces uncomfortable questions about the consequences of strongly held religious beliefs, and, like Antigone, he can inspire analogies to terrorists and others who are willing to die for what they believe.

At the same time, it is important to help the students move beyond a potentially simplistic view of More: much of the learning of the class comes from students' struggle with More's evident complexity, the manner in which he, unlike previous protagonists, can commit himself to several moral objectives and employ different modes of moral reasoning. That is why *A Man for All Seasons* concludes the module on moral reasoning, and through it students learn vital lessons about being able to reason from a variety of moral perspectives, even if, like More, they end up choosing one of these as dominating the others.

The class concludes with a brief discussion in which students are asked to draw conclusions – lessons learned – both from *A Man for All Seasons* and from the module on moral reasoning.

A way of opening the discussion

Thomas More was born in 1478. When he was 7, Henry Tudor, Earl of Richmond, defeated and killed Richard III. Henry succeeded to the throne as Henry VII – the first Tudor, who, until his death in 1509, introduced stability to England after the disastrous Wars of the Roses between the houses of York and Lancaster.

More's early years were calm and prosperous. His father, John More, was a semi-wealthy merchant (a mercer, i.e., in the cloth trade), a stalwart in the Mercers' Guild, the most powerful guild in England – he was what we'd call plugged in. John More was also a lawyer, rising to Justice of the King's Bench (a big deal) along the way. More's schooling was of the upper-crust sort, enabling him to mingle with equally plugged-in folks.

From a socio-political point of view, the merchant and lawyering classes had achieved social respectability – they could go up as well as appreciate "the down." Unlike France, where things were more fixed, this class was seen as integral to the learned society, which comprised an extensive swath of people: churchmen; aristocrats; merchants. It was also a time when women occupied a (relatively) high estimation. This was due, in part, to the economic structures of the times, which were changing from relatively fixed guilds to trans-national businesses – it was really globalized for its time. Women (wives and daughters of merchants) were called into action to deal with businesses and laws changed, in consequence, to allow women to inherit businesses in certain cases.

Young Tom followed his solid early education with graduate work in law at Lincoln's Inn in London. By all accounts a stellar pupil, he was skilled in learning and, particularly, in oratory. He was also attracted to the Church and lived for four years in a monastery as a lay brother. He subsequently married his first wife, who in six years bore him four children, three of whom – female – survived (including Margaret of the play). His wife died in childbirth and More almost instantly married Alice – years his senior, from a very wealthy family, and who (unlike her portrayal in the movie, but implied in the play) was sharp, witty, fully his equal, though without formal education.

Getting back to the Tudors: in 1509, at the age of 18, Henry VIII succeeded to the throne following his father's death; he married Catherine of Aragon at the time of his succession. More's eventual association with Henry was inevitable: More's rise in power – he became, for example, Speaker of the House of Commons in 1523 – powerful connections, law cases, scholarship, all put them on a path of connection. We pick up the story roughly in 1530, after Henry (now 39) and Catherine had been married for 21 years. Thomas More is 52. (He is killed in 1535, at the age of 57.)

1 UNDERSTANDING THE CONFLICT (20')

In the opening discussion, you will ask students to lay out the substance of the disagreements between Thomas More and Henry VIII. The conflict encompasses a wide range of facts and themes, and it will take students several passes to get at the essentials: who has the authority to make decisions over matters such as marriage, legitimacy of heirs, and religious doctrine; indeed, who determines the nature of religious practice and belief? The discussion is structured as a conflict between Henry's "position" and the "other side" – More's actual position is laid out in a succeeding discussion.

For the moment, it is crucial for students to appreciate the pressures that are on Henry, on England, and on the Roman Catholic Church. Students familiar with English or religious history find this highly engaging. To others, it can seem like a bit of a slog. To confront the resistance, you may find it helpful to ask these students what relevance any of this has to matters they regard as important. Student responses are thoughtful (see below for examples); ground them and give them motivation to pursue a fuller understanding of the conflict.

Questions driving the discussion are in bold

Before we get to Thomas More, let's discuss the issues. What, exactly, is this conflict about?

It is useful to start at the most concrete level, the initial decision that is being debated. The question dividing More and Henry (and Henry and much of the rest of Christendom) is who gets to decide whether Henry can divorce his wife Catherine – the Pope or Henry himself. This initial conflict evolves, over time, into a decision for More (and all other Englishmen of rank) as to whether he will swear an oath of allegiance to Henry, now Supreme Head of the Church in England.

What is Henry's position?

Students find it relatively easy to lay out Henry's position on the debate, weaving together the facts of Henry's situation, his rationale for divorcing Catherine, and, in order to do this, his need (and perceived right) to declare himself head of the Church in England.

Henry argues on religious grounds that he should be allowed to divorce his wife of twenty-one years because he had married his brother's widow, which is forbidden in the Bible. His "mortal soul" is in danger, because he violated God's law. Proof of this is that all of the sons born to Catherine die – a clear sign to Henry that God is punishing him for his transgression.

In matters of state, Henry references the disastrous and lengthy Wars of the Roses, arguing that it is vital to produce an heir, or the country will once again fall into chaos. Catherine has proved to be unable to bear healthy male offspring and must be replaced by someone who can.

Henry received papal dispensation to marry Catherine in 1509, so in 1530 the Pope is unwilling to reverse the decision and annul the marriage or to allow other Catholic clerics to do so. In response to this dilemma, Henry offers to appoint an archbishop who will approve the marriage. When this offer is refused, Henry claims that he is justified in breaking with the Church, and by "natural right" an Act of Supremacy is passed by Parliament, and he is appointed Supreme Head of the Church in England.

What is the "other side"?

The other side of the argument is not as clearly depicted in the play or the movie, so it is sometimes harder for students to describe. If they appear stuck, you can advise students simply to follow the outlines of the first argument, and to construct the alternative point of view.

In this position, the divorce should not occur because the Pope forbids it. Henry's marriage to Catherine is sanctified (and unbreakable) by virtue of the first papal dispensation. If need be, a bastard could succeed to the throne (a precedent was set by William the Conqueror, who ruled from 1066–1087, among others[6]), but the Church-approved marriage should not be undone. Henry cannot appoint himself (or be appointed) Supreme Head of the Church in England – he has not the authority to do so. Only the Pope, appointed by role to be the direct descendant of St. Peter, is authorized to stand for God's will on earth.

Why is Henry so upset? Why is the divorce so important to him?

As depicted in the play, Henry is a sincerely religious man who cares about church doctrine, his soul, and the inviolability of an oath taken. **Why, then, is Henry willing to break with Rome?** Students respond by referring to Henry's fear of a return to anarchy. He is, after all, only one generation away from the Wars of the Roses. They will also add, of course, that he is in love with Anne Boleyn.

What does the divorce stand for? What is really at stake here?

You can deepen the discussion by asking students to consider the broader implications of the debate between the Pope and Henry. Some insightful students have responded with great clarity. "This is a debate over moral authority and moral legitimacy." "By law Henry can be named the head of the Church, but the real conflict is over who has the authority and legitimacy to establish the structure and content of religious life in England." Students may reflect on the different sources of authority claimed by the respective parties: God-based authority of the Church as defined historically, opposed by the God-claimed authority of royalty – the authority of the state at that time.

A helpful probe to ask students is **What kind of issues would get decided on?** In short, why does this matter? They offer good answers. "This is not just a question of affairs of state." The "life of everyday people hangs in the balance," along with many of the most important decisions that affect them: marriage, divorce, inheritance, religious practice and belief, or, as one student put it – "what the people were living *for*."

What relevance – if any – do these facts and tensions have to the world you know and care about?

By this point in the discussion, some students may very well be reconsidering their commitment to the "Moral Leader" course, and wondering if they had somehow stumbled into a course in English history or religion. If you sense this, it can be helpful to ask about the relevance of the debate that has been laid out.

Students answer with perhaps surprising candor and concern: "We think a lot about how to have faith and be in the world." "We worry about any political leader who imposes his religious convictions on the populace" (with references to events around the globe). "This conflict is relevant to anyone who needs to decide how far to go in the name of their own beliefs: What are you willing to die for?" You can also ask students to compare their concerns to Henry's, who may, by now, be perceived to have a real problem on his hands: "He needed an heir and didn't want to be damned."

2 ANALYSIS OF MORE'S POSITION (15')

Having examined the conflict, you next ask students to describe and analyze More's position on it. Students will speculate on More's motivations, so in this discussion it is important to ask them to focus and defend their description of More's position with passages from the play. How does More describe his reasoning?

Let's now turn to More's position. How did he see the conflict between Henry and the Church?

At More's trial he is confronted by Richard Rich, who falsely testifies that More made treasonous remarks, suggesting that Parliament "had not the competence" to make Henry Supreme Head of the Church in England.[7] Since the penalty for treason is death, the implications of these manufactured charges are clear to More. Having no reason to hold his silence any longer, he explains his objections to the Act of Supremacy in clear terms (quoted in the opening of this chapter). Many students find, and reference, this explanation of More's views; but, if they don't, you should ask them for their understanding of this passage.

What are More's faith-based arguments? What about the law? What arguments does he make based on the law?

More argues that the Act of Supremacy is religiously blasphemous – "directly repugnant to the Law of God" – and legally illegitimate, since the Church's immunity from state power is protected in the Magna Carta (the foundation of English legal beliefs) and by Henry's oath of office. Some students offer a wonderfully nuanced understanding of how More brought together law and religion: "He tried to make good on each, and used them to reinforce each other."

What core beliefs underlie More's judgment of the Act of Supremacy, offered in the closing acts of the play?

A commitment to the rule of law

More's commitment to the rule of law is evident throughout. As Bolt observes in his introduction, "If 'society' is the name we give to human behavior when it is patterned and orderly, then the Law . . . is the very pattern of society. More's trust in the law was his trust in his society; his desperate sheltering beneath the forms of the law was his determination to remain within the shelter of society."[8] More chastises his impetuous son-in-law, Roper: "This country is planted thick with laws from coast to coast – man's laws, not God's – and if you cut them down – and you're just the man to do it – d'you really think you could stand upright in the winds that would blow then? (*Quietly*) Yes, I'd give the Devil benefit of law, for my own safety's sake."[9]

Using the complexity of the law to defend himself

But More's commitment to the law was based on more than self-preservation or even the preservation of England. He appeared to revel in its intricacy, seeing the law as a reflection of the wisdom and complexity that humans are capable of. There is no contradiction or embarrassment to More in attempting to use the law to protect himself. If the language of the oath required by the Act of Succession created a loophole for him to exploit, he would exploit it, believing that the finding of such loopholes was as much a part of legal process as the drafting and enforcing of laws.

More defends the attempt to find such a loophole in religious terms as well. He says to his daughter Margaret:

> God made the *angels* to show him splendor – as he made animals for innocence and plants for their simplicity. But Man he made to serve him wittily, in the tangle of his mind! If he suffers us to fall to such a case that there is no escaping, then we may stand to our tackle as best we can ... But it's God's part, not our own, to bring ourselves to that extremity. Our natural business lies in escaping.[10]

The fusion of religious belief and self

While More demonstrates consistent commitment to the institution of the Catholic Church, in Bolt's depiction of him, his religious convictions are intimate, human, and movingly personal. The *I* that is More and the *I* that believes are one and the same. Some students describe this identity this way: by being true to himself, More is "being religious" because for him there was no space between himself and God. Speaking to Norfolk, More says, "Affection goes as deep in me as you think, but only God is love right through, Howard, and *that's* my *self.*"[11] Similarly, oaths and oath taking are a demonstration of personal and spiritual truth for More; he asks (of Margaret) "What is an oath then but words we say to God?"[12]

Most of our protagonists had a great deal of difficulty operating from different moral perspectives simultaneously – they had to choose. What enabled Thomas More to argue from the standpoint of both law *and* religion?

Students will begin to speculate on the type of person Thomas More was. Where Antigone, Creon, and Stevens (to name some likely counter-examples) all seemed to be single-tracked thinkers, Thomas More was multi-faceted. "He's smarter than most people – that helped him think about the situation the way he did." Students may mention the complexity of More, which, again, can be probed. **What kind of complexity is this? Can you define it?** The purpose of this line of inquiry is not to sum up More, or even fully to define complexity (see the Themes and Questions for some thoughts on this), but to stimulate students to consider the kind of personal attributes that may enable individuals to engage in multiple forms of reasoning.

3 MORE'S APPROACH TO THE CONFLICT (15')

The discussion moves from state and religious doctrine and policy to action. How, in light of the debate, did Thomas More respond? This discussion asks students to examine More in his multiple roles, enabling them to see the *effects* of his moral reasoning.

More didn't have the luxury of just thinking about the conflict with Henry; he was forced to act. Let's try to understand his situation as he might have seen it. What were More's responsibilities? How did he understand them?

Students describe More's multiple roles and responsibilities: a respected (and honest) judge thoroughly versed in the law; a devout Catholic and student of the Church's teachings; a favorite of the King and close friend of members of the nobility such as Norfolk – More spans the political and religious worlds that are increasingly at odds in Henry's England. More is, as well, a family man, an apparently devoted father and affectionate husband. The roles consist of obvious commitments and nearly irreconcilable tensions.

Appointed Chancellor against his wishes (and those of his family), More is charged with responsibility for upholding the laws of England. No stranger to affairs of state (but still, possibly, naïve or wishful), he assumes the role with the understanding that Henry would not involve him in the "marriage question." Henry fails to respect this commitment when More's silence on the marriage question and related issues of state and religious policy becomes increasingly intolerable, appearing to offer unspoken criticism of Henry and his actions.

These facts are clear, and students are asked in this discussion to describe how More responds to the hostile and increasingly dangerous reaction to his (presumed) opinions.

This conflict stretched out over years. What options did More have? Which did he take?

Students begin with the Chancellorship, recalling that More only takes the role because Henry promises to keep him out of the divorce conflict. More's actions as Chancellor were those of any senior courtier. He is not above hosting a surprise supper for Henry, or of attempting to distract him through flattery when they argue over the divorce. More resigns the Chancellor post when the Law of Supremacy is passed – a law he could not support. More gives up writing – a wrenching decision for a public intellectual who wrote important treatises on education, religion, and civic society, and who was in constant communication (by the standards of those times) with other leading scholars.

More searches for loopholes in the oath the new Law of Succession required – for ways to take it that would not cause him to contradict his beliefs. Despite the entreaties of his daughter and his wife, More keeps his counsel, at no time disclosing the opinions that he held of Henry's divorce, marriage to Anne Boleyn, or actions as Supreme Head of the Church in England.

More breaks with his friend Norfolk, advising him to keep his distance: he is, by that point, "dangerous to know." More spars with Cromwell and others who question him, defending his silence and refusing to be drawn into incriminating statements. Under interrogation, it becomes clear that More anticipated inquiry into his affairs, and he is able to produce copies of important documents that undermine several attempts to catch him in a treasonous posture.

How big a conflict was this for More? What was he giving up by his silence?

Students create a long list of More's sacrifices: position, wealth, and prominence; influence over Henry; a loving family whom he loves; a life of the mind. The conflicts that More faced were large and terrible. He appeared to enjoy his life greatly. He was troubled by his refusal to give the King what he wanted, and worried that he put his family and friends at risk.

In your view, how hard did More work to avoid his fate?

Most students conclude from this examination that More worked hard, mightily hard, to avoid his eventual fate. Significantly, most agree that More did not appear to be rushing toward martyrdom. This is important in light of More's eventual canonization by the Catholic Church. Without this detailed inquiry into his actions, it would be easy (too easy) for some students to dismiss More as a religious extremist. This does not prevent some students from casting his actions in those terms, and all of them speculate on his motivations.

Despite all of this hard work, More failed. How do you understand what happened? Why did it end the way it did?

In the end, More was caught in a situation that he could not control, even with all of his talent, intelligence, and agility. But students may point out a "true fact" – were it not for Richard Rich's perjury and lies against him, he may very well have succeeded.

4 JUDGMENT OF MORE'S DECISIONS AND ACTIONS (35′)

While many students find much to praise in More, this is by no means a universal consensus, and you will find a considerable variety of opinion on him. This discussion allows students finally to judge More.

Is this enough to die for? As you see it, should More have acted as he did?

The discussion is structured as a debate between those who support More's decisions and actions, and those who do not. Somewhat uniquely in the course, More inspires some students to report confusion: "What am I to make of such a person, and to take from his story?" More is a complicated figure, and his actions raise troubling questions.

Probes for "Yes" position

How important are these issues – really? What makes them important enough to die for? Isn't this moral self-indulgence – frittering away his influence for personal and selfish ends?

Students support More's decision, affirming that, yes, this was worth dying for, for a number of reasons. "I had real admiration for him. It's so hard to stay consistent to your beliefs – it's impressive that he could do that." Others point to the lasting legacy of More's actions: "He had enormous influence on the Catholic Church as an example of faith and belief; he is someone to look up to because he was real." Moreover, More's beliefs have independent merit, since they were (at least in his view) consistent with the "Law of God" and with the laws of England. Students also realize the force of logic for More – some see him as compelled to act by his own reasoning process. This argument relates to another one, more personal and psychologically grounded. One student proposed that, through the conflict with Henry, More discovered who he was – the core of himself: "To deny that would be death; to validate it, he has to die."

Other students see attributes in More that they would appreciate in any senior statesman. He is pragmatic *and* principled, able to hold strong views, but not impose them, or even wish to have them known. He is admired for the ways in which he tried to make good on his multiple duties and obligations: "More used his silence to let people know what he thought, without putting his family at risk." The lengthy description of evasive actions he took prompts some to declare that "More did all that he could; he could not have done any more."

Probes for "No" position

Is it wrong to put loyalty to God over loyalties to King and family? What would you advise More to do in the face of such strong beliefs? What did these beliefs mean to More?

More's critics charge that he failed to honor competing obligations – to his family and to his King. Who but More, they argue, would have been able to stop Henry in his drive to Anglicize the Catholic Church in England? Other students assert the view that More's death was a waste – and wouldn't change anything. More's priorities are challenged, with some students taking him to task for the apparently low level of priority assigned to his family; "I'm disappointed in him. He might not have thought he had other obligations, but I did – he just gave up on them." And More is criticized for inconsistency. To save her life, he urges his daughter Margaret to swear to the oath he will not take. If his beliefs are worth dying for, the students contend, then everyone should die for them, including his family. If they are not worth dying for, he shouldn't die for them either.

More puzzles and angers some students by what they see as his passivity. He makes it clear that he has no intention of acting in a way to influence others. Why is he willing to simply hold beliefs and not communicate them?

The transition to moral leadership

A Man for All Seasons extends students' understanding of what moral reasoning is and how it works, and also serves as a segue to the final module on Moral Leadership. Students begin, unaided, to range over the terrain of that topic.

More is alternately praised or condemned for how well he reads his environment – a topic to be explored in the next class on Machiavelli's *The Prince*. Students sometimes debate whether More would qualify for the term "moral leader." What some see as passivity, others characterize as a smart move, enabling him to stay loyal to Henry while holding in private views that are no longer tolerated; More defends the right not to to have to disclose what he believes. And, while criticized by some, he is admired by others for not "getting all heroic" and trying, instead, to make good on multiple obligations for as long as he could.

5 REFLECTIONS (20′)

More generates powerful emotions, which you can build on by providing students with a chance to go up a level of abstraction and consider the lessons they have taken from More and this final examination of moral reasoning. I give students five minutes in two-or-three-person buzz groups and then devote fifteen minutes to group discussion.

This is our last class on moral reasoning. What lessons do you take out of Thomas More's story and what we have been discussing?

Students are very thoughtful at the end of this class. Here are some examples of comments.

"One of the things that enabled More to do what he did was that he was so clear about what he believed in. I don't even know the moral categories I should be thinking in, and I'm afraid that without the ability to think about issues in advance I'll make the wrong decision and end up hating myself for it."

"I had criticized More for not exhibiting moral reasoning but now I don't think that's true. I think he knew what he believed – in fact, his beliefs were layered like a wedding cake: God and Church were the foundation and the biggest layer, then Henry and the law, then family, and then others. So he could know, if he had to choose, which was his core belief."

"I've concluded that if you're going to be moral you'd better not be a leader. If you're going to be a leader, you'd better not be too moral. If you're going to try to be a moral leader, you'd better be prepared to know what you would be willing to die for, because you might just have to do that."

"We think in our lives that we're going to see a lot of gray – not a lot of black and white situations that would call for the ultimate sacrifice from us. There were many church-going Catholics who found themselves able to sign the oath. What More did was to make the gray into black and white. I wonder what situations might cause us to do the same."

"I can't think of anything that I know I would be willing to die for except my family. More isn't realistic as a role model – he's an aspiration – a wish or a hope."

One student admitted: "I'm as confused as ever. What am I to take from this story?" Others responded: "When to be flexible and when to hold firm." "You learn about your heart – the part of you that you don't yield." "You learn about your self." "Would you call that 'conscience'?" "I don't know; conscience can be manipulated . . ."

And so we are ready for Machiavelli, and for Moral Leadership.

The conflict

More's position

More's actions

Is this enough to die for?

Reflections

Figure 11.1 A Man for All Seasons *roadmap*

Henry VIII   Catholic Church

                              Thomas More

Laws of England   Family

Figure 11.2 A Man for All Seasons *board plan*

NOTES

1 Robert Bolt, *A Man for All Seasons*, New York: First Vintage International edition, 1990, p. 65.
2 Ibid., p. 91.
3 Ibid., pp. 159–160.
4 The 1534 Act of Supremacy established Henry VIII as head of the English church, separating it from Rome, and founding the Anglican religion.
5 More was found guilty of treason based on the false testimony of an early protégé, Richard Rich. Many believe that, had it not been for Rich's perjury, More's silence on the Act of Supremacy and on Henry's marriage to Anne Boleyn might have been successful in saving his life.
6 William the Conqueror (1066–1087) was the son of the Duke of Normandy and a French tanner's daughter named Arlette. Other examples include Harold I (1035–1040), whose father Canute (1016–1035) had two "wives" simultaneously, the first of whom, Harold's mother, he may never have married. Source: David Hilliam, *Kings, Queens, Bones, and Bastards: Who's Who in the English Monarchy from Egbert to Elizabeth II*, Stroud: Sutton Publishing, 1998, pp. 21–22, 27, 212.
7 Bolt, op. cit., p. 156.

8   Ibid., p. xvi.
9   Ibid., p. 66.
10   Ibid., p. 126.
11   Ibid., p. 122.
12   Ibid., p. 140.

Moral Leadership Class Plans

Moral Leadership Module Map: Themes and Learning Points

Central theme	Text and setting	Storyline	Learning points
Exercising authority	*The Prince*, by Niccolò Machiavelli Sixteenth-century Italy	A handbook of advice for new leaders	How to obtain and maintain power Public versus private morality Relationship between leaders and followers
Earning legitimacy	*The Secret Sharer*, by Joseph Conrad 1890s off the coast of Siam	A new captain's struggle to establish himself in his first command	Procedural legitimacy Technical legitimacy Moral legitimacy
Balancing benefits and harms	*Truman and the Bomb*, compilation Japan, Second World War Excerpts from *Just and Unjust Wars*, by Michael Walzer	US President Harry S. Truman's decision to use the atomic bomb and its consequences	Leaders and advisers War as a rule-governed activity Judging leaders' moral decisions
Taking a stand	*Personal History*, autobiography of Katharine Graham 1970s America, recalled Excerpt from *A Good Life*, autobiography of Ben Bradlee	The leadership of *Washington Post* publisher Katharine Graham during the investigations of the "Pentagon Papers" and Watergate	Moral courage Power of moral legitimacy Moral consistency
Assuming leadership	*American Ground: Unbuilding the World Trade Center*, by William Langewiesche Post-September 11th USA	How a small group of city bureaucrats and engineers came to manage the "unbuilding" of the World Trade Center	Willingness to act Power of technical expertise Learning to manage moral impacts

Chapter 12

The Prince

Exercising authority

IN THE ACTIONS OF ALL MEN, and especially of princes, where there is no court of appeal, one judges by the result.[1]

...

A prince, therefore, need not necessarily have all the good qualities I mentioned above, but he should certainly appear to have them. I would even go so far as to say that if he has these qualities and always behaves accordingly he will find them harmful; if he only appears to have them they will render him service. He should appear to be compassionate, faithful to his word, kind, guileless, and devout. And indeed he should be so. But his disposition should be such that, if he needs to be the opposite, he knows how.[2]

...

... it is far better to be feared than loved if you cannot be both ... Men worry less about doing an injury to one who makes himself loved than to one who makes himself feared. For love is secured by a bond of gratitude which men, wretched creatures that they are, break when it is to their advantage to do so; but fear is strengthened by a dread of punishment which is always effective. The prince must none the less make himself feared in such a way that, if he is not loved, at least he escapes being hated. For fear is quite compatible with an absence of hatred; and the prince can always avoid hatred if he abstains from the property of his subjects and citizens and from their women[3] ... So, on this question of being loved or feared, I conclude that since some men love as they please but fear when the prince pleases, a wise prince should rely on what he controls, not on what he cannot control. He must only endeavor, as I said, to escape being hated.[4]

...

None the less, so as not to rule out our free will, I believe that it is probably true that fortune is the arbiter of half the things we do, leaving the other half or so to be controlled by ourselves.[5]

THE PRINCE: THEMES AND QUESTIONS

The requirements of leadership

Machiavelli begins the second half of *The Prince* by reminding readers of his purpose: "[S]ince my intention is to say something that will prove of practical use to the inquirer, I have thought it proper to represent things as they are in real truth, rather than as they are imagined."[6] Students thus begin the third and final module with an immediate immersion in **one of the most clear-eyed and realistic descriptions of the requirements of leadership ever written.** Following on the discussion of Thomas More, **Machiavelli's handbook is a dash of cold water**, a warning that connecting moral leadership to the ideas explored in the modules on moral challenge and moral reasoning will require real work.

Yet Machiavelli and More[7] were contemporaries: they were born within ten years of each other – Machiavelli in 1469, More in 1478, and their most famous written works emerge at nearly the same time – manuscript copies of *The Prince* are in circulation in and beyond Florence by 1516, the year of publication of More's *Utopia*. But their views could not be more different on where authority comes from and what it should be used for. **The challenges More faced were within an evolving but familiar context: secular authority stems from religious authority; straight lines can and must be drawn between King, Pope, and God.**

Machiavelli bursts on to this scene with an astounding first sentence: "All the states, all the dominions under whose authority men have lived in the past and live now have been either republics or principalities. Principalities are hereditary, with their prince's family long established as rulers, or they are new."[8] And, later, **"But now we come to the other case, where a private citizen becomes the ruler of his country . . . by the favour of his fellow citizens."**[9] **God, the Church are nowhere to be found; to Machiavelli, the state's authority is squarely** *self-derived*. The context of leadership is thus profoundly new and modern, one of the reasons why *The Prince* continues to be so relevant, so endlessly quoted and cited by those who concern themselves with leadership.

Exercising authority

The module on **moral leadership** is structured around **a pair of twinned challenges** that leaders face, that we shall characterize for the students as **exercising authority** and **earning legitimacy**. *The Prince* provides an initial mapping of this terrain, predominantly focused on the leader's power.

It begins with a detailed description of various ways in which authority over a state can be secured, describing the particular requirements of each setting or condition of leadership ("new principalities acquired by one's own arms and prowess," as opposed to, for example, "new principalities acquired with the help of fortune and foreign arms"); **the manual then goes on to specify strategies that will allow the leader's authority to be sustained** – advice that is useful for new princes in any situation. **A leader's authority is exercised for one purpose only: to gain and maintain control over a state.**

The purity of this goal allows the task of exercising authority to be studied on its own terms. We are uncluttered by objectives that might cloud our ability to understand and press **the moral questions that come with a leader's exercise of power: What is permissible? What is required? What, if anything, is prohibited?**

Machiavelli's realistic and surprising answers to these questions are unsettling. Very little seems to be prohibited, while much that is ordinarily regarded as impermissible (lying, for example, or reneging on a commitment) is described as not just allowable, but advisable for a leader intent on maintaining her power. **In what students will recognize as a profoundly utilitarian view, Machiavelli justifies all manner of actions by their results. Students are thus forced to consider the tension that leaders face in selecting ends and means**, a theme that will resonate and be explored with increasing depth in each of the classes in this module.

Further, students find that, even if run by an absolute ruler, the state Machiavelli imagines contains attractive features. Late in the manual, Machiavelli refers to these more aspirational qualities: the state has been "adorned and strengthened . . . with good laws, sound defences, reliable allies, and inspiring leadership."[10] And "Nothing brings a man greater honour than the new laws and new institutions he establishes. When these are soundly based and bear the mark of greatness, they make him revered and admired."[11]

Earning legitimacy

And what of the task of earning legitimacy? That is fundamentally an undertaking that concerns itself with the relationship between leaders and their followers. Students find that **Machiavelli's prince is surprisingly beholden to "the people."** The oft-quoted maxim that it is better to be feared than loved[12] is frequently unaccompanied by its addendum: but, above all, do not be despised or hated[13] – often with disastrous results for leaders who miss this critical insight. Machiavelli's prince is repeatedly reminded that his power is only maintained with the consent of the governed. This is not consent as we understand it, backed by rights, laws, and procedures that enable it to be bestowed. But consent it is, and **students find that even a purely instrumental view of leadership requires a functioning relationship between the leader and the led.**

Raising questions

For all of these reasons, students are ambivalent about *The Prince*. Machiavelli was the first to describe the tensions and temptations common to organizational settings, whether they are in states, cities, or individual institutions. Students recognize from their own experiences that Machiavelli's advice can lead to success: many are drawn to the realistic strategies he presents for amassing and maintaining power and to his depiction of power relationships. **Students thus face a question of application: Can this work be treated as a pick list – a menu of options – or must it be accepted whole cloth?** This raises other, more fundamental questions about assumptions. **What is Machiavelli's view of man? How central is this view to the successful adoption of his recommended strategies and tactics? In their quest for moral leadership, is this a view students feel they can adopt?**

STUDENT ASSIGNMENT

READINGS: *The Prince*, by Niccolò Machiavelli.

In chapters I–XIV, the first half of *The Prince*, Machiavelli describes the various circumstances by which a prince can obtain power over a state; he offers strategies tailored to each situation, as well as advice on how to manage the martial resources necessary to the task of securing power. In chapters XV–XXVI, the book's second half, Machiavelli offers more general advice focused on the prince's behavior toward his subjects and allies.

1   As you read *The Prince*, ask yourself what kind of leadership Machiavelli is depicting.

2   What lessons can be learned from the first half of the book? Are these useful to leaders today?

3   What are the most important lessons from the book's second half?

4   This book has variously been called a "handbook for thugs" and a "justification for public morality." What do you think?

5   What is the relevance of this book to the exercise of moral leadership?

CLASS PLAN OUTLINE: DISCUSSION BLOCKS

1 Why Begin the Module on Moral Leadership with *The Prince*? (20′)

2 What Lessons Are Offered in the Initial 14 Chapters? (15′)

3 What Are the Main Themes and Assumptions of the Book's Second Half? (40′)

4 How Do You Evaluate the Advice in This Handbook? (30′)

CLASS PLAN OVERVIEW

Many students will be familiar with *The Prince*. It is a staple of secondary and undergraduate education for many of the same reasons that it has enthralled readers for the last five hundred years. And the study of Machiavelli is a virtual industry: the last comprehensive bibliography of *modern* criticism and scholarship related to Machiavelli, completed in 1990, featured three thousand works.[14] Machiavelli's maxims are quoted in newspaper editorials and opinion pieces, and the label "machiavellian" is imbedded in popular culture as shorthand for manipulation and abuse of power. So the challenge for instructors is to set this work in a new context – to help students move beyond their preconceived notions to explore some potentially surprising ideas.

The opening comments for instructors provide historical background for students, many of whom are unfamiliar with the tradition of "mirrors" – handbooks or written rules to guide the conduct of leaders. This sense of history is important, allowing students to fit their search for a definition of moral leadership into a stream of inquiry stretching over thousands of years.

In the opening block you ask students a question they may have mulled over as they read the text: **Why start a module on Moral Leadership with *The Prince*?** Students are pushed beyond simple and obvious answers ("So we'll know what *not* to do") to consider what a serious study of leadership would consist in, and what role *The Prince* might play in it.

The next two blocks (one on each half of the book) are consistent with the methodology of the course and ask students to describe and analyze before they judge. This in-depth discussion of Machiavelli's ideas requires students to push beyond familiar passages to the context in which Machiavelli views power, and the assumptions on which his theory of leadership is built. The lengthy analysis of *The Prince* will help students come closer to the lived reality of power, with a better understanding of how it is amassed, maintained, and potentially lost.

The final block allows students to judge the work, and usually this splits the group. Many students are drawn to Machiavelli's understanding of power politics and leadership dynamics, while others are appalled and even alarmed at the seductive nature of Machiavelli's ideas. The question of whether the manual should be viewed as a philosophy or a pick-list of ideas brings this conflict out in the open, and students struggle with the role of tactics – means – in the pursuit of even worthwhile ends.

A way of opening the discussion

Our purpose in this last module of the course is for each of us to develop our own working definition of moral leadership. We will build on prior sessions and look at how moral challenge and moral reasoning work in the lives of individuals with broad responsibility for others.

We are not alone in this search. It is a focus of today's work, The Prince. *As we begin, it is helpful to appreciate how ancient the search is for rules to guide the conduct of leaders.*

Back as far as recorded history goes (e.g. three thousand years ago, during the early dynastic eras in Egypt), king-fathers provide leadership tips to their presumed heirs, who were generally, but not always, the oldest of their sons. We have the documents! The advice is Prince-*like: the focus is on managing the masses, keeping powerful groups in check (priests, courtiers, barons, et al.) and proper conduct in peace and war.*

The tradition of stipulating what government should look like is at least as old as Plato's Republic *(the first half of the fourth century BC). Leaders and followers (citizens) are fully addressed in such works, whose aim is both descriptive and instructive; the ideal state is depicted.*

As Anthony Grafton points out in his excellent introduction, at the time of Machiavelli's writing, Florence considered itself to be a revival of the Roman Republic. During that Roman time, influential citizens, like Cicero (100 BC), were fully conversant with Plato. In Rome it was customary to declaim on what good government looked like. The Roman love of law, its most lasting creation, was fully explored in these speeches, particularly the emphasis on duties (obligations, responsibilities) of leaders and citizens.

In an introduction to a different edition of The Prince, *Dominic Baker-Smith asserts that the spiritual or religious progenitor of works such as* The Prince *is St. Augustine's the City of God, begun in [4]13, "3 years after Alaric and his Gothic army had captured Rome and humiliated the former capital of the* world."[15] St. Augustine's argument, simply put, was: "If Rome could be corrupted and disintegrate then there was no hope of an ideal society on earth: the city of this world was doomed to frustration. The only society that can match human aspiration is the city of God, centered on Christ, which will only be realized at the end of time. In this life, the believer is a pilgrim, journeying to a sublime but posthumous future . . . Action in the city of this world was inevitably judged in light of its reference to the city of God."[16]

The genre of "mirrors" or handbooks for princes reaches a peak in the sixteenth century with the completion between 1513 and 1516 of three works: Machiavelli's The Prince, Sir Thomas More's Utopia, and The Education of a Christian Prince by the Dutch writer Erasmus.

Erasmus shows how thoroughly these two strands, the civic or political and the spiritual or religious, are joined in contemporary thinking in Machiavelli's time. According to Erasmus, the chief guarantee of political success of the ruler is his probity, or righteousness and high principles. He writes: "Whenever Kings invite wisdom to their councils and cast out those evil counselors – ambition, anger, greed, and flattery – the commonwealth flourishes in every way."[17]

Enter Machiavelli – with a vastly different view of what political success depends on, and how leaders need to behave.

1 WHY START WITH *THE PRINCE*? (20′)

The first question is designed to enable students who may very well be familiar with *The Prince* to examine it in a new light. They must step away from individual passages and their own reactions (past or current) to consider the relationship between *The Prince* and the "Moral Leader" course of study. Why is this a good place to start an examination of *moral* leadership? This is an intriguing question that students enjoy answering; some appear to have thought about it while reading Machiavelli's text. I find it helpful to ask students initially to answer the question in small discussion groups, suggesting that at this point in the course they should change seats and talk the question over with someone they don't normally sit next to.

Questions driving the discussion are in bold

Let's start with a question that you may have considered as you read the book in preparation for class: Why start a module on Moral Leadership with *The Prince*?

Student responses to this question are an early indication of their analysis and reactions to *The Prince* in the context of "The Moral Leader." One student commented that *The Prince* provides a baseline for the study of moral leadership by describing what leadership looks like absent morality. Others build on this, suggesting that the first half of the treatise describes how to obtain power over a state, while the second half describes how to sustain it. Student understanding that this is a book about power is vital; *The Prince* enables an examination of the pursuit and maintenance of power without the possibly blinding familiarity of modern corporate, political, or organizational settings.

Students often quote Machiavelli's intent to show the world as it is, rather than how it is supposed to be. They propose that *The Prince* enables us to examine leadership in a realistic context, and not be too idealistic about it. "He describes things that leaders have to do. We like to think we can be virtuous and never do other people harm, but the world is not like this. This is the most realistic view we could have."

This point will resonate through the last module. Students want to examine moral leadership as a real, potentially achievable state; they don't want the exploration to devolve into a feel-good exercise that has little to do with the requirements of exercising leadership in real organizations. Some students add to this the view (to be examined later in the discussion) that people haven't changed in their essentials since Machiavelli's time. They propose that they and their peers will have the same reactions to leadership as when Machiavelli was writing. In this sense, they say, the work is timeless.

Other students use the question to begin to lay out their own view of the themes that are most salient in the text. One student observed, "Machiavelli makes room for the individual in morality. It's too easy to think of morality as only pertaining to what we do on behalf of others. In the figure of the prince, Machiavelli puts the individual front and center, and allows an exploration of where the self fits into moral action." A larger number of students hold an opposing view, and describe their surprise at how prominently the people (i.e., the governed) figure in the prince's world; they comment on the relationship that must be maintained between a prince and the people if he is to stay in power.

As with many such discussions in the course, there are no particularly right or wrong answers to the question; its aim, instead, is for students to begin to consider how to link morality with the art and practice of leadership.

2 THE FIRST HALF: OBTAINING POWER OVER A STATE (15′)

The next discussion invites students to examine the ideas on leadership put forth in what is being viewed as the first half of *The Prince*: chapters I–XIV. Early on I taught *The Prince* focusing only on the better-known second half of the text. The addition of the first half allows for a fuller and more informed discussion in which students can reflect on the context of Machiavelli and his work.

This section of the book could be looked at as an anachronism. What general lessons can be discovered from this review of strategies for obtaining power over a state?

Situational leadership

Students find a variety of generalizable lessons in the first half of Machiavelli's text. To many, the most striking lessons derive from the diverse situations in which a prince can acquire power. For Machiavelli, what leaders do and how they act depends on the circumstances by which they come to power. Machiavelli's detailed depiction of the various conditions under which power over a state can be obtained provides a wealthy array – a veritable catalogue – of types of states extant in sixteenth-century Europe.

Some students observe that they get a much richer understanding of leadership by examining it through the variety of states Machiavelli describes, since each state-type requires its own strategy and corresponding tactics. Situational leadership, as it would become known in contemporary studies, recognizes the necessity of adapting one's leadership style and actions to the particulars of a given situation.[18] Students point out that the method is generalizable, even if the exact types are not.

There are still tyrants

Students sometimes lament the close correspondence of conditions in their home or native countries to those Machiavelli describes. They observe that tyrants continue to come to power through "crime and force of arms." To these students, Machiavelli's observations are no anachronism, and they report learning (and recognizing) strategies and tactics of such modern leaders.

How to manage conflict

Students also relate the chapters concerned with quelling conflict or containing local populations to recent or current events. Referencing conflicts in Algeria, Vietnam, Afghanistan, and Iraq, students note that contemporary political leaders would have been well served if they had heeded Machiavelli's warning that by sending troops into states far from home, "[the] prince does far more injury because he harms the whole state by billeting his army in different parts of the country, everyone suffers from this annoyance, and everyone is turned into an enemy."[19]

Most of the situations Machiavelli describes require the prince to obtain power through force of arms. But in chapter IX he describes a "Constitutional Principality." What do you make of his assertion that a "private citizen" can become a prince through the support of his fellow citizens?

You will want to bring to student attention one of the most intriguing – and surprising – lessons of the book's first half, laid out in chapter IX, which is devoted to the "constitutional principality." Machiavelli begins this chapter by describing what he refers to as "the other case," "where a private citizen becomes the ruler of his country neither by crime nor by any other outrageous act of violence but by the favour of his fellow citizens (and this we can call a constitutional principality, to become the ruler of which one needs neither prowess alone nor fortune, but rather a lucky astuteness)."[20] This lucky astuteness, students learn, lies primarily in attending to those whose goodwill the constitutional prince needs for support – his citizens, divided by Machiavelli into the camps of the nobles and the people.

One student pointed out that Machiavelli's argument is as true in modern organizations as in the sixteenth century: it is easier to gain power through the nobles, but to maintain it the prince needs the support of the people. Many students link the constitutional monarchy and a ruler's need for support to Machiavelli's own situation. Jokingly, they call The Prince "the longest cover letter"[21] ever written, and identify it as a lengthy appeal to Lorenzo de' Medici, whose favor Machiavelli had hoped to win, with the possibility of a return to a life of action at the de' Medici court. Students argue that, as a new prince, de' Medici would be bound to appreciate the advice Machiavelli offers, and that the variety of situations described in the first half of the book validates the more general advice offered in the second.

Other students disagree. Even an up-and-coming family like the de' Medici would not want the path to power to be laid out so clearly, with the implication that anyone could be a prince, and that princes can be made – and unmade – by the people. These students see danger in what Machiavelli wrote, and find in this chapter an explanation of why his treatise was received so poorly by its intended patron.

How did reading the first part of The Prince influence your understanding of the second part?

"I understand the climate and instability that Machiavelli was living in, and can now see why stability – just preserving power – was so important." "I found myself agreeing much more than I would have thought to ideas in the second half of the book because the ideas in the first part were so clearly laid out." With this context in mind, students are better-prepared to discuss the second half of the text.

3 THE SECOND HALF: GENERAL LESSONS FOR LEADERS (40′)

If the first half of *The Prince* is devoted to describing how power over a state can be won, the second half details how it can be sustained over time. In these chapters, Machiavelli lays out his philosophy of leadership and it is a surprising one, for his time or any other. The thrust of this discussion is for students to lay out the central elements of this philosophy, to grasp, among the details and specific articles of advice, the big ideas Machiavelli is proposing. Some of these ideas are now so central to the canon of leadership theory and observable practice that it is difficult to appreciate how novel they were at the time. Other ideas continue to shock, exciting strong responses. You will want to remind students that this discussion is focused on making sure that Machiavelli's main insights into leadership are clear. The discussion block that follows will give them an opportunity to express their reactions to *The Prince* and to link their understanding of Machiavelli's ideas to the pursuit of a workable definition of moral leadership.

If you were stopped by a fellow student and asked what were the most important ideas from Machiavelli – what would you say?

Probably the most fundamental idea students identify is Machiavelli's premise that leadership of public institutions requires its own philosophy and rules. According to this view, public leaders, and especially new leaders, need to exercise force; they may also need to engage in tactics that are questionable on strictly moral or ethical grounds. Machiavelli insists that behaving well or admirably is the first and preferred strategy, and that these other tactics are only to be engaged if required: "he should not deviate from good, if that is possible, but he should know how to do evil, if that is necessary."[22] Machiavelli's leader needs a flexible disposition – the ability to exercise his dark side (the "beast")[23] if circumstances demand it.

These reassuring comments are belied, however, by the many examples that Machiavelli provides. From them, it appears that public leaders don't need just occasionally to stray from commonly agreed upon standards of behavior, but, rather, that there is a public morality for leaders that is fundamentally different from the private morality that motivates individuals.[24] Machiavelli writes, "I would even go so far as to say that if he has these [moral] qualities and behaves accordingly, he will find them harmful; if he only appears to have them they will render him service"[25] and "he will find some of the things that appear to be virtues will, if he practices them, ruin him, and some of the things that appear to be vices will bring him security and prosperity."[26]

What assumptions does Machiavelli make about the nature of "man?"

Machiavelli appears to delight in turning conventional moral arguments on their head: parsimony, rather than generosity, best serves a leader; cruelty, rather than compassion; not keeping one's word is preferable to keeping it, "because men are wretched creatures who would not keep their word to you."[27] Indeed, the assumptions made by Machiavelli of man – "ungrateful, fickle, liars, and deceivers, they shun danger and are greedy for profit"[28] – suggest that a respectful relationship between the leader and the led is impossible, a futile hope that would render a leader powerless if pursued. One student recognized the centrality of these assumptions, observing that everything that Machiavelli prescribes flows from his view of man.

Machiavelli draws a distinction between being feared and being hated. What would the line between these two look like? Can a leader really be feared but not hated?

If these points sketch many of the broad outlines, there are important details to be filled in. One of the pivotal arguments made by Machiavelli (and one frequently misquoted and therefore misunderstood) is his famous dictum: "far better to be feared than loved if you cannot be both."[29] What is often left out from references to this teaching is its essential corollary: "The prince must none the less make himself feared in such a way that, if he is not loved, at least he escapes being hated."[30]

Students are quite taken with the distinctions Machiavelli draws, and can be asked to flesh out how they understand these differences.

Why it is so important for a leader to avoid being hated? If you have already decided that it is acceptable (desirable even) to be feared, why stop there?

One student responded by observing, "As feelings, love and hate are mirror images of each other. We cannot say why we love who we do, or hate who we do, but fear is cognitive, based on reasons of which we are often painfully aware." Other students support this view, suggesting (as Machiavelli does) that control of love or hate lies within the individual who is doing the loving or hating, while fear lies within the power of the individual who instills it in others. Students add, fear stops an individual from acting, while hatred impels them to act. This last point was reinforced with a reference to Antigone, who, the student claimed, at the moment of hate, was "beyond fear" of Creon and motivated to act.

Some students find Machiavelli's premise unappealing, even if they understand it. "Isn't anyone bothered by this personally?" one asked. "If I had a choice between living in an organization where I'm motivated by hope versus fear, I'd choose hope."

Students move easily during the discussion from the state Machiavelli describes to organizational settings they are familiar with. The relevance of the text is never in question, and where the preceding module reinforced a view that moral reasoning is cognitive *and* emotional, through *The Prince* students begin to explore the emotional as well as the cognitive mechanisms of leadership. This exploration raises important questions. Some are questions of intent: **What motives should a leader appeal to, and why?** Others are more practical: **What actions would lead to being feared but not hated?**

Is this distinction useful, and not just interesting?

To avoid hatred, Machiavelli warns that a leader must abstain from the women of citizens, and their property, "because men sooner forget the death of their father than the loss of their patrimony."[31] He appears to understand the danger of temptation – "a prince who starts to live by rapine always finds pretexts for seizing what belongs to others"[32] – and the injunctions to avoid being hated continue through the text. Their rationale? A prince must avoid being hated because of the power of the people, who guard him against conspiracies within, and who ("[i]n our times") are the "most powerful"[33] faction he leads.

Leaders often have to contend with situations outside their control. How does Machiavelli view "fortune?" What must a leader do (or not do) in light of how fortune operates?

Machiavelli reminds the new prince that there are circumstances beyond his control. Indeed, to a modern reader schooled in theories of leadership that attribute heroic powers to leaders of states with millions (or a billion) citizens, and near-magical powers to leaders of global organizations, Machiavelli is surprisingly tempered in his view of the limits of a leader's power.

He writes, "so as not to rule out our free will," fortune "is the arbiter of half the things we do, leaving the other half to be controlled by ourselves."[34] Fortune exists, and "the one who adapts his policy to the times prospers, and likewise the one whose policy clashes with the demands of the times does not."[35] Given this uncertainty (and in language certain to arouse some readers), Machiavelli urges that it is "better to be impetuous than circumspect; because fortune is a woman and if she is to be submissive it is necessary to beat and coerce her."[36]

One student complained, "I'm troubled by the inconsistency between the first part and the second. The first part looks very cut-and-dried, but all of a sudden, in the second part, fortune rules half of what affects us – and we need to adapt ourselves to changing circumstances." Another responded, "It's a big deal to give fortune or free will half of control. This was a time of Reformation, of taking religion out of the hands of the Pope – a time for individual interpretation. Events are no longer preordained or in someone else's control." And another, "The difference is in time. The first part of the book is about taking over a state and that's a relatively short-term event – one year or so. But the second part is about preserving power – that's endless, so fortune kicks in, times change, and we need to be able to adapt to changes."

All of the actions of the prince are dedicated to maintaining control over the state. How does Machiavelli describe the goal here: what is the ideal state that a prince creates?

Students divide on this question. Some accept the description offered by Machiavelli of the prince having a "twofold glory, in having founded a new state and in having adorned and strengthened it with good laws, sound defences, reliable allies, and inspiring leadership."[37] Students who agree with this argument describe the state as one in which people are free to pursue their own ideas and to live their own lives. Students note the context of the Italian city-states of Machiavelli's time, whose weakness and instability would render such an ordered society all the more appealing.

Other students disagree. Machiavelli's prince is not concerned about the type of state that is established, only with amassing and maintaining power. The few descriptions of the ideal state in the text show how unimportant its exact composition is. This is not statesmanship, but the pursuit of personal power, raw and unadorned.

4 EVALUATION (30′)

Finally, you invite students to share their evaluations of the advice offered to leaders by Machiavelli. The text arouses strong reactions, and students are frequently torn – among themselves and often within themselves. Machiavelli's ideas resonate as familiar and practical, and even students who reject them try to split the difference and come up with a way of appropriating some of the more useful concepts without accepting all of them.

How do you evaluate the advice in this handbook? In what ways is this an accurate picture of how the world works? What is left out? Is the advice that is offered to leaders useful? Sound?

The Prince wins many fans among students for its practicality and the realism of its worldview. "I see from reading this that my leadership style – which I try to make inclusive and transparent – is not appropriate in all situations, and will cause me to fail sometimes." "My boss should have done some of these things," remarked another. "If you lead, you must be willing to do these things," commented a third student, active in campus affairs. Many students come to class with heavily underlined editions and are able to reference numerous useful tips about leadership and organizational life they found in Machiavelli's text.

And, indeed, scholars of the modern organization such as Robert Jackall describe the world in Machiavellian terms. The modern corporation is a "patrimonial bureaucracy," "the organizational form of the courts of kings and princes. There, personal loyalty was the norm, not loyalty to an office. In a patrimonial bureaucracy, one survives and flourishes by currying favor with powerful officials up the line who stand close to the ruler."[38]

To students familiar with the reality of organizational life, Machiavelli appears to offer a guide for how to lead an organization *and* a guide for how to survive its predictable tensions. *The Prince* teaches how to play the game, and reminds students that they can easily be put in a situation where they will respond as Machiavelli describes. The world and its occupants do not appear to have changed; much that is written is still relevant.

Other students are more neutral. They view the text as an example of utilitarian thinking: what it looks like when you work backward from an end to the means to get there. One student observed, "*The Prince* is an example of what it can look like if you have one goal (the state); it shows how all of your actions can be aligned to be consistent with that goal. But if you are motivated by other goals and ideals (say, for example, community), then it is not that helpful; it's not complex enough." Another added, "This is a great first-cut analysis: Here's what I'd need to do to accomplish my goal. Then I'd conduct a second analysis – let me apply moral reasoning and look for other ways to get there."

To some, *The Prince* shows the dangers of utilitarian logic: "Machiavelli assumes you can predict outcomes. He's been criticized at times for being too simplistic. There are too many situations in which events will not turn out as he predicts. Moreover, if you are thinking in utilitarian terms and are wrong, you'll be wrong in a really big way, because you're making big bets on what will happen."

Finally, there are students who reject Machiavelli's ideas outright. "It's way more cynical than I want to be," said one student, adding, "I'm willing to take my chances on being treated badly." Another responded: "I'll meet you there. It may happen a few times, but not all of the time." Students argue over whether it is possible to create a system in which Machiavelli's logic is not the prevailing view. Other students defend their rejection as being grounded in human rights, the "inalienable right to develop myself as I want to, without anyone directing me."

How did you think of this handbook: as a system or as a pick-list? Can you pick or choose from this book?

One of the most interesting dilemmas presented by *The Prince* is whether it is possible to have a single reaction to the text, given its mix of apparently useful guidance with suggestions that are, to many students, simply awful. Some students find a total system of leadership in *The Prince*, in which tactics flow directly from clearly laid out assumptions – all of the pieces fit together. If you don't accept the assumptions, they argue, you won't be able to follow the prescriptions Machiavelli lays out. Others push back: you don't need to do all of these things, but some of them are helpful and good.

Do you agree with Machiavelli's assumptions about the nature of "man?"

The *Trifles* class hammered home the importance of separating facts from assumptions, and students can be asked whether they believe the assumptions that Machiavelli makes are true, particularly assumptions about the nature of man. Machiavelli justifies many of the prince's actions on the strength of these assumptions, and students can be asked whether they, too, are willing to view others as "ungrateful, fickle, liars, and deceivers"[39] and, as some students point out in critiquing the text, as fundamentally unable to grow and change. Students who maintain that these assumptions apply at least some of the time can be probed: **What do these assumptions imply about a leader's actions – if people are really like this, how should a leader behave?**

Now that we've looked at this work in detail, let's return to the question we began with. What is the relevance of this book to the study of *moral leadership*?

"This is a perfect place to start moral leadership, since leadership requires the use of power. This is about power – how to get and preserve it, a necessary condition of leadership."

Other students return to the relationship between the leader and the led in connecting *The Prince* to moral leadership. While Machiavelli disdains the masses, he repeatedly acknowledges how dependent the leader is on followers to maintain his hold on power. This is the opening foray into the students' exploration of legitimacy, and while Machiavelli sets a low bar – not to be hated – it is a bar none the less.

One student concluded, "This is not a good analogy to a modern corporation. Leaders need more from us than just passive acquiescence (the product of fear) – we need to be motivated positively." And thus students are ready for their next class, which explores the ways in which leaders earn legitimacy.

Why start with *The Prince*?

Part I: acquiring power

Part II: preserving power

Evaluation

Figure 12.1 The Prince *roadmap*

Part I: acquiring power	Part II: preserving power
Main ideas	*Main ideas*
Situational leadership	Public leadership vs. private morality
Managing conflict	The nature of man
Constitutional principality	Loved / Feared/ Hated: how different?
	Fortune
	The ideal state

Figure 12.2 The Prince *board plan*

NOTES

1 Niccolò Machiavelli, *The Prince*, New York and London: Penguin Books, 1999, p. 58.
2 Ibid., p. 57.
3 Ibid., p. 54.
4 Ibid., pp. 55–56.
5 Ibid. p. 79.
6 Ibid., p. 49.
7 The analysis of Machiavelli's original conception of governance and its comparison to the context of Thomas More comes from Barbara Feinberg, whose collaboration on "The Moral Leader" course is described in the Preface.
8 Machiavelli, op. cit., p. 5.
9 Ibid., p. 31.
10 Ibid., p. 78.
11 Ibid., p. 84.
12 Ibid., p. 54.
13 Ibid., p.54.
14 Silvia Ruffo Fiore, *Niccolò Machiavelli: An Annotated Bibliography of Modern Criticism and Scholarship*, Westport, Conn.: Greenwood Press, 1990.
15 Dominic Baker-Smith, Introduction to *The Prince*, New York: Everyman's Library, Alfred A. Knopf, 1992, p. xiii.
16 Ibid. pp. xiii–xiv.
17 Ibid., p. xiv.
18 For example: Fred Fiedler, *A Theory of Leadership Effectiveness*, New York: McGraw-Hill, 1967; Paul Hersey, *The Situational Leader,* New York: Warner Books, 1984; and Kenneth Blanchard, Patricia Zigarmi, and Drea Zigarmi, *Leadership and the One Minute Manager: Increasing Effectiveness through Situational Leadership*, New York: William Morrow & Company, Inc., 1985.
19 Ibid.
20 Ibid., p. 31.
21 To a résumé or curriculum vitae.
22 Machiavelli, op. cit., p. 57.
23 Ibid., p. 56.
24 See Isaiah Berlin, "The Originality of Machiavelli," in *Against the Current: Essays in the History of Ideas,* New York: Viking Press, 1980, pp. 25–79, for a compelling analysis along these lines.
25 Machiavelli, op. cit., p. 57.
26 Ibid., p. 50.
27 Ibid., p. 56.
28 Ibid., p. 54.
29 Ibid., p. 54.
30 Ibid., p. 54.
31 Ibid., p. 54.
32 Ibid., pp. 54–55.
33 Ibid., p. 66.
34 Ibid., p. 79.
35 Ibid., p. 80.

36 Ibid., p. 81. This passage can (and has) inspired discussions of the eternal topic, "Is this what women want?" I allowed one such discussion to unfold to see what course it would take. Students made some interesting progress on the image they had of the prince (more a father than a husband) – but they did not even agree on that characterization. The topic did not last long, and students returned to the analysis of the second half of Machiavelli's text on their own.

37 Ibid., p. 78.

38 Robert Jackall, *Moral Mazes: The World of Corporate Managers*, New York: Oxford University Press, 1988, p. 11.

39 Machiavelli, op. cit., p. 54.

Chapter 13

The Secret Sharer
Earning legitimacy

IT MUST BE SAID, too, that I knew very little of my officers.
. . . But what I felt most was my being a stranger to the ship; and if all
the truth must be told, I was somewhat of a stranger to myself. The
youngest man on board, (barring the second mate), and untried as yet
by a position of the fullest responsibility, I was willing to take the
adequacy of others for granted. They had simply to be equal to their
tasks; but I wondered how far I should turn out faithful to that equal
conception of one's own personality every man sets up for himself
secretly.[1]

. . .

"There's a ship over there," he murmured.

"Yes, I know. The *Sephora*. Did you know of us?"

"Hadn't the slightest idea. I am the mate of her—" He paused and
corrected himself. "I should say I *was*."

"Aha! Something wrong?"

"Yes, very wrong indeed. I've killed a man."

"What do you mean? Just now?"

"No, on the passage. Weeks ago. Thirty-nine south. When I say a
man—"

"Fit of temper," I suggested, confidently.

The shadowy, dark head, like mine, seemed to nod imperceptibly
above the ghostly gray of my sleeping suit. It was, in the night, as though
I had been faced by my own reflection in the depths of a somber and
immense mirror.

"A pretty thing to have to own up to for a Conway boy," murmured
my double, distinctly.

"You're a Conway boy?"

"I am," he said, as if startled. Then, slowly . . . "Perhaps you too—"
. . .

I walked to the break of the poop. On the overshadowed deck all hands stood by the forebraces waiting for my order. The stars ahead seemed to be gliding from right to left. And all was so still in the world that I heard the quiet remark "She's round," passed in a tone of intense relief between two seamen.

. . . The foreyards ran round with a great noise, amidst cheery cries. And now the frightful whiskers made themselves heard giving various orders. Already the ship was drawing ahead. And I was alone with her. Nothing! No one in the world should stand now between us, throwing a shadow on the way of silent knowledge and mute affection, the perfect communion of a seaman with his first command."[2]

THE SECRET SHARER: THEMES AND QUESTIONS

The novel responsibility of command

The Secret Sharer extends the exploration of moral leadership and its twinned tasks of exercising authority and earning legitimacy through the story of a young captain facing the "novel responsibility of command." The discussion of *The Prince* focused largely on the leader's exercise of power and authority; *The Secret Sharer* class is designed to explore the second task, allowing an examination of the many ways in which *legitimacy* can be understood.

The first and most salient theme to students personally is of **leaders new to their role**. Machiavelli wrote from the outside in – schooling the new prince in strategy and tactics; Conrad writes from the inside out – narrating in the captain's own voice his concerns and fears. For aspiring leaders, the story is **a roadmap of the step change to a "position of highest authority."**[3]

Based on the example of Conrad's captain, this roadmap includes distinctive features: the loneliness of command; the requirement to become familiar with the capacities of the new institution and its members; the correct perception that one is being tested; and the need to establish oneself as leader.

Like *Blessed Assurance*, *The Secret Sharer* is focused on a moment of transition, and, it, too, provides a window into the psychology of transition – in this story, the psychology of assuming leadership. The captain's internal dialogue is born of the self-consciousness of a new leader – the need to watch and weigh each act. Novice leaders are on an internal hunt for strengths they fear they don't have, and for weaknesses they are certain they do.

Procedural legitimacy

But, where Machiavelli's prince must wrest his position and authority from a reluctant state, **Conrad's captain-narrator arrives on the scene appointed by his ship's owners, and cloaked in the extensive powers given to captains by the laws of the sea**. In the terminology of the time, mercantile ship captains were called "masters," understood first in the sense of masters of their craft, fully experienced with knowledge attested to by superiors under whom they had served, and licensed by bodies such as the British Board of Trade. Captains were also literally masters on board their ships, expected to maintain order, to protect the ship and its cargo, and to see to the health and welfare of the crew.[4]

So Conrad's captain begins his leadership challenge from a very different starting point from Machiavelli's prince. Students can examine the benefits of **procedural legitimacy, the legitimacy that comes from authority bestowed by clear and recognized processes**, such as the election of a president by a country's citizens, or, in this case, the lawful appointment of a leader by a ship's owners. Procedural legitimacy provides a framework within which authority can be exercised, a shared understanding of the nature and scope of the captain's powers and obligations and the corresponding rights and duties of the crew.

But, from the time of his arrival on board, Conrad's captain is beset by doubts about his ability to master his ship, its crew, and, most of all, himself. His early, faltering actions appear to be proof that **procedural legitimacy is necessary but not a sufficient condition for leadership**. The remainder of the story provides a vehicle for students to explore what else legitimated leadership entails.

The challenge

As readers familiar with *The Secret Sharer* know, the captain is confronted on his first night of command with a staggering challenge. A naked swimmer comes to the side of the ship while the captain is alone on watch. The swimmer, Leggatt, claims to have escaped from the *Sephora,* where he served as first mate. He fled to avoid being turned over to civil authorities and tried for the murder of a fellow seaman. Leggatt does not deny the murder; he justifies his act as necessary, part of the successful effort he undertook to keep the *Sephora* from going under during a ferocious storm.

The captain must respond to Leggatt's sudden and clearly unexpected arrival. His formal duties are clear: as captain he is bound by maritime and civil law to hand Leggatt over to civil authorities or to the captain of the *Sephora*. Instead, on the strength of shared sympathy with Leggatt and a common conviction that no land-based jury could understand the obligations and stresses of marine officers responsible for a ship in near-fatal conditions, he decides, intuitively at first, and then with increasing planning, to save Leggatt. This impels the captain to take three pivotal actions: first, to engage in a nerve-racking and complicated process of hiding Leggatt in his own cabin; second, lying to the *Sephora*'s captain who comes in search of the escaped officer; and, third, putting his ship and crew at risk by sailing close enough to shore for Leggatt to swim to an island far from the reach of colonial authorities. These actions provide the context within which the captain's pursuit of legitimacy as a leader is worked out.

Technical legitimacy

If the captain enjoys procedural legitimacy without effort, he appears to search for ways to establish **technical legitimacy, the legitimacy that comes through demonstrated competence at the specific tasks required by his role.** But his search is complicated by the decision to take Leggatt on board, and the machinations required to keep Leggatt hidden make the captain appear increasingly indecisive, quixotic, and incompetent.

All of this is background to the captain's final decision to sail close enough to shore for Leggatt to make his escape. The decision is described as a test of will, with the captain relying on his (apparently) superior understanding of the capabilities of the ship and its crew to enforce such a risky and potentially fatal maneuver. The crew greets the successful execution of this action with "cheery cries," relieved, at last, to have a potent demonstration of the captain's expertise. **From Machiavelli students learn that results matter. Technical legitimacy takes this requirement one step further, and shows the relationship between a leader's skill and the expectation of willing actions from followers.**

Moral legitimacy

But, just as procedural legitimacy is a necessary but not sufficient condition for moral leadership, so, too, is technical legitimacy. The crew may have gained some measure of trust in the captain's ability to master his craft, and he may believe that he has attained "the perfect communion of a seaman and his first command,"[5] but, when asked, students are reluctant to describe the captain as having attained legitimacy. **The captain is seen as lacking *moral* legitimacy, the legitimacy earned by pursuing moral ends, for moral motives, through moral means.**

The first problem is that the captain's technical legitimacy is built on a lie. While the crew may believe that the captain is trustworthy, he is far from that to readers who understand the complete story, since the captain claims that the reason they need to sail close to shore is to catch more favorable winds. And this lie is eclipsed by the more disturbing lies the captain makes to the captain of the *Sephora* and to his own crew when he claims that Leggatt is not on board.

The second and more damaging problem comes from the captain's decision to favor Leggatt's interests over those of his own command and crew. The situation poses moral questions for the captain: Could Leggatt obtain a fair trial in a civilian setting? And, even in the face of a potential miscarriage of justice, what actions are morally justifiable?

The captain undermines his moral adequacy to assume command by repudiating his duties to uphold civil and maritime laws, and, most tellingly, by his readiness to put the lives of his crew and his owners' ship at risk to help Leggatt to safety. This does not appear to be the kind of moral complexity students admired in Thomas More, but, rather, a callous disregard for lives placed in his care and a preference, based on class prejudice, to favor one life over many.

At the same time, the captain must prove – to himself and to his reluctant and doubting crew – the ability to exercise his authority. Using the situation with Leggatt to accomplish this task can be construed as Machiavellian in a positive sense, a willingness to use an opportunity that was available to establish the authority essential to leadership. For these reasons, *The Secret Sharer* is no simple morality play, but a multi-layered tale that leaves questions open about the relationship between leaders' authority and their legitimacy – questions that will be pursued in the next three classes.

STUDENT ASSIGNMENT

READING: *The Secret Sharer,* by Joseph Conrad.

1   What leadership challenges did the captain face *before* Leggatt arrived at the ship?

2   Why did the captain hide Leggatt? Do you agree with his decision to do so?

3   Think about the captain's relationship with his crew. Has he been able to establish legitimacy? Why or why not?

4   What lessons do you take from this story about the "novel responsibility of command"?

CLASS PLAN OUTLINE: DISCUSSION BLOCKS

1 Responsibilities of a New Leader (25′)

2 The Captain's Decisions (20′)

3 Optional Discussion: Alternative Interpretations (10′)

4 Judgment (20′)

5 Is the Captain Now a Legitimate Leader? (20′)

6 Lessons about the "Novel Responsibility of Command" (10′)

CLASS PLAN OVERVIEW

Despite (or perhaps because of) its depth and complexity, *The Secret Sharer* is not a story that students easily warm to. Some students enjoy its explicitly literary aspects, symbolic events, psychological portrait, and tight, compact prose. Others find the story maddeningly ambiguous, and the captain hesitant, insecure, and unappealing. As with *The Remains of the Day*, this story cuts a little too close to the bone; students, many of them aspiring leaders, find it frightening to be confronted with the emotional burdens of the ascent to leadership.

The class plan has been devised to build a bridge between those aspects of the story that are most accessible – the characteristic problems of a young, new leader – and the events that follow. The initial block asks students to describe the problems faced by the captain *before* Leggatt comes on board. Through this discussion, students develop empathy for the captain, and a fuller appreciation of the context in which his search for legitimacy takes place. Students are also asked to reflect on their own leadership experiences, and this question provides another bridge – linking the problems they have experienced in establishing themselves as leaders with those of the captain.

The second block is an analysis of the captain's decisions and actions, and it is conducted in the same way as the class on *Trifles*: students are asked first to describe the facts about Leggatt as they know them, and then to compare those facts to the storyline that the captain appears to have constructed that inspires him to save Leggatt. The difference in perspectives is striking, and builds a foundation to use in analyzing the captain's decisions.

211

There is also a brief, optional section on "alternative interpretations" that has been designed to let students express some of their own questions about Leggatt. Conrad's depiction of the captain's shaky psychological state is so compelling that students sometimes wonder whether the captain hasn't simply made up Leggatt to be a source of comfort and inspiration for the decisiveness that leadership demands. If such questions are raised, it is helpful to bring them out in the open, since they allow students to develop a deeper description of the captain's emotions than they might reach otherwise. Eventually, one of the students or the instructor observes that while Leggatt may appear to be a figment of the captain's imagination, his existence is validated by the captain of the *Sephora,* who comes to seek Leggatt and, if found, to bring him to justice.

The heart of the class plan is the exploration of the captain's legitimacy. The idea that there are types of legitimacy is a new concept for most students, and helps explain the many ways in which the term is used. Students are quite energized (incensed even) in their judgment of the captain, so the block in which they describe their reactions to his decisions is usually quite lively. Finally, there is a last block on personal reflections that allows students to attain some measure of closure on this complex story and to draw broader lessons from it.

1 CONTEXT: RESPONSIBILITIES OF A NEW LEADER (25′)

The opening discussion is designed to help students approach the text by empathizing with the plight of the captain. Asking students to take some time (it can be as long as five minutes) to write down their answers to the opening question allows them to bring in many more details than if they just answered the question when posed. The discussion also reinforces one of the principal learnings from *The Prince* – context matters: leaders' actions are shaped, in part, by the conditions under which they come into their role.

A way of opening the discussion

This is our second story about a new leader, and Conrad has written a complex psychological tale about the moment of transition to a role of highest authority. Let's start by trying to understand the nature of the leadership challenge faced by the captain-narrator. Take a few minutes and write down your answer to this question:

Questions driving the discussion are in bold

What are the most important elements of the leadership challenge faced by the captain in Conrad's story *before* Leggatt comes on board?

Students usually do an excellent job of describing what they understand as the most important elements of the captain's context and situation.

Fulfilling responsibilities

Many begin with the unique responsibilities of a ship's captain: thousands of miles from others, a captain's crew depends on him more than is common in nearly any other organizational setting. Students appreciate that this is a particularly demanding type of leadership to assume, carrying with it multiple duties: successful execution of the ship's commercial venture on behalf of its owners; leadership and guidance of the ship's officers; maintenance of the physical condition of the ship and of the health, well-being, discipline, and productivity of the crew.

The captain's situation

All leaders work within the structure of established rules and practices, but a captain is nearly unique in being recognized as the sole arbiter of what is lawful on his ship. A captain's duties run outside the vessel as well. He is charged to uphold the laws of the sea and is equally answerable to civilian authorities.

Students then typically move to the particulars of the captain's situation. They note his unfamiliarity with the crew, which has been together for eighteen months prior to his arrival. This circumstance, trying enough, is compounded by the captain's youth. He is by his own account the second-youngest man on board, and must supervise older officers and a crew with substantially more experience.

The captain also knows nothing of the prior captain or the practices that were common aboard ship. Students note this as a serious disadvantage, since an experienced leader in a new assignment might purposefully fashion himself to be either similar to, or deliberately different from, the prior commander.

Students with boating experience will remark that the captain is unfamiliar with the ship, not knowing its capacities or how it would behave under various conditions of sea and weather. Then there is, of course, the fact that this is the captain's first exposure to a "position of fullest responsibility " – his first command.

Students infer from these facts a number of challenges that the captain must surmount. Many reference the captain's admission that he is a "stranger to himself,"[6] and students can be probed: **In what sense did he see himself as a stranger; what didn't he know?** They frame their answer carefully: the captain seems confident in his technical skills; what he is not sure of is how he will respond to this level of command. One student observed that if the captain could "know himself," he'd be able to learn how to take charge of the ship.

Establishing himself as leader

Other students claim that the captain's most pressing challenge is to establish himself as leader in the eyes of the crew. The rigors of life at sea require unquestioning obedience to a captain's orders, and the crew needs to be able to trust the captain in his role. The captain is painfully aware of this requirement for success, and some students claim that it colors his early actions and the crew's reactions to him.

In this regard, the students debate whether the captain's first action – taking the first night watch himself – was consistent with the goal of establishing his standing with the crew. Some students admire the act, arguing that it was needed to give the captain time to get used to the ship and to the responsibility of command. They add that the order, clearly a novel command that the officers and crew did not expect, showed the captain as forceful, with unique thought processes that those on board would have to learn.

Other students disagree, arguing that the captain simply proved himself to be capricious and insensitive to the common practices of the ship. Likening the decision to mistakes typical of inexperienced leaders, one student observed that the captain gave an order when he could have asked a question, and took the watch himself when he could have delegated this relatively unimportant task to one of his officers.

Who here has had a position of leadership similar to that of the captain? What additional insights can you provide about the nature of assuming your first position of command over a group or an institution/entity? [*Note:* this can be in any context: professional, extra-curricular, etc.]

Many students identify with the situation of the captain, and are usually quite open in sharing their experiences with the step-change to leadership. They relate stories of the requirement (like the captain's) to supervise older and more experienced members of a group or organization, and describe various strategies that they devised to accommodate and shape the reactions of more experienced workers to their leadership. Asking questions, rather than commanding; explaining, rather than demanding – the students' tactics reflect contemporary understanding of how leaders operate, as well as practical instincts driven by necessity. Students also identify with the captain's insecurity. One especially candid student said, "I was worried, like the captain, that I wouldn't make the right decisions. Sometimes I didn't and that made it worse. I don't feel I ever figured out how to be capable as a leader."

But even as the students tell their own stories they remind themselves of the differences between their leadership roles and the captain's. "What's different here is that lives are at stake." "*I* could tell them 'I don't know why I was chosen; I don't think I'm any better than you,' but the captain couldn't do that."

2 THE CAPTAIN'S DECISIONS (20′)

The next discussion moves from the context of the captain's situation as a new leader to the decisions he made. The purpose of this block is for students to examine the captain's actions in detail and to understand, from his perspective, why he acted as he did. The discussion starts with fact-finding, a critical part of the moral reasoning process. In a discussion reminiscent of the *Trifles* class, you will first ask students to lay out what appear to be the essential facts of Legatt's situation. You will want to record their answers on the board. You then ask them to describe the captain's view of these facts and the process by which he appears to have arrived at his decisions. This analysis links moral challenge and moral reasoning to leadership, and enables students to explore how the captain makes decisions under conditions of responsibility for others.

We know the captain took enormous risks in hiding and saving Leggatt. Why did he do that? How does he justify his actions? Let's start with fact finding. What are the "pure facts" about Leggatt as we know them? Let's try to get as clear and unbiased a view of the facts as we can.

The students will describe these facts: the naked Leggatt approaches the captain's ship from the water, having swum there, and is allowed by the captain to come on board. Previously chief mate on the *Sephora*, Leggatt has escaped that ship where he was imprisoned by its captain for murdering a seaman. Leggatt was being held on the *Sephora* until he could be brought to shore to be tried for his crime by civilian authorities.

215

How would the captain tell Leggatt's story? What would he stress?

Some students are very effective at channeling the captain and reconstruct Leggatt's situation as the captain might have described it: "Leggatt, a forceful and effective chief mate, assumes command of the *Sephora* when his own captain proves unable to manage the ship through a terrific storm. Stressed nearly beyond endurance by the need to keep control of the crew and the ship, Leggatt is challenged by a seaman, a long-time troublemaker whose questions and attitude threaten the safety of all on board. In the rush of the moment, Leggatt murders the seaman. Leggatt's quick-wittedness, courage, and decisive actions enable the *Sephora* successfully to ride out the storm.

Rather than acknowledge responsibility for his own failings and commend Leggatt for saving the ship and its crew, the weak and fearful captain of the *Sephora* insists on bringing Leggatt to land to stand trial for murder. Leggatt is right in thinking he would never get a fair trial: no land-based authority could ever appreciate the danger that the seaman posed, or the necessity of Leggatt's action.

These quite different accounts of Leggatt's circumstances, actions, and prospects set the context for the captain's decision-making. But behind the second storyline is a set of questions next put to the students:

Why was the captain so positively disposed to Leggatt? Why did he believe his story?

Many students recognize the tension Conrad sets up between the captain's affinity for Leggatt, a bond forged by class, station, and common schooling at Conway, the British academy for training officers in the merchant marine, and the captain's distance from his own officers and crew. Intimations of class prejudice are close to the surface, and students struggle over why the captain is so quick to believe Leggatt's side of events, and, even more important, why he is willing (by the story's end) potentially to sacrifice the crew and his command to see Leggatt to safety. "He judged Leggatt solely on the basis of white teeth," remarked one student, angrily. "No seaman would ever have white teeth!"

While the captain refers to Leggatt as his double, students point out that the differences between them may be even more important in understanding the captain's decisions. Leggatt seems to possess a preternatural confidence, and the contrast between the captain's hesitancy and self-doubt and Leggatt's belief in the necessity of the actions he took in saving the *Sephora* is striking. Even more, Leggatt is capable of using force (one aspect of exercising authority) in carrying out his duties. At the end, the captain also proves able to impose his will on his own crew, and many students argue that the captain believes Leggatt because he admires him. Rather than seeing Leggatt as his double, he is, in fact, his ideal, the captain he would like to be.

How would you describe the captain's moral reasoning – the process he uses to arrive at his decisions?

Here, student opinions differ. Many students claim to see no evidence of moral reasoning at all – or of reasoning, for that matter. From his first decision to allow Leggatt to come on board, the captain seems to act unconsciously – one decision leads to another without evidence of conscious direction.

Some students taking this view will argue that the captain had an obligation to find out whether his view of the facts was true, and they criticize him for not verifying the facts of Leggatt's situation with the captain of the *Sephora*. They also criticize the captain for being more driven by psychological needs than by any sense of moral duty or obligation; his acts are emotional, not moral.

Other students disagree, saying that the captain appeared to believe that he had two duties. One duty was to Leggatt, given the similarities in background between them. A student likened it to the moral duty of a mother to a son – a duty based on personal connection. In the captain's reasoning, this duty trumped the other, more abstract and general obligation that he had to the crew, justifying his decision to save Leggatt.

Were there other realistic options, given the captain's desire to help Leggatt?

Some students sketch a scenario in which the captain brings the crew and officers into his confidence, letting them know of Leggatt's presence on board, and of his commitment to save him. But most students predict that this strategy would have a low likelihood of success, since it is not at all clear that the officers and crew (no "Conway boys" among them) would support the captain's actions. They might even mutiny.

More practical options include holding Leggatt prisoner until the captain's ship reached England, or, even easier, turning Leggatt over to the captain of the *Sephora* when he came on board. Students are highly critical of the captain for not at least considering these options, which leads them to a more general discussion of how they evaluate the decisions the captain made.

3 OPTIONAL DISCUSSION: ALTERNATIVE INTERPRETATIONS (10′)

Conrad depicts the psychological stresses of the ascent to leadership so powerfully that some students question whether Leggatt is real at all, or whether he is, instead, a fiction of the captain's imagination. It can be helpful to allow these alternative interpretations to be discussed, particularly if they appear to interfere with the students' ability to take the story at face value. This should be a short discussion, however, more to clear the air than totally to satisfy those who hold to this interpretation.

Some of you seem to find the storyline of *The Secret Sharer* improbable. How do you understand the captain's actions?

Students offer different interpretations of the rationale behind the captain's decisions regarding Leggatt. They sometimes create a new backstory: the captain had himself killed someone before; like Leggatt, he was guilty of murder and couldn't turn Leggatt in without turning himself in. Others take a symbolic view: Leggatt was "washed clean" of his crime by the sea – the sea is a rebirth for Leggatt; by allowing him to reach the captain's boat, the sea proved he should be saved.

Many, however, offer more psychologically grounded interpretations. The most common of these is that the captain has in some fashion constructed or created Leggatt to gain control over his new situation. In this view, Leggatt provides an alter ego for the captain to engage with – a stronger and more decisive alternate self, a model to emulate and learn from.

Other students will usually push back on these interpretations of Leggatt as a creature of the captain's fancy. They argue that Archbold, captain of the *Sephora* who comes in search of the escaped chief mate, provides third-party corroboration of Leggatt's existence and story. They point out that the waters were warm enough to swim in, that Leggatt was reputed to be a champion swimmer, and that the distance from the *Sephora* to the captain's ship was not beyond Leggatt's physical capabilities. Some diehards may continue to argue that if the captain was truly crazy he could have made up Archbold and the search for Leggatt, but few are willing to take the argument that far, and the discussion usually moves on.

As a transition, you may note that these interpretations are a tribute to the spectacular job Conrad has done of depicting the psychological pressures of the step-change to leadership. Students may want to add this insight to their growing understanding of the leadership role, a warning, possibly, of what to expect as they assume a position of "fullest responsibility" themselves.

4 JUDGMENT (20′)

Having described the context of a new leader and the captain's decision-making process, you now ask the students for their evaluation of the captain's actions. This discussion is divided into two parts: a general assessment, and then a more particular inquiry into whether students believe the captain has achieved legitimacy in his role. The majority of students tend to be quite critical of the captain's decisions, so you will want to support those who take a different point of view, or challenge the apparent consensus yourself.

We've spent a lot of time trying to understand these actions from the captain's point of view. What do you think? Do you agree with what he's done? Let's try to separate out the actions for judgment:

- The captain's initial decision to take Leggatt on board
- The decision to hide Leggatt
- Lying about Leggatt's presence
- Bringing the ship close to shore so Leggatt could swim to safety

Most students accept that the captain's first decision, to take Leggatt on board, was morally defensible – in fact, even morally required. However, the three subsequent decisions arouse considerable criticism, with few students taking the captain's side. The captain is criticized (described as "morally reprehensible") for lying to the crew about Leggatt's presence, and, even more strongly, for putting the crew at risk to enable Leggatt to escape as close to shore as possible. The captain is accused of logical inconsistency: if Leggatt is such a strong and capable swimmer, why guide his ship so close to shore?

Students also criticize the captain for dereliction of duty. They argue that he signed on to abide by the code of the sea, a code that he immediately abandons in his first act of any real significance as captain. Some fair-minded students (or the instructor) may interject:

The captain appears to be being held to a different standard than that of Stevens, butler in *The Remains of the Day*. In that class, many of you argued that Stevens should abandon the butler's code of loyalty and refuse to support immoral actions such as Lord Darlington's firing of the Jewish maids. The captain is trying to prevent what he sees as a miscarriage of justice. What is different here?

Students respond: lives are at stake. The captain's code reflects his duty to the whole crew, and not just to a single person, no matter how similar their backgrounds.

In the captain's defense, a few students point out that Leggatt's actions may very well have been necessary, and that he did appear to have saved the *Sephora*. However, this justification of Leggatt's actions does not usually persuade the bulk of students, who separate what Leggatt may have done, from the captain's actions in saving him.

Well, but can't we say at the end of this that, "All's well that ends well"? Leggatt is helped, presumably to safety and a new life. The captain has assumed command. He is even cheered on by the crew. What's wrong with this picture?

The argument that offers the strongest support for the captain is utilitarian; *The Secret Sharer* ends on a surprisingly upbeat note given the tension and *Angst* of the story. The captain is serenaded by the crew with "cheery cries," and he is satisfied, nearly exultant, with the simultaneous success of dispatching Leggatt close to his island destination and having exerted his will over a reluctant and doubting officer and his crew.

Students are by this point familiar with the strengths and weaknesses of utilitarian logic, and some may ask: How much should consequences matter? If the ship had been wrecked, or Leggatt drowned, the captain would have been immoral and a failure. Is evaluating him on the basis of consequences sufficient as a *moral* judgment?

5 IS THE CAPTAIN NOW LEGITIMATE IN HIS ROLE? (20′)

The utilitarian argument is a natural segue to this discussion block, in which students are asked whether they believe that by the end of the story the Captain is now legitimate in his role. This is an important discussion that introduces the second major theme of the module on moral leadership; the captain's status at the end of the story gives students an example on which to test their ideas about legitimacy and how it is earned.

The captain reflects at the end of the story that he believes he has established "the perfect communion of a seaman with his first command." In fact, it could be argued that he is now legitimate, a captain not just in title but also in the eyes of his crew. Do you agree? Is he now a leader who is legitimated in his role?

Technical legitimacy

Students acknowledge that the captain appears to have pulled off a feat of significant technical skill, demonstrating capability in handling his new ship in a dangerous and even potentially fatal maneuver. And some allow as how this technical skill will be welcomed by the crew, since the captain had previously demonstrated only a certain capricious willfulness. The dependence of the crew on the captain's judgment and seamanship is undeniable, and without such a demonstration they may very well have been reluctant to serve under him. In this way, students describe the crews' "cheery cries" as cries of relief, even more, perhaps, than of good cheer.

Moral legitimacy

But where students credit the captain with technical capability or legitimacy – proof that he could handle the boat and its officers and crew – they none the less maintain that he is not a "legitimate" leader. The language formerly used in the course to describe moral challenges, a language of right versus wrong and right versus right, is transformed in student arguments into a language of ends and means. This translation of moral challenge into the domain of leadership – the choice of ends and of the means to attain them – was achieved during the discussion of *The Prince*. There, the fundamental moral argument and debate was whether the prince's end – obtaining control over a state – was worthwhile, and whether the means that were proposed to achieve this end were morally tolerable.

In a similar vein, students argue that the captain does not deserve the title of legitimate leader because of the means he uses to achieve his ends. Lying to the crew about the need to sail close to the shore is one such questionable means. Even more serious is the captain's command to sail perilously close to the shore, endangering the lives of the crew, as well as the ship and her cargo, for Leggatt. Thus students argue that legitimacy has several meanings, and they reserve the designation of *legitimate* for leaders whose ends and means pass tests of moral acceptability.

Summary comments on earning legitimacy

Rather than wait for the end of class to make closing comments, you may find it easier to summarize the three types of legitimacy at the end of this discussion, capturing the headings (Procedural Legitimacy; Technical Legitimacy; Moral Legitimacy) on the board and linking them to individual student comments. The typology is helpful to students, providing them with a framework to use in their analysis of the remaining texts in the module, and in their course papers.

6 LESSONS ABOUT THE "NOVEL RESPONSIBILITY OF COMMAND" (10′)

The Secret Sharer is a rich and complex story, raising issues for students who are concerned about the step-change to leadership. Time permitting, it is helpful to put students into buzz groups to discover the lessons and insights they have gained about the "novel responsibility of command" and then to have a brief discussion of their ideas.

What lessons do you take from *The Secret Sharer* about the "novel responsibility of command"? What questions are you left with?

"This story raised a question for me of how far we should be willing to go to establish ourselves as legitimate in the eyes of our followers. Is it OK to lie – to use immoral means – to get the legitimacy we need?"

"I saw that legitimacy isn't gained just once. The captain, like any leader, will need to keep delivering in order to be perceived as legitimate. There will be an ongoing series of tests to pass – not just one."

"This story is a reminder to me of how easy it is to slip into making decisions that favor or privilege people like us. In the captain's case, his similarity to Leggatt was obvious, but in other situations it can be more subtle. But it's still bias."

"I'm struck by the loneliness of leadership."

These reflections are a segue to the next class, which focuses on one of the hardest – and loneliest – leadership decisions ever made: US president Harry Truman's decision to use the atomic bomb against the Japanese during the Second World War.

Responsibilities of a new leader

The captain's decisions
- Fact-finding
- Rationale
- Process

Judgment

Is the captain "legitimate"?

Figure 13.1 The Secret Sharer *roadmap*

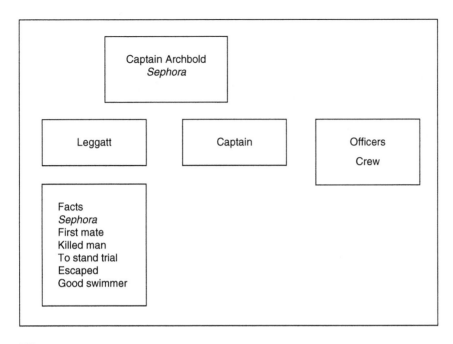

Figure 13.2 The Secret Sharer *board plan*

NOTES

1   Joseph Conrad, *The Secret Sharer*, New York: Dover, 1993, p. 84.
2   Ibid., p. 113.
3   Ibid., p. 84.
4   A captain's powers over the crew were not absolute, however, and the nineteenth century saw a gradual lessening of the captain's power, and a shift of maritime laws in favor of the interests of the crew, lending even greater urgency to the need for a new captain to establish himself as leader. A. G. Course, *The Merchant Navy: A Social History*, London: Frederick Muller Ltd, 1963, pp. 220, 235.
5   Conrad, op. cit., p. 113.
6   Ibid., p. 84.

Chapter 14

Truman and the Bomb
Balancing benefits and harms

THE MORAL REALITY OF WAR is divided into two parts. War is always judged twice, first with reference to the reasons states have for fighting, secondly with reference to the means they adopt.[1]

. . .

Mr Tanimoto found about twenty men and women on the sandspit. He drove the boat onto the bank and urged them to get aboard. They did not move and he realized that they were too weak to lift themselves. He reached down and took a woman by the hands, but her skin slipped off in huge, glovelike pieces. He was so sickened that he had to sit down for a moment. Then he got out of the water and, though a small man, lifted several of the men and women, who were naked, into his boat . . . On the other side, at a higher spit, he lifted the slimy living bodies out and carried them up the slope away from the tide. He had to keep consciously repeating to himself, "These are human beings."[2]

. . .

Henry L. Stimson, Secretary of War

Memorandum for the President, July 2, 1945, on proposed program for Japan:
. . . A question then comes: Is there any alternative to such a forceful occupation of Japan which will secure for us the equivalent of an unconditional surrender of her forces and a permanent destruction of her power again to strike an aggressive blow at the "peace of the Pacific"? I am inclined to think that there is enough such chance to make it well worthwhile our giving them a warning of what is to come and a definite opportunity to capitulate. As above suggested, it should be tried before the actual forceful occupation of the homeland islands

is begun and furthermore the warning should be given in ample time to permit a national reaction to set in.[3]

...

President Harry. S. Truman

The final decision of where and when to use the atomic bomb was up to me. Let there be no mistake about it. I regarded the bomb as a military weapon and never had any doubt that it should be used. The top military advisors to the President recommended its use, and when I talked to Churchill he unhesitatingly told me that he favored the use of the atomic bomb if it might aid to end the war.

In deciding to use the bomb I wanted to make sure that it would be used as a weapon of war in the manner prescribed by the laws of war. That meant I wanted it dropped on a military target. I had told Stimson that the bomb should be dropped as nearly as possibly [sic] upon a war production center of prime military importance.[4]

TRUMAN AND THE BOMB: THEMES AND QUESTIONS

Balancing benefits and harms

The third class in the module is centered on **one of the most difficult moral leadership decisions of the twentieth century:** the decision of US President Harry S. Truman to use the atomic bomb in 1945 in the Allies' war against Japan. This decision moves beyond the historical and hypothetical considerations of state power described in *The Prince,* and the anguished search of one new leader for legitimacy laid out in *The Secret Sharer,* to a situation with unmistakable stakes and worldwide consequences. **It places students firmly in the role of needing to evaluate what does, and does not, constitute an act of moral leadership.** And it puts a spotlight on the twin tasks of exercising authority and earning moral legitimacy.

The leader as process designer

The class features two very different kinds of readings. The first is a compilation of readings, *Truman and the Bomb,* which marries excerpts from John Hersey's *Hiroshima,* an account of the impact of the atomic bomb on the city of Hiroshima, with a selection of historical and autobiographical accounts of the decision-making process that led to the use of the bomb.

225

The *Hiroshima* excerpts begin and end the case, and provide graphic details that force upon students the human costs of the bomb, as well as statistical data on its effect. The historical and autobiographical writings provide a chronological window into the decision-making process of the advisors to Harry S. Truman, the arguments they mounted, opposing points of view, as well as Truman's own account of his decision.

While by no means exhaustive, this reading allows students to enter into an analysis and judgment not just of Truman's decision but of the process he used to come to this decision, and the quality of the advice he was given. **Most of us think of leaders as sole decision-makers, but this reading lays out a vital theme for moral leadership: the leader as designer of the *process* through which decisions with moral and ethical stakes are made.** This theme will be picked up and continued in the class that follows.

Leadership as a rule-governed activity

The second reading is a series of excerpts from political scientist Michael Walzer's 1977 classic, *Just and Unjust Wars*. Written in response to the Vietnam War, Walzer's aim was to study war as a "rule-governed activity,"[5] through contemporary historical examples and with reference to medieval and modern "just war" theory. His premise, important to the "Moral Leader" course and to students' development, is: **"For war is the hardest place: if comprehensive and consistent moral judgments are possible there, they are possible everywhere."**[6] This is the rationale for including the Truman reading in the "Moral Leader" course, and students use Walzer's framework to shape and bolster their evaluation of Truman's decision.

Walzer lays out the two primary categories by which wars are judged.[7] **The first is *jus ad bellum*, or justice *of* war, which is concerned with questions of ends: "[*j*]*us ad bellum* requires us to make judgments about [what constitutes] aggression and self-defense."[8] The second category is *jus in bello*, or justice *in* war, which is concerned with questions of means:** "*jus in bello* [is] about the observance or violation of the customary and positive rules of engagement."[9]

The historical examples Walzer uses to exemplify and analyze these principles are compelling, including his own assessments of Truman's decision to use the atomic bomb, and the precedent-setting firebombing of civilians in Dresden by the Allies earlier in the war. Equally important to students' intellectual development, Walzer's book shows what it looks like to reason morally – to work through the meaning and application of principles, such as the positive rules of war, to specific situations. Walzer's text is a consistent and coherent illustration of judgment based on moral principles.

STUDENT ASSIGNMENT

READINGS: *Truman and the Bomb*, HBS Case. *Just and Unjust Wars*, by Michael Walzer.

1   Did Harry Truman demonstrate moral leadership in his decisions about the atomic bomb? Why? Why not? Please note that this question involves thinking about the decision-making process and the analysis of options that led up to Truman's decisions.

2   In considering the Walzer reading, do you think it is reasonable to think about war as a rule-governed activity? Why or why not?

CLASS PLAN OUTLINE: DISCUSSION BLOCKS

1 Situation Analysis and Fact-Finding (25′)

2 Analysis of Advisors' Recommendations and Truman's Rationale (25′)

3 Do You Agree with Truman's Decision? (40′)

4 Leaders and Moral Rules (15′)

CLASS PLAN OVERVIEW

This is one of the students' favorite classes. Harry Truman's decision is the kind of large-scale, life-and-death choice that many students think of when they first consider the concept of moral leadership. Students are familiar with this decision and are highly energized coming into the discussion. Left to their own devices, they would begin immediately to debate the merits of the Truman decision.

Instead, the class method, which students are familiar with by this time, is to build slowly toward this moment of judgment. This approach is particularly crucial in this class, where students labor under the "hindsight effect." The lethality of the atomic bomb and the horrific consequences of radiation poisoning are now well-known facts. To understand the situation as Harry Truman experienced it, students must be carefully brought back to the knowledge base and emotional–political context of late spring, 1945. The careful laying out of facts on the ground, and then of the arguments that Truman's advisors and the President himself offer for his decision, re-creates for students a sense of the requirements and ethos of the time.

Since the bomb was used on the Japanese, the case raises the question of race, particularly in a class where an open atmosphere for such discussions has been cultivated. Students often will ask whether the atomic bomb would have been used on white Europeans. It is important to support these questions, which often come up somewhat casually and without great force, since these are troubling and risky issues to surface. Students explore this issue well, contributing important insights, such as the fact that the atomic bomb was developed by the Allies and the Germans to be used against *each other*. Asian students will often have their own family stories of prejudice or internment to offer, providing a rich personal context for the debate.

The readings from *Just and Unjust Wars* are particularly useful, for two reasons. First, on the specifics, Walzer advances the argument that the Allied bombing of Dresden was the first and precedent-setting example of a highly lethal attack devised solely for its effect on innocent civilian lives and morale. Second, the Walzer reading lays out the rationale for the "rules of war," including the immunity of noncombatants, and provides a grounded intellectual framework and vocabulary for addressing these questions, as well as the more general topic of the rules which leaders should allow to constrain their exercise of authority.

A way of opening the discussion

From our previous classes it should be clear that the characteristic context of moral leadership is moral decision-making under conditions of responsibility for others. And nowhere is that context more urgently descriptive than of leaders during times of war.

The typical mental model that many of us have of moral leadership is some version of "loneliness at the top." And, in fact, the Truman reading begins with such an observation from Harry Truman himself:

> *The Presidency of the United States carries with it a responsibility so personal as to be without parallel.*
>
> *Very few are ever authorized to speak for the President. No one can make decisions for him. No one can know all of the processes and stages of his thinking in making important decisions. Even those closest to him, even members of his immediate family, never know all of the reasons why he does certain things and why he comes to certain conclusions. To be President of the United States is to be lonely, very lonely at times of great decisions.[10]*

At the same time, we see laid out in the reading an elaborate infrastructure of decision support: administration officials, such as Henry Stimson, Truman's secretary of war, other advisors, the Interim Committee, a scientific panel, individual experts, all of whom are dedicated to helping advise Truman on the decisions that he needed to make. So while Truman had final responsibility for making the decision – and that is the inescapable fact of leadership – he did not come to his decision unaided.

This is an important picture to fix in your mind, both now and later, because it closely resembles the life of a leader in any walk of life, with final responsibility for decisions, but with a process – and people – who aid in that act.

I'd like us to start by first laying out the facts, and then move to the view of the decision that this collection of advisors created over time. We'll then move

229

specifically to Truman and his decision. In terms of flow, we'll first analyze the Truman decision without judgment, and then move to your assessment of it.

As we begin our fact-finding, let me offer some facts that are outside the case, but very helpful in setting a context for it.

First, with regard to the European theater of the war. Roughly at the time that the case begins, Supreme Allied Commander Dwight Eisenhower has declared: "The mission of this Allied force was fulfilled at 0241, local time, May 7th, 1945." Here are the facts on the ground in Europe:

- *20 million Soviet soldiers and civilians have died of privation or in battle*
- *8 million British and Europeans died or were killed, as did 5 million Germans*
- *Nazis murdered 6 million Jews in ghettos and concentration camps*
- *Manmade death had ended 39 million human lives prematurely*

Harry Truman assumed the presidency from Franklin Delano Roosevelt on April 12, 1945. Roosevelt had served as President for 13 years. As of April 12:

- *16 million men and women are serving in the US armed forces*
- *200,000 US soldiers died in the war in both theaters*
- *900,000 US casualties (killed, wounded, missing, prisoners)*
- *The rate of US casualty: 900/day – nearly 7,000/week[11]*

1 SITUATION ANALYSIS AND FACT-FINDING (25')

This discussion is designed to help students imaginatively place themselves back to roughly April 1945, the point of Harry Truman's assumption of the US presidency and the beginning of his involvement in deliberations on whether, and how, to use the atomic bomb. Part analysis of facts provided, the discussion also allows students to add their own perspectives on the situation facing the Allied leaders as the European theater was closing down, while fighting in the Pacific theater continued unabated. At the end of the discussion, students should be able to engage in a more informed and empathetic assessment of the decisions Truman faced.

In this class, it is particularly important to counteract the "hindsight effect" – the tendency to let knowledge of subsequent events bias the evaluation of decisions made before such events had occurred. So let's try to work our way back to the knowledge base that Harry Truman and Allied officials charged with the conduct of the war would have relied on in the spring of 1945.

Questions driving the discussion are in bold

From the readings, what facts do you think are particularly important to the decision about whether or not to use the atomic bomb?

The analysis usually touches on a number of topics: the situation in Japan; the history of the atomic bomb; political tensions within and among the Allies; Truman's ascendance to the US presidency. As these and other topics are covered, it is useful to ask students for their analysis: *What are the implications of these facts for the decisions that Harry Truman had to make?*

The situation in Japan

Many students start their analysis with Japan. She is characterized as a ferocious enemy, whose armed forces will (in the words of Secretary of War Henry Stimson) "fight literally to the death,"[12] as may her civilian population. In reviewing the situation, students experience the same difficulties Allied planners faced in separating facts from assumptions, so you will want to challenge the "fight to the death" argument for facts that support this view. Students may respond with details of Japanese battles, such as the battle for the island of Okinawa, in which 110,000 of the 120,000 soldiers who fought died rather than be taken prisoner.[13] Japan's cruelty in waging war in China may also be referenced as well.

But, while a fierce and highly focused combatant, students cite Stimson's memo to point out that, by April 1945, Japan had no allies and her list of enemies was long: the Anglo-American forces, rising opposition in China, and the growing threat of Russia. Still boasting an army of 5 million and 5 thousand suicide aircraft, Japan was none the less weakened militarily: her navy was nearly destroyed, and she was vulnerable to blockade. Presumably in response to these weaknesses, the Japanese had made tentative proposals through Soviet mediators for a negotiated peace that would have included keeping some captured territory. Truman and other planners would have to weigh these competing views of Japan and determine which was stronger: the will to fight or the will to end the war.

In justifying the bombing, students will cite the importance of Japan's initial "sneak attack" on the United States at Pearl Harbor, and the fact that the two eventual bombsites were military targets: Hiroshima contained an army post, and Nagasaki navy and industrial resources.

The history of the atomic bomb

Students will review the history of the atomic bomb, including its origin in an arms race started by the Nazis; they will also often refer to the motivation of German scientists who emigrated to the United States to ensure that their new homeland would be the first to have a deployable atomic weapon. Timing was important: the bomb was not ready for use until after the Allies had won the war in the European theater. Scientists in several countries had knowledge of the science and technology that led to the bomb's development; it was unlikely that the bomb would remain the exclusive province of the US and the UK for long. Students also note how much was not known about the atomic bomb at the time that Truman needed to make a decision, and reflect on the difficulty in making a decision when "you don't know what you don't even know."

The political context

The political situation in 1945 is also critical to the decision. After four years of war, the American public was impatient for an end to that country's sacrifice in lives and treasure. Students often find the statistics on casualties and war dead stupendous, particularly in light of more recent conflicts. Russian territorial ambitions were also becoming clear, and some students may point to Russia's 1945 Berlin offensive and occupations of the Eastern Front as the beginning of the Cold War between the United States and Russia. Decision-makers in Washington were looking ahead to the growth in Russian power, and the post-war geopolitical balance was a conscious concern and rationale for action.

Harry Truman, a new leader

Finally, students point to the personal situation of Harry Truman. Linking this class to the prior one, they point out that Truman is a new leader, who, like the captain in *The Secret Sharer*, needs to establish legitimacy in his role. While Truman's procedural legitimacy is clear (vice-presidents hold their positions in order to become presidents when needed), his technical legitimacy and moral legitimacy were not yet established. Truman had been kept far from the conduct of the war, and, in particular, from the development of the atomic bomb, of which he was entirely unaware. The decision regarding the bomb would be his first major act of leadership, and it is hard to imagine a more significant or visible indicator of his leadership abilities and moral fitness to lead than the decision it represented.

2 ANALYSIS OF ADVISORS' RECOMMENDATIONS AND TRUMAN'S RATIONALE (25′)

In the second discussion you will ask students to lay out the arguments that Truman's advisors, and Truman, put forth on the use of the atomic bomb. This is a vital discussion, asking students to review the various rationales that were presented. You will also ask students to describe their understanding of the decision process that was used to arrive at the final conclusion. A major theme of the Moral Leadership module is that leaders are responsible not just for the outcome of decisions with moral or ethical stakes, but also for the processes that they put in place for making these decisions. To hold off the nearly irresistible urge to add their own opinions to those of the advisors and Truman, you may want to remind students that in the discussion that follows they will be able to present their own assessment of Truman's decision.

What were the arguments for using the atomic bomb? Which of these arguments were strategic, and which tactical?

Arguments for using the bomb were plentiful, and students easily review the major themes. As a strategic military weapon, Truman's advisors were convinced that the bomb would have immediate psychological impact on the Japanese leadership, persuading them to surrender unconditionally, something they had not yet agreed to do. The advisors also looked to the long-term impact of the bomb as a factor in intimidating Stalin and the Russians in their drive for power in a post-war world. Tactically, it was argued that using the bomb would end the war sooner than an invasion of the Japanese mainland, and with considerably less loss of life and cost for the Americans (principally) but also for the Japanese.

What assumptions were these arguments based on?

There were important assumptions underlying these arguments, and students should be pressed to lay them out. One essential assumption was that the bomb was a legitimate weapon of war; in fact, it appears that the use of the atomic bomb as a weapon was never seriously questioned, even though longer-term concerns of how to manage a post-bomb world were acknowledged.

A related assumption (and one that presumably justified the view of the bomb as a legitimate weapon of war) was that the Germans were prepared to use it against the Allies and would have done so if they had completed its development before they were defeated. In this sense, the Allies were first to use the bomb nearly by accident. A third assumption was that the American public would want the bomb used, tired as they were of war and eager for resolution.

Advisors also believed that the bomb had diplomatic value, but only if the bomb were used in a visible fashion, one that demonstrated its true capabilities and potential for destruction. Finally, advisors assumed that the bomb could do what prior military engagement and increasing casualties could not – get the Japanese leadership to surrender unconditionally.

Which of the arguments were lodged on moral grounds – what kind of moral theories were appealed to?

There were moral arguments launched as well. The bomb was a humanitarian solution to the end of the war, with a seeming certainty for less loss of life than a protracted land invasion – a utilitarian argument. Further, the United States had moral superiority through being the victim of the unannounced Japanese attack on Pearl Harbor; this was defensive, not offensive, war. Finally, using obligation-based reasoning: the nation's leaders had a duty to protect its citizens.

What arguments were raised against using the bomb?

Students will often review all of the pro-bomb arguments without any reference to anti-bomb arguments, testimony to how one-sided the advocacy was. In the case text, the only substantial arguments against the use of the bomb were made by Niels Bohr, whose contribution was to set conditions for the development and use of the bomb that anticipated its role in the post-war world.[14] Bohr's suggestions predate Truman's decision by a year, and they were rejected.

Why was there so little opposition to this decision? What factors led to such one-sided decision-making?

Students understand that the process they are describing does not represent a serious search for alternatives, and they can be asked why the advocacy for the use of the bomb was so one-sided. They will attempt to reconstruct the effect of the war on those responsible for policy, reaching for psychological dynamics such as "group think,"[15] a pervasive war logic that drove out any kind of non-war thinking. They may speculate that the advisory boards were stacked with pro-bomb supporters, although this is a relatively weak argument, given the credentials of the boards' members as described in the case.

Some students have pointed out that the decision-making groups were composed of Americans only, and that there were no people with more distance, such as European allies, to weigh in on the decision. This, too, is belied by the advice given to Truman by Churchill, who strongly supported the use of the bomb (see below). Others make a similar point differently, noting that there were no religious leaders or ethicists involved, and therefore no alternative viewpoints to scientific and military considerations.

Should there have been more debate? What could have been done to create more balance? Is the unanimity in this situation desirable or harmful?

Students are divided on their responses. On the one hand, they acknowledge the danger of such one-sided thinking. On the other, some are leery of introducing complexity during war. Isn't this the time for clear (and therefore possibly one-dimensional) direction – not debate?

What did Truman add to this thinking? What were his assumptions? How did he justify his actions?

Some students refer to Truman's address to the nation quoted in the Walzer reading as evidence of his belief that the United States had a morally defensible right to attack the Japanese, based on the Japanese attack on Pearl Harbor. Others describe his reliance on his advisors ("The top military advisors to the President recommended its use"[16]) and on Churchill, who "unhesitatingly told me that he favored the use of the atomic bomb if it might aid to end the war."[17] Even Stalin told Truman that he hoped the Americans would make "good use of it against the Japanese."[18]

Truman's contribution rests more on the conditions he set for the bomb's deployment than on any unique argument for (or against) its use. As described in the opening quote, Truman said he wanted to "make sure that [the bomb] would be used as a weapon of war in the manner prescribed by the laws of war. That meant I wanted it dropped on a military target ... a war production center of prime military importance."[19] Whether students agree that these conditions are met will be covered in the next discussion, which asks them to describe their judgment of Truman's decision.

3 DO YOU AGREE WITH TRUMAN'S DECISION? (40')

Students are divided about Truman's decision, and in this discussion it is helpful to know what positions students are taking. If students use name cards, you can ask them (for example) to leave their name cards on the horizontal if they are supporting the decision, but to put them on the vertical if they are in opposition.

Although their reasons for either agreeing or disagreeing with Truman's decision differ, personal context and history (country of origin, ethnic identification) matters more in this class than in many others. But the discussion is not simply a rehearsal of predictable reactions, and you will hear eloquent attacks and defenses from some surprising quarters. None the less, the weight of hindsight is heavy, and students are sometimes too ready to agree with the decision in light of its relatively positive outcome.

By this point in the course students are used to exercising their moral imagination. In addition to offering their agreement or criticism of Truman's decisions, some may be eager to discuss what they wish Truman had done and to share thoughts on other ways to end the conflict between the Allies and the Japanese.

Do you agree with Truman's decision?

Students who support Truman's decision make a variety of arguments. Most rely, in one form or another, on the utilitarian calculus established by Truman's advisors. While horrible, the atomic bomb was less costly, not in its immediate effect on the citizens of Hiroshima and Nagasaki, but on the millions of other Japanese and the Americans who would otherwise be forced to fight them. Students appreciate the context, arguing that it is hard to criticize the decision without considering the momentum effect of so much loss of life, over such a long period of time, and at such a heavy cost.

Some supporters will ask those who oppose the use of the bomb how different is this from what has come before? They will argue that the moral line of attack against civilians had already been crossed, citing Churchill's policy of terror bombing of German cities, established in 1940.[20] The firebombing of Dresden by the British in the spring of 1945 is often brought up as an extreme example of a concentrated effort aimed at killing large numbers of civilians without regard for military necessity.[21] Supporters of the bomb also cite the American firebombing of Tokyo, which killed over 100,000,[22] claiming the atomic bomb was cheaper: two planes and (ironically) "two guys with bad dreams" instead of 100 or more US pilots at risk.

Probes for "Yes" position

Do you agree with all of the decisions that were made? How do you defend the use of the second bomb on Nagasaki?

Supporters should be challenged to defend why it was necessary to bomb both Hiroshima and Nagasaki. Supporters of Truman will insist that he "did exactly what he had to do," convincing the Japanese by the use of the second bomb in such close proximity to the first that the Americans had lots of bombs and would keep on using them. Students also argue that it seemed highly unlikely that the Japanese would have surrendered without the second bomb, since they barely made the decision with it.

Supporters may also argue that the Japanese were "not rational" since they didn't give up even after the terrible firebombing of Tokyo in March 1945. Facing such an enemy, Truman need not be bound by the rules of war, since his enemy wasn't capable of rational thought. Students will debate this point, describing the different attitude toward life and honor of the Japanese. The Japanese moral code would require that adherents fight far longer than might be expected, and therefore a different approach was needed to shake them out of their traditional way of thinking.

Did you agree with the decision not to issue a warning to Hiroshima?

Students opposing Truman's decision sometimes argue that at least (some) modern terrorists issue warnings, and that, had such a warning been used, an evacuation of Hiroshima might very well have ensued, allowing the bombing to be conducted with significantly less loss of life. Students schooled in the history of the Japanese campaign will note that leaflet barrages were used to warn citizens of Tokyo before that city was firebombed.

What would you have done if you were in charge of the decision – would you have issued a warning?

You will want to find at least one place in the discussion to ask students to put themselves in the role of decision-maker. As a tactical decision, the issuance of warnings is a good possible topic, since it is easier to imagine making this decision than the far more momentous one of dropping the bomb itself.

Students are divided on the topic of warnings. Some find it unconscionable that no warnings were issued, arguing that even a single life saved would have made the warning worthwhile. Others argue that the bombing was particularly effective because it was a surprise, and that the Allies couldn't afford to dilute the message of the bomb by advance warning. Some are concerned that a warning becomes a moral crutch, allowing the bombing nation (or decision-maker) to escape guilt because they can argue that they had warned the population. Students also debate the efficacy of warnings – debating not whether they should be used, but whether they are effective in saving lives.

Probes for "No" position

Which of the decisions do you disagree with? There was significant effort made to apply "just war" rules as they understood them: they rejected Kyoto as a bomb site because of its cultural significance; looked for targets with military importance. What do you object to in what they did?

Students opposed to the use of the bomb marshal their own arguments. Some focus less on the bomb and more on its target. They argue that it is wrong to kill civilians; following Walzer (or their own thoughts on the matter), they stress that people have a right not to be treated as military if they are not. "Soldiers sign up to die, civilians don't." This often starts a debate about whether conscripted soldiers should be viewed as voluntarily – or involuntarily – engaged in combat. Some find this a compelling distinction; others, while acknowledging the difference, say that at times of war a soldier must be treated as a combatant (even if a reluctant one) and a civilian as a noncombatant (even if an enthusiastic war supporter).

Did the Allies give enough time between the first and second bombs for real decision-making to take place? [Hiroshima bombing: August 6 – Nagasaki bombing: August 9]

Other students disagree with the tactics of the decisions, arguing that there should have been a longer period of time between the bombing of Hiroshima and that of Nagasaki. The day or so that was given was not long enough to allow any kind of real decision-making to take place, particularly given the prior intransigence of the Japanese and the requirement to push the decision up to the most senior Japanese war leaders and even to the Emperor. From the standpoint of moral reasoning, the bombing of Nagasaki is viewed as more morally reprehensible than the original decision at Hiroshima, since the horrible reach and impact of the first bomb would by then have been at least partly known.

One student complained that Truman appeared to realize that the atomic bomb was a historic and unprecedented weapon. She wished that he had done something to acknowledge this realization, but he seemed, instead, to treat the bomb as simply a tactical and conventional weapon. This is an example of students' exercising their moral imagination – a search for alternatives to the decisions that Truman made. If such an admission is made, students can be pressed:

What would you have wanted Truman to do?

In response to this question, one student sketched out a scenario: use the atomic bomb to flatten a Japanese mountain. A small number of farmers might die, but the Japanese could have seen the power of the bomb without all of the killing.

Other students say they would have wanted the United States to exhaust all possibilities before using the atomic bomb. For example, unconditional surrender may have been politically desirable but did not appear to be militarily required; insisting on it was proof that the Americans did not negotiate in good faith or make a serious attempt to limit Japanese casualties. Students sometimes even question the efficacy of violence altogether, citing the example of Gandhi and Martin Luther King, Jr. and the perhaps surprising potency of nonviolence as a policy for resistance and change.

Did Truman demonstrate moral leadership?

The final question asks students to step back from the particulars of the decision and attempt to develop a point of view on what moral leadership consists in. Is the definition of moral leadership simply a different way of stating "these are decisions I agree with," or is there some characteristic set of activities, effort, or motivation that the leader demonstrates, separate from the moral rightness or wrongness of their decisions?

This is an important but potentially subtle point, and one that may or may not fit into the discussion the group has been engaged in. If spirits are high, there may be a temptation to rehash arguments previously made; if your group moves in that direction, you will want to push on to the last discussion. But some groups may be able to respond to probes such as:

If Truman had satisfied himself that he was acting in the world's best interest, had thought it through, did not underestimate the impact of what he did ... isn't that moral leadership? What is missing here?

Some students may criticize Truman for not trying hard enough to look for alternative points of view, or for other ways in which the process of decision-making could have been more rigorous. Others disagree, concluding that he showed enough effort, with enough attention to principles and consequences, and enough concern for all of the parties involved, to have his decision qualify as moral leadership.

4 LEADERS AND MORAL RULES (15')

The last discussion moves to a higher level of generality, and asks students to consider more broadly the relationship between leaders and moral rules.

The Walzer reading was chosen specifically for the point of view it presents on war as a rule-governed activity, with rules that specify boundaries for *jus ad bellum*, or justice *of* war – questions of ends, and *jus in bello*, or justice *in* war – questions of means.

Students are not uniformly fond of Walzer's logic, which contradicts their own mental models of war, fighting, and the rules that should bind a leader's actions in times of great, even ultimate, stress and challenge. It is useful for students to discuss their reactions to the specifics of Walzer's argument, as well as to his more general theses. This is not just so students can more knowledgeably debate issues of war and its conduct (topics, lamentably, of even more salience than when this reading was originally assigned), but also because in the course we are making what Walzer would call a "domestic analogy." If leaders can be governed by moral rules in time of war, then certainly it is reasonable to ask what rules should govern their actions in the nonmilitary domains they normally inhabit.

Walzer describes war as a rule-governed activity, and points out that "War is always judged twice: first with reference to the reasons states have for fighting, secondly with reference to the means they adopt."[23] It's hard to imagine a way of thinking that is more different from Machiavelli's view of war and leadership, which emphasizes flexibility, responsiveness, and few if any limitations on action. In your view, is Walzer's structure a helpful way to think about war and how it is managed and led?

Students are assigned eighty pages in Walzer's book, and many choose to read all of it. It is not possible to do justice to his arguments here, but an overview of the main points may help in understanding how students will approach this discussion.

War as a social creation

Walzer asserts that war is a "social creation,"[24] consisting of rules of engagement that are developed by individuals and whole societies. War does not break out, people who take certain acts start it; war is not an uncontrollable force, it is guided by individuals and states to further their own goals. Wars are "judged twice," first with regard to their purpose – the ends they are dedicated to achieving, and second, with regard to their conduct – the means that are used to pursue them. "Just war" theory is described by Walzer as a "necessary guide to democratic decision-making"[25] since it is only citizens in democratic societies who are able to engage in the debates that shape the social understanding of war and the rules and conventions that govern it.

The legalist paradigm

In describing the "ends" of war, Walzer sketches out what he calls the "legalist paradigm," which outlines key tenets under which modern wars are fought, e.g., "There exists an international society of independent states."[26] "This international society has a law that establishes the rights of its members – above all the rights of territorial integrity and political sovereignty."[27] "Any use of force or imminent threat of force by one state against the political sovereignty or territorial integrity of another constitutes aggression and is a criminal act."[28] "Aggression justifies two kinds of violent response: a war of self-defense by the victim and a war of law enforcement by the victim and any other member of international society."[29] He then proceeds to fill in these general tenets, and to revise and extend them, through reference to specific situations: When is it permissible to launch a preemptive war? Under what conditions is intervention permissible?

The second half of "just war" theory, which deals with the conduct of war, is especially relevant to the debate about Truman and the use of the atomic bomb. When, if ever, is it permissible to use such a weapon? Does "just war" theory make any allowances for the kind of indiscriminate killing that an atomic bomb produces? Or for the circumstances faced by Truman and the Allied commanders at the end of the war with Japan?

War is hell

Walzer's answers to these quesions are at odds with several of the mental models that students have about war. The first of these is referred to in the text by its shorthand, "War is hell," a description offered by US General William Tecumseh Sherman, whose infamous burning of the city of Atlanta during the US Civil War stands as a hallmark of violence in a supremely bloody conflict. "In his view, war is entirely and singularly the crime of those who begin it, and soldiers resisting aggression (or rebellion) can never be blamed for anything they do that brings victory closer. The sentence *War is hell* is doctrine, not description. It is a moral argument, an attempt at self-justification."[30]

In opposing "War is hell," Walzer argues that actions taken in the name of war must be independently justified on moral grounds. Thus, a "just war" can be fought unjustly, and it is certainly possible to wage a war "justly" even if its objectives are not morally sound.

Many students accept the "War is hell" doctrine, and challenge Walzer's rules for self-restraint as unnatural and self-defeating. They ask, "Didn't the US learn from Vietnam not to go in for a limited war? Wasn't that the lesson of that conflict?"

The sliding scale of judgment

A second mental model that is contradicted by "just war" rules is what Walzer refers to as the "sliding scale" model,[31] which sets limits on rules of engagement according to the conduct of soldiers, or (for civilians) of their leaders. Student criticisms of the Japanese as irrationally persistent, or as morally bereft because of the unannounced attack on Pearl Harbor, or as guilty of enormous crimes in their own conduct of the war, are all reflections of a sliding-scale model of moral judgment.

"Just war" rules, on the other hand, are premised on a moral equivalence of lives. The rules of "just war" conduct do not stipulate different standards of engagement for enemy combatants than for one's own troops, or for enemy civilians (noncombatants), regardless of actions taken by them or their leaders. "Just war" rules also state, categorically, that the deliberate targeting of civilian noncombatants is morally wrong.

A supreme emergency

So what, then, constitutes a situation in which a weapon of war such as an atomic bomb might be used? Walzer is no antiwar ideologue and he lays out a description of a "supreme emergency," which, he asserts, is the only context in which the right of noncombatant immunity (the rights of civilians not to be targets of attack) can be overridden. A supreme emergency is defined by two criteria, both of which must be present: imminence of danger and seriousness of danger. "If we are to adopt or defend the adoption of extreme measures, the danger must be of an unusual and horrifying kind."[32]

To clarify what a supreme emergency consists in, Walzer contrasts Churchill's decision to firebomb German cities in 1940 with Truman's decision to use the atomic bomb in 1945.

In defending the first decision, he argues that Nazism constituted "an ultimate threat to everything decent in our lives,"[33] and that the situation in 1940 was "a time when victory was not in sight and the specter of defeat ever present. And it was made when no other decision seemed possible if there was to be any sort of military offensive against Nazi Germany."[34]

The Japanese war, on the other hand, was "a more ordinary sort of military expansion, and all that was militarily required was that they be defeated, not that they be conquered and totally overthrown."[35] Walzer argues that it was the American insistence on unconditional surrender, and the likely options that would be required to secure it, that created the "necessity" to use the atomic bomb. That political aim, while desirable, did not justify the use of the bomb. "In the summer of 1945, the victorious Americans owed the

Japanese people an experiment in negotiation. To use the atomic bomb, to kill and terrorize civilians, without even attempting such an experiment, was a double crime."[36]

In your view, is Walzer's structure a helpful way to think about war and how it is managed and led?

Some students reject Walzer's arguments out of hand. "I don't see why or how the means of war matters. All that matters is whether to fight the war in the first place. I just don't buy the reality of an unjust war fought justly." Others push back: "You're spending too much time on the less common situation where the unjust war is clear. It's much more common for each side to perceive that they are fighting a 'just war' so it really matters how they fight it."

Many students are troubled by the notion of a "supreme emergency," and see it as a contradiction that allows Walzer's carefully built-up edifice of "just war" rules to be breached. Others point out that the argument is based on drawing a hard line between Nazism and the Japanese, and a distinction between the desperate situation of the British in 1940 with the situation facing the soon to be victorious Americans in 1945. If you don't accept these distinctions, they argue that Walzer's argument against the use of the atomic bomb falls apart.

As a civilian, I have been struck by the fact that the strongest supporters of Walzer's arguments are students with prior military experience: "These rules really matter if you are a soldier. How you think about how you conduct yourself in fighting is important, as are rules to match the level of force to what is used by the enemy." "Why? asked another student. "Dead is dead." The soldier-student replied, "The rules are what make it war – not murder."

If there are no military students in the class, I will put the point to students:

In other classes where there have been students with military experience, they've tended to support Walzer's approach to war as a rule-governed activity. Why do you think they'd do that?

Using empathy and their moral imagination, students will discuss the importance of a military life as a profession, with its own code of conduct that must be followed. Others are able to imagine the choices that soldiers face, and the need for rules to govern them in conditions of extreme stress.

Even with their objections, many students are taken with the thesis that leaders should operate within a set of moral rules. Their struggle is more with the details of the arguments, and the ways in which their own views coincide with or differ from Walzer's.

But wars are not the only context in which leaders can be expected to consider the aims they pursue, and the means to achieve them. The theme of leadership as a rule-governed activity will be continued in the next class, which focuses on the leadership of *Washington Post* publisher Katharine Graham during the "Pentagon Papers" and the Nixon Watergate scandal.

Fact finding

Analysis of arguments

Judgment

Is war a "rule-governed" activity?

Figure 14.1 Truman and the Bomb *roadmap*

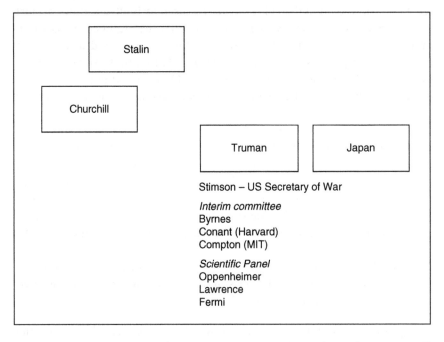

Stalin

Churchill

Truman

Japan

Stimson – US Secretary of War

Interim committee
Byrnes
Conant (Harvard)
Compton (MIT)

Scientific Panel
Oppenheimer
Lawrence
Fermi

Jus In Bello
Justice *In* War: Means

Jus Ad Bellum
Justice *Of* War: Ends

Figure 14.2 Truman and the Bomb *board plan*

NOTES

1 Michael Walzer, *Just and Unjust Wars: A Moral Argument with Historical Illustrations*, New York: Basic Books, 1977, 2000, p. 21.
2 John Hersey, *Hiroshima*, New York: Alfred A. Knopf, 1998, pp. 60–61.
3 Henry L. Stimson (1867–1950), Secretary of War under President Roosevelt from July 1940 to April 1945 and under President Truman from April to September 1945, was in overall charge of the United States atomic development program. This section by Stimson is excerpted from *On Active Service in Peace and War*, by Henry L. Stimson and McGeorge Bundy. New York: Harper & Brothers, 1947, p. 621.
4 Harry S. Truman, *Memoirs by Harry S. Truman, Vol. I: Year of Decisions*, Garden City, NY: Doubleday, 1955, pp. 419–420.
5 Walzer, op. cit., p. 36.
6 Ibid., p. xxiii.
7 In *Arguing about War*, New Haven, Conn.: Yale University Press, 2004, Walzer establishes a third and new category for moral judgment of the conduct of war: *jus post bellum*, or justice *after* war. See, for example, p. xiii and pp. 18–22. Written in response to more recent conflicts than those covered in the 1977 *Just and Unjust Wars*, including the 2003 US war in Iraq, Walzer takes up the issue of "war's endings" and the criteria that should be used to judge the situation following the conclusion of hostilities, including the condition of the state and efforts that are made to restore it to a functioning level.
8 Walzer, 2000, op. cit., p. 21.
9 Ibid., p. 21.
10 *Truman*, op. cit., p. ix.
11 David McCullough, *Truman*, New York: Simon & Schuster, 1992, p. 354.
12 Stimpson and Bundy, op. cit., p. 418.
13 Walzer, op. cit., p. 266.
14 Martin J. Sherwin, "The Atomic Bomb and the origins of the Cold War" US Atomic-Energy Policy and Diplomacy, 1941–1945," *The American Historical Review*, **78**, 1973, 954–960.
15 Scott Plous, *The Psychology of Judgment and Decision Making*, New York: McGraw-Hill, Inc., 1993, p. 203.
16 *Truman*, op. cit., p. 419.
17 Ibid.
18 Ibid., p. 416.
19 Ibid., p. 420.
20 See Walzer, op. cit., p. 253.
21 Ibid., p. 261.
22 Ibid., p. 266.
23 Ibid., p. 21.
24 Ibid., p. 24.
25 Ibid., preface to the third edition, p. xvi.
26 Ibid., p. 61.
27 Ibid., p. 61.
28 Ibid., p. 61.
29 Ibid., p. 62.
30 Ibid., p. 32.

31 Ibid., pp. 228–232.
32 Ibid., p. 253.
33 Ibid., p. 253.
34 Ibid., p. 258.
35 Ibid., p. 258.
36 Ibid., p. 259.

Chapter 15

Katharine Graham: *Personal History*

Taking a stand

Katharine Graham

Fritz was on the other end of the [phone] line. He told me about the argument between the lawyers and the editors over whether to publish the next day, outlined the reasoning on both sides, and concluded by saying, "I'm afraid you are going to have to decide."

I asked Fritz for his own view; since he was so editorial-minded and so decent, I knew I could trust his response. I was astonished when he said "I guess I wouldn't." I then asked for time to think it over, saying, "Can't we talk about his? Why do we have to make up our minds in such haste when the *Times* took three months to decide?"

At this point, Ben and the editors got on various extensions at Ben's house. I asked them what the big rush was, suggesting we at least think about this for a day. No, Ben said, it was important to keep up the momentum for publication and not to let a day intervene after getting the story. He also stressed that by this time the grapevine knew we had the Papers. Journalists inside and outside were watching us.

I could tell from the passion of the editors' views that we were in for big trouble on the editorial floor if we didn't publish. I . . . remember Phil Geyelin's response when I said that deciding to publish could destroy the paper. "Yes," he agreed, "but there's more than one way to destroy a newspaper."

. . . I was extremely torn by Fritz's saying that he wouldn't publish . . . [A]fter all, he was the lawyer, not I. But I also heard *how* he said it: he didn't hammer at me, he didn't stress the issues related to going public, and he didn't say the obvious thing – that I would be risking the whole company on this decision. He simply said he guessed he wouldn't. I felt that, despite his stated opinion, he had somehow left the door open for me to decide on a different course. Frightened and tense, I took a big gulp and said, "Go ahead, go ahead, go ahead. Let's go. Let's publish." And I hung up.[1]

. . .

Ben Bradlee
We did know that the Pentagon Papers experience had forged forever between the Grahams and the newsroom a sense of confidence within the *Post*, a sense of mission and agreement on new goals, and how to attain them. And that may have been the greatest result of the publication of the Pentagon Papers.

After the Pentagon Papers, there would be no decision too difficult for us to overcome together.[2]

. . .

Katharine Graham
I have often been credited with courage for backing our editors in Watergate. The truth is that I never felt there was much choice. Courage applies when one has a choice.[3]

KATHARINE GRAHAM: *PERSONAL HISTORY:* THEMES AND QUESTIONS

Discretionary action

Up until this point, the challenges faced by leaders in the Moral Leadership module appear largely as *situational imperatives.* Whether it is the requirement to establish authority for a new prince, the need to establish command and legitimacy in the eyes of doubting crew members of a ship, or the tragic necessity of determining how a war will be waged, each of the three preceding leaders were forced, in one way or another, to act through the requirements of their role and situation. The question in each class was whether the authority that comes with leadership was exercised in ways that could be viewed as moral, and whether the leader's actions served to enhance, or detract, from the legitimacy necessary to their role.

Kay Graham's challenges – the Pentagon Papers and the Nixon Watergate investigation – were more voluntary, and **push the context in which moral leadership is examined to discretionary situations in which a leader has to choose whether, and how far, to act on the basis of principle.** Defending the truth is one such principle, and the class allows students to explore the **importance of truth in a democracy, and to debate the boundaries of** investigation, truth telling, and disclosure in times of war. These are not abstract questions for a newspaper, and the stories of the Pentagon Papers and Watergate lead to a deeper understanding of the additional requirements that come with leading an organization that has a moral, as well as an intrinsic and self-sustaining, purpose.

Moral courage

Students are assigned a lengthy excerpt from Graham's autobiography, *Personal History*, covering the Pentagon Papers and Watergate, as well as a chapter from the autobiography of Ben Bradlee, the *Post*'s managing editor under Graham, on the Pentagon Papers. These accounts overlap and allow students to examine in detail Graham's rationale for her actions, and the impact of those actions on people inside and outside her organization.

While strong arguments can (and will) be made in favor of the actions that Graham took at the *Post*, equally strong and perhaps even more persuasive arguments can be made for not stepping forward in either of these situations. In this sense, Graham's story is one of moral courage, an attribute that is featured in works such as *Antigone, Blessed Assurance,* and *A Man for All Seasons,* but here is examined in the context of organizational leadership. The Graham and Bradlee readings enable students to explore the multiple obligations that leaders hold, and to debate the weight that should be given to moral principles that at the same time embody the organization's mission *and* put the organization at risk, perhaps for its very existence.

The process of decision-making

Like *The Secret Sharer* and the Truman case, these materials also provide a minute-by-minute depiction of actual decisions being made, and students have an opportunity to assess the *process* of decision-making that the leader follows. The decision to publish the Pentagon Papers must be made by Graham as she is surrounded by warring factions of lawyers, editorial staff, business managers, and trusted advisors. Students are reminded that leaders have choices about how much, or how little, to involve others in critical decisions. They also see the ways in which organizations *pull* leaders into decisions, an inescapable feature of their authority and role.

Graham stands for the principle of a free press in choosing to publish the Pentagon Papers – a moral end. The decision creates a foundation of moral legitimacy for her leadership and for the *Post* as an organization, as the quote from Bradlee at the beginning of this chapter indicates.

But, where the Pentagon Papers incident focuses on a single decision of whether to publish, the Watergate investigation shows the slow, tense, and

249

draining process of pursuing moral ends without any assurance that these ends will, in fact, be obtained. **The students' view of moral leadership is deepened by seeing a situation in which staying the course and moral consistency are critical; students come to understand that leaders must support direction as well as set it.**

Enforcing moral means

A large part of consistency comes in assuring that the means that organizations employ are as moral as the ends they choose. The *Post* sets a series of ground rules for determining which facts it will publish, and punctilious adherence to these rules is as much a demonstration of the organization's and its leaders' morality as the decision to pursue the Watergate investigation in the first place. These rules echo the distinctions drawn by Walzer between the rules that govern the ends of war and those that govern its conduct. Students come to see that **moral consistency is grounded – takes its shape in – the rules that are created to pursue chosen goals.**

STUDENT ASSIGNMENT

READINGS: *Personal History*, by Katharine Graham, pp. 433–508. Chapter 13 from *A Good Life*, by Ben Bradlee.

1   The Graham reading presents us with two distinct episodes: the Pentagon Papers and Watergate. In what ways are the challenges in these situations similar? In what ways are they different?

2   What is your assessment of the choices Graham makes in response to these two situations?

3   At the conclusion of the assigned Bradlee chapter, Ben Bradlee recounts: *"After the Pentagon Papers, there would be no decision too difficult for us to overcome together."* What does he mean by that?

CLASS PLAN OUTLINE: DISCUSSION BLOCKS

1   Risk Analysis of Pentagon Papers Decision (25')

2   Assessment of Graham's Pentagon Papers Decision (30')

3   Differences between Watergate and the Pentagon Papers (15')

4   Assessment of Graham's Leadership during Watergate Investigation (20')

5   Is This Moral Leadership? (15')

CLASS PLAN OVERVIEW

This is a lively class, with a straightforward and logical discussion flow. There are, none the less, two issues to manage. The first is the complexity of the situations and decisions facing Graham and the *Post*, in particular, the numerous parties from the *Post* organization as well as members of the Nixon government involved in the Watergate investigation.

The first time I taught these materials I was asked by an international student to identify the high points and most important events of the Watergate situation. In typical Harvard Business School fashion, I turned to the class and asked who was willing to summarize the facts. After a lengthy silence (not rare, or even troubling, usually) one of the students observed that I was the only person in the room who was "old enough to have lived through the situation," and hence it would be best if I would do the honors. After thanking the student for making it easy for me to identify one of the recipients of the required "lowest category" rankings on the forced grading curve, I was compelled to realize how confusing the facts are that Graham describes. The timeline of Watergate events in the student textbook should help. You need not memorize these events, but should definitely feel free to refer students to the chronology if questions of fact and sequence emerge, as they occasionally do.

The second issue is a potential thread of gender bias that can wind its way through the discussion. It is hard for many students to appreciate how isolated Graham was as a female leader at the helm of her company since such roles, while still not common enough, are no longer the absolute exception they were in Graham's time.

Further, Graham is a remarkably candid chronicler, and students have more data than they are used to having about a real (as opposed to a fictional) leader's insecurities and doubts. In fact, one of the great triumphs of the autobiography is the picture that emerges of Graham rising above these very human feelings, feelings that are not at all unexpected for a woman of her time in the nearly unique position of leadership that she held. These feelings would have been justified under any circumstance, and are even more understandable in light of the nature of the enemies, including President Nixon, who attacked Graham and the *Post*.

Student bias can be revealed in unduly harsh and critical assessment of Graham's actions that does not take these contextual factors into account, and a tendency to ascribe nearly all business-like concerns and sensitivities to Bradlee. These last are not surprising observations, since Bradlee writes far more than Graham about the competitive situation facing the *Post* and his own objectives to establish the paper's reputation to be on a par with *The New York Times*. Female students tend to side more with Graham, and male students tend to be more critical of her decisions, in particular the apparently impetuous "Let's go" decision to publish the Pentagon Papers quoted at the beginning of this chapter. These divisions are not hard-and-fast; many male students are as appreciative and admiring as some of the women of the long slog of leadership that was required to manage the Watergate investigation.

The context-setting information provided in the student textbook goes some way toward providing the necessary background to offset these incoming perceptions. The question of Graham's gender, and its impact on her leadership style and actions, is addressed directly in the discussion of the Watergate investigation. The question is purposefully introduced in that section so students can draw on their assessment of Graham's actions in both the Pentagon Papers and Watergate, which feature very different types of leadership challenges.

A way of opening the discussion

The two episodes at the Washington Post *highlighted in our readings – publishing the Pentagon Papers and pursuing the Watergate story – happened some thirty years ago, and yet they resonate strongly with current events.*

Then, like now (2007), the United States was bitterly divided over moral values and political affiliation.

Then, like now, a war fought far away, in alien geography, was increasingly seen by a large portion of the country as being waged for unclear reasons.

Then, like now, under the rubric of national security, many citizens grew concerned that their constitution-derived rights were being jeopardized. Then, like now, the media felt the executive branch's sting.

But two things were very different then, both relevant to our discussion, and embodied in Kay Graham. The first is that women were essentially non-existent in positions of leadership – in any arena; the second is that the style of leadership Graham exhibited is nearly extinct, or at least in severe decline.

It's hard to remember, with the United States having its second female secretary of state, and women serving in 2005 and 2006 as Chancellor, Executive President, and Prime Minister in Germany, Liberia, Chile, and South Korea,[4] how unthinkable it was in the mid-1960s for a woman to occupy a leadership role, when Graham took the Post's *helm (in her mid-fifties). As we contemplate US firms such as eBay, Hewlett-Packard, Xerox, Lucent, Avon . . . the list of Fortune 500 corporations that have been headed by women, we have to understand that this, too, was nearly inconceivable.[5]*

Indeed, Katharine Graham was the first woman to head a Fortune 500 company.

In one sense, she inherited that position. The paper was owned by her father and subsequently run by her husband. He committed suicide – she discovered his body. Yet, against much advice and after much soul-searching, she took charge.

It was she who built a paper of little consequence into a force of political nature – making the company highly profitable en route.

Graham's leadership style mixed being a boss and being a host, and her dinner parties were legendary – combining the powerful and the interesting, the young and the old, the "in" and the "out."

The Post, *in its editorial on Graham's legacy (July 18, 2001), captured this side of her leadership:*

> *[S]he hosted presidents (including the incumbent) and generals and secretaries of state. She liked doing these things – Mrs Graham knew the pleasure of gossip, and she believed, among other things, that Washington should be fun – but there was a serious aspect to them too.*
>
> *Beneath the high-society veneer was an old-fashioned patriotism: a belief that liberals and conservatives, Republicans and Democrats, even politicians and journalists, shared a purpose higher than their differences and so ought to be able to break bread together. Her credentials for bringing people together were strengthened by her scrupulous refusal to use her interests (not to mention this editorial page) to advance her personal or corporate financial interests.*

In today's business and political world where transparency is often equated with separation, we look at someone attempting another approach.

So let's see how these two differences – and the similarities – play out in our analysis of Graham's leadership in the Pentagon Papers and Watergate.

253

1 RISK ANALYSIS OF PENTAGON PAPERS DECISION (25')

Some students are tempted to treat the decision by Graham to publish the Pentagon Papers as a no-brainer, so this turns out to be a critical and hard-working discussion. The question allows students to explore the many risks the decision posed to the *Washington Post* and to Graham, its publisher. Even more important, the Pentagon Papers decision sits within a broader context, and students find themselves debating the nature of press freedom, the role of the press in a democracy, and the relationship between the "fourth estate" (the press) and government.

Questions driving the discussion are in bold

Let's start with the Pentagon Papers [June 13, 1971]. As we know, the pivotal point in this incident came in a phone call to Graham, asking her to decide whether to publish articles analyzing the Pentagon Papers. Risk analysis is an important type of situation analysis – a way of looking at the facts through the lens of risk and reward. What were the risks *of* publishing the Pentagon Papers?

Legal risks

First, there were substantial legal risks. At the time of Graham's decision, *The New York Times* had been enjoined from publishing the Pentagon Papers, so if the *Post* published articles related to the Papers the newspaper could be seen as defying the law and disrespecting the court. Moreover, because the Pentagon Papers concerned the Vietnam War, which was in full force at the time, the *Post*'s lawyers were concerned that the paper could be liable under the US Espionage Act for publishing information that might endanger national safety and aid a wartime enemy. Violation of the Espionage Act was a criminal offense, and if convicted as a felon under the act the *Post* corporation would have to give up its TV licenses.

Business risks

There were also substantial business risks – risks to the financial viability of the firm. The *Post* was about to go public with a $35 million stock offering. If the underwriters could establish that the *Post* was violating the terms of its prospectus to publish a newspaper "dedicated to the community and national welfare,"[6] they would be released from their obligation to buy and resell the company's public shares. Added to this possible loss was the far more damaging potential loss of revenue associated with its three TV stations – another $100 million.

Many students also point out the serious reputation risks faced by the *Post*. The *Post* had obtained roughly 4,400 of the 7,000 pages of the Pentagon Papers – a large, but not complete portion of the source material. It was attempting to do in twelve hours what *The New York Times* had taken three months to do – write newspaper articles that accurately reported and analyzed the facts laid out in the Papers. If the reporting resulted in a serious violation of national security, or even if they got some of the facts wrong, the impact on the *Post's* reputation could be devastating.

Political risks

There were also political risks. Refusing the request not to publish would enrage the new Nixon administration, closing off potential sources of information. Moreover, these risks were not just organizational. Graham faced personal risk in defying or at least challenging the President, Supreme Court, and Attorney General of the United States. She might even be jailed for treason under the Espionage Act.

Moral risks

There were also moral risks in publishing. The *Post* could be seen as causing damage to US national interests. Even more important, perhaps, the *Post* would be trading its future financial viability as an operating company, encompassing duties to employees, the public (and soon its shareholders) for its right to publish the Pentagon Papers. While it is conventional to see these as purely business issues, they are moral duties as well. Students can be asked:

How do you think these business duties should be weighed against the *Post's* duty to defend freedom of the press? How can duties that appeal to different principles (and parties) be sorted out?

What were the risks of *not* publishing?

Students are quick to point out that there were significant risks in *not* publishing as well, often quoting the *Post* editor who claimed during the internal debate, "[T]here's more than one way to destroy a newspaper."[7] Students describe the view of the *Post's* reporters and editors that the decision to publish was a defense of press freedom, and the likely alienation of newsroom staff that would result from a decision not to publish. There was

255

also reputation risk to the *Post* in not publishing, since Bradlee's efforts to put the *Post* on a footing equal to *The New York Times* would be seriously undermined. And moral arguments were made as well. Bradlee insisted, "Not publishing the information when we had it was like not saving a drowning man or not telling the truth."[8]

Graham and Bradlee both describe the events that led to *The New York Times* being unable to publish the Pentagon Papers.[9] After the *Times* refused US Attorney General John Mitchell's request to stop publishing articles related to the Pentagon Papers, "the U.S. Justice Department went to court and got an injunction against the *Times*, restraining a newspaper in advance from publishing specific articles, for the first time in the history of the republic."[10] What is "prior restraint" of the press, and why did Graham and Bradlee regard it as so problematic?

The concept of *prior restraint* may confuse some students, so it is helpful to ask what it means. One student responded rather angrily to another, who had asked about it, "Prior restraint is censorship! The government is deciding what a newspaper can publish." Another added an important distinction: news media can be found guilty of libel, or slander, or of endangering the national interest, but all of these would be cases that would be brought *after* publication of a story (or showing of a broadcast) had been made. Prior restraint is taking action before publication and, as such, has been regarded as a violation of the First Amendment of the US Constitution. That amendment states, "Congress shall make no law . . . abridging the freedom of speech, or the press."[11]

Do you agree with the position they took – that prior restraint of the press is always bad? Why or why not? How about in this situation?

Bradlee and the rest of the *Post* editorial staff regarded freedom of the press as trumping even US national security. Students can be asked if they agree; they will differ in their opinions.

Some students, showing considerable trust in the classification of documents by the US government (and possible naïveté), claim that the Papers were classified "for a reason." The risks to national security are too great to allow media leaders to be given the right to publish classified material like the Pentagon Papers, especially against the express wish of the executive branch, and particularly in times of war. Many students also fear bias in the press, claiming that newspapers will follow their own ideology and interests, rather than those of the nation.

Others push back. One reasoned, "A democracy should be willing to risk even the safety of its soldiers so that the country they die for is worth dying for." The context of the times is also cited. By 1971, the undeclared Vietnam War had been going on for ten years. Hundreds of thousands of US soldiers had gone to fight; thousands had died. Students argue that information put out by the US government had lost credibility, so a defense of the public's right to know was reasonable, even necessary. Some also point out that the Pentagon Papers refer to historical events; in fact, the article the *Post* was rushing to print covered a decision made in 1954. What possible relevance could this article have to national security and to events in Vietnam in 1971?

2 ASSESSMENT OF GRAHAM'S PENTAGON PAPERS DECISION (30')

Having debated the risks and stakes of the decision, students are now ready to tackle how well, or poorly, they believe Graham handled it. A very powerful introduction to this discussion is to ask a student to read first Bradlee's and then Graham's description, which is a minute-by-minute account of the decision and her thoughts as she made it. (The Graham excerpt I have students read is reproduced as the first quote in this chapter.) This recitation moves the discussion from a debate about a decision anyone could have made to the particular setting and process of Graham's decision-making and leadership. Students disagree, markedly, on their response.

Bradlee and the others certainly knew who had to make the final call on this set of competing risks. Bradlee's language is telling: he referred to "the ultimate showdown with Kay Graham;"[12] "a Fail-Safe telephone call with Kay;"[13] and, finally, "Show Time."[14] We are at the actual moment of decision-making. Let's read [out loud] how Bradlee (page 316) and then Graham (page 450) describe this moment, and then get your reactions.

What is your assessment of this process, and of Graham's leadership?

Regardless of whether the prior discussion seemed to tilt in favor or against publication, many students are highly critical of Graham's decision and of how she made it. "Awful," one student commented. "Too quick." "In the middle of a toast." "Clearly, she gave it no thought." Some students don't glimpse any evidence of reasoning; they would have liked to see Graham consciously weighing the risks, as they have just done. Graham is also criticized for not worrying enough about getting the facts right. It was "impossible" to go through 4,400 pages in one day, even with an army of experienced and knowledgeable reporters and editors. Graham's own political convictions are also questioned. She never seemed to like Nixon, even at this early stage in their relationship.

Other students strongly support Graham, describing her as doing a great job as a leader. "She had all the resources available to her – reporters, lawyers, editors – that's why it could take just five minutes to decide." "She trusted the people she surrounded herself with." "She was sensitive to nuance, and could distinguish between strong advice and an opening for her to use her own judgment."

What principles did Graham invoke in her decision? What was her rationale? Let's look at what Graham says, herself, about her rationale (page 457).

You will want to ask students how Graham describes her own rationale, which she laid out in a speech at the end of 1971.

> [W]e believed from the start that the material in the Pentagon Papers was just the kind of information the public needed in order to form its opinions and make its choices more wisely. In short, we believed the Papers were so useful to a greater understanding of the way in which America became involved in the Vietnam War that we regarded their publication not as a breach of the national security, as the administration claimed, but, rather, as a contribution to the national interest – indeed, as the obligation of a responsible newspaper.[15]

What is Graham saying about citizens in a democracy? In what ways is the publication of information like the Pentagon Papers a contribution to the national interest? How does Graham define the obligation of a "responsible newspaper"?

Students can be asked to parse Graham's argument. Citizens in a democracy have rights and duties to make choices, and these choices need information if they are to be made wisely. Consequences are improved, and better public decisions are made, if informed citizens are engaged in the political process. Newspapers not only have the right to publish freely, they have duties to inform the public.

Were the rights and duties of a newspaper that Graham claimed unbounded? What rules did the *Post* use in working with the Pentagon Papers?

Students who take the position that Graham was insufficiently mindful of managing the risk of the Pentagon Papers can be asked whether the right that Graham claimed was unbounded. Did the *Post* use any rules in working with the Pentagon Papers?

The answers (sometimes hard for students to locate; see pages 455–456 of the text) were that the *Post* did not have in its possession, nor would it publish, any information from the volumes that US Deputy Attorney General Richard Kleindienst was concerned about. The *Post* also followed its standard policy against publishing information "based on intercepted intelligence, or signal intelligence, or cryptography [information purposefully disguised] in general."[16] The role of rules – and the specific rules enacted – will be revisited with greater force in the discussion of Watergate.

3 DIFFERENCES BETWEEN WATERGATE AND PENTAGON PAPERS (15′)

The next brief analysis serves as a transition between the assessment of Graham's leadership during the Pentagon Papers crisis and her leadership of the extensive Watergate investigation.

What were the most important differences between Watergate and the Pentagon Papers?

Students usually cite time as the first important difference. Two weeks after Graham made her "Let's go" decision to publish, the US Supreme Court ruled that the government had not "met the heavy burden of showing justification,"[17] on grounds of national security, for continued restraint of publication of the Pentagon Papers. Watergate, by contrast, dragged on for three years.[18] And with this lengthy time period came complexity. Students point out that, with Watergate, Graham faced not a single decision, but an endless stream of them.

Second, students note that while the Pentagon Papers required the analysis of historical materials, a large bulk of which were already in the hands of the *Post* and its reporters and editors, Watergate required investigative reporting. In fact, many regard Watergate as having established a new model of investigative reporting, the hallmark of which was uncertainty, a step-by-step pursuit of the truth, without ever being certain just where or when the pursuit would end.

The sources of information were also quite different. The Pentagon Papers were a detailed and exhaustive history of the Vietnam War, compiled at the request of the US government. Watergate, by contrast, depended for many of its tips and corroboration from Deep Throat, a mysterious and possibly unreliable source.

The Watergate investigation also put Graham and the *Post* squarely at odds with the Nixon administration. The Pentagon Papers covered decisions about the Vietnam War made before Nixon's presidency, but the Watergate break-in was not only made on Nixon's watch, but led, nearly from the start, to individuals at increasingly higher levels in the Nixon administration, ending, of course, eventually at Nixon himself.

How would you compare the level of risk between the two situations?

There is little debate about these main points of comparison, but students often differ on their assessment of the relative risks of the two situations.

Most argue that the Watergate investigation was more risky, since it was focused on an administration that would do nearly anything (dirty tricks, lies, exerting influence over governmental regulatory agencies) to protect itself. Watergate was also an inherently risky investigation. Unlike the Pentagon Papers, whose value and provenance had been vetted by *The New York Times*, the *Post* was pursuing the story of the Watergate break-in on its own. Without other newspapers on the hunt, it was not clear whether there was really any "there, there."

Some students dispute these views, however, arguing that the Pentagon Papers' substantial risks to the financial viability and legal standing of the *Post* were far greater than the Watergate investigation. The worst that would happen with Watergate, they maintain, is that the story would die and the *Post* might look as if it had pursued it wrongly and perhaps out of bias.

4 ASSESSMENT OF GRAHAM'S LEADERSHIP DURING WATERGATE (20′)

Having established some of the main differences between the Pentagon Papers and Watergate, you then ask students to assess Graham's leadership during the Watergate investigation. The several-year timeframe allows a much more detailed examination of Graham's leadership than with the Pentagon Papers decision, and students debate how she, and Bradlee, managed the *Post* organization through it all.

In your view, how well did Graham handle the Watergate investigation?

Unlike the Pentagon Papers decision, over which students are quite split and negative views may dominate, many students admire Graham's handling of the Watergate investigation. Supporters sometimes begin with the differences in atmosphere. Watergate was more impressive because there was not a "big, emotional context," just a steady drive to pursue the truth. Under Graham's leadership, the *Post* was pursuing a moral end, and students often revisit what was at stake in the Watergate investigation: democracies need the truth and visibility to how their leaders make decisions. Nixon's involvement in the illegal Watergate break-in raised questions of a sliding scale: If he was willing to sanction that act, what else would he feel free to do? These are questions that fit well within the themes of the course, inviting an examination of the ways in which Richard Nixon exercised his authority – what power he had and how he chose to use it.

We know that unlike the Pentagon Papers, which lasted only a few weeks, the Watergate investigation took over two years, and was marked by increasingly ferocious opposition. How did Graham (and Bradlee) sustain the *Post* through it all? Let's see if we can separate the leaders here: What was Bradlee's role – what did he do? What was Graham's role?

Students readily discern the different roles that Graham and Bradlee played in managing the Watergate investigation. Bradlee was the charismatic leader; in Woodward's words, "There was always a sense that Bradlee was our leader. He's the guy who's planting the flag."[19] Graham's leadership was exercised in less visible ways, and you'll want to ask the students to become specific:

What, exactly, did Graham do?

Graham's risk-taking on behalf of press freedoms in the Pentagon Papers stand-off established a strong base of legitimacy for her with the *Post* organization, as shown in Ben Bradlee's quote at the beginning of this chapter. She became increasingly visible as the public defender of the Watergate investigation; she was the guardian at the gate, willing to go to jail to protect the paper and its sources. Graham took upon herself the burden of maintaining communication with the Nixon administration and with others whose opinion of the *Post*'s actions were important to the paper's viability.

But most students point to Graham's largely behind-the-scenes support as what really mattered. "She stood behind her editors and reporters, letting Bob Woodward and Carl Bernstein know she believed in them, and then let them do what they did best." Students observe that this was a great incentive, to be allowed to work on the best story ever; what any newspaper person would want.

Other students are more critical and raise questions of why Graham was so trusting. For example, they ask, didn't she have an obligation to know the identity of Woodward's source, Deep Throat, on whom so much seemed to depend?

Students will parse their answer carefully, citing contemporary examples. To avoid the risk of a fabricated story, perhaps Bradlee or some other *Post* editor should have been told the identity of the source. But, as publisher, Graham would not be expected to control, or even to have specific knowledge of, the sources her reporters relied on.

Were there rules here? What "means" did the *Post* use to pursue its ends?

Graham championed the rules that were used in the Watergate investigation: "The best we could do while under such siege, I felt, was to keep investigating, to look everywhere for hard evidence, to get the details right, and to report accurately what we found."[20] Students will readily point to Graham's description of the rules that were devised to promote accuracy in reporting:

> First, every bit of information attributed to an unnamed source had to be supported by at least one other, independent source . . . Second, we ran nothing that was reported by any other newspaper, television, radio station, or other media outlet unless it was independently verified by one of our own reporters. Third, every word of every story was read by at least one of the senior editors before it went to print, with a top editor vetting each story before it ran.[21]

In what ways were these rules important? Why did they matter?

Students will cite a number of reasons of why the rules mattered, from the most basic: "it's the truth; we have to know it's right," to the more prudential: the political consequences of being wrong were enormous. Some students draw an analogy with the Walzer reading from the Truman class: "The rules Graham set were like the rules of war – they set the boundary within which they could act." Others extend this view: "Because of the rules – you could act more aggressively as a reporter."

How exactly does that work? I would have thought it goes the other way – reporters could be more aggressive when they *don't* have rules.

One student responded that establishing rules is a moral act that is always driven by context. Since Watergate was an exploratory investigation that depended on sources who refused to be identified, it required far more stringent fact-checking and rules of corroboration than those used to govern the reporting on the Pentagon Papers. "The rules build confidence. I know I'm going to be backed up with all of these procedures, and I know I have to meet these tests. If I'm a reporter, that allows me the certainty of knowing how to push into uncertainty."

Just as the captain in *The Secret Sharer* was characterized by his youth, Graham's gender is an unmistakable fact. How would you weigh the gender factor as an influence on Graham and her actions, or on how she was perceived?

Some supporters of Graham admire her for "not giving up on her identity as a female while still being a leader." Students disagree about the ways in which Graham integrated traditional female roles into her management: "Was that *all* that she could do – give parties? Her job became her – we don't want that." Other students, while admiring the integration of Graham's personal and professional lives, stress the differences in the times between their current situation and 1969, when Graham assumed the unique role as her industry's only female publisher. They also note the remarkable social distinction of Graham and her friendships with public figures, adding, "We couldn't replicate what she did, even if we wanted to."

Students also comment on Graham's use of letter writing and back channels. Some admire her attempt to keep open lines of communication with members of the Nixon administration. Others are more neutral, describing her as shrewd and wondering why someone like Henry Kissinger would still talk to her after all the stories that the *Post* ran about Nixon and Watergate.

In *Personal History* students get as close to a real leader as they do at any point in the course, so you will want to surface as many of these ambiguities as possible. Giving students an opportunity to examine how Graham operated, and what they admire and criticize in her actions, is an important grounding for the work they are doing in defining moral leadership for themselves.

Graham said that "Courage applies when one has a choice,"[22] and that she "never felt she had much choice,"[23] since there was no single decision to make. So she was not courageous in her own view. Do you agree?

Students will agree, in part, with this assessment. They will note that the Watergate investigation involved a nearly endless series of decisions to keep pursuing the story along its multiple paths. In this way, it did not offer the same opportunity to take a stand as Graham did in approving the publication of the Pentagon Papers. But most students disagree with Graham about the larger point. They claim that she did display courage, not once, but over and over again, and in the face of enormous pressure on her as a publisher and as an individual. "Impressive," many conclude.

5 IS THIS MORAL LEADERSHIP? (15′)

The last brief discussion leads directly from students' assessment of Graham's leadership, particularly during Watergate, to put the course question: Is this moral leadership? The opening discussion is framed from the standpoint of Machiavelli to help the students step back from the Watergate analysis and to consider Graham's leadership more generally. The most important question is the second: What new elements about moral leadership have you learned from Graham? – which students respond to in buzz groups and then in open discussion. Often most of the main points have come out through the prior discussions and from these questions; but, if they have not, you can conclude by asking students whether, in their view, Graham has demonstrated moral leadership.

If Machiavelli could have constructed a setting to explore his concepts in twentieth-century American business life, he would have been hard pressed to find a better example than the story of Katharine Graham. Threatened by powerful enemies with almost infinite resources and a willingness to use them, the *Washington Post* needed to defend itself from attacks while it pursued an investigation of those in power. How would Machiavelli evaluate Graham? What would he think of her performance as a leader?

This is an engaging question for students, and leads them to reinforce their appreciation of some of the surprising strengths of Graham's leadership: her ability to persevere in the face of relentless opposition; her use of informal communication and other means to defend herself. Like Machiavelli, Graham believes in luck and is the first leader openly to acknowledge the role it played in her success. Students are divided on the topic, some wondering if it is "female modesty" or insecurity that allows Graham so easily to give credit to forces outside her control, while others see her comments as a realistic assessment of the challenges the *Post* faced and the factors that contributed to their resolution.

What has Kay Graham *added* to your definition of moral leadership? What new elements do you see in her leadership that are different from the leaders we have studied?

"This is what it looks like when you start with a moral decision – to affirm your duty to provide the news/truth. All business decisions flowed from that and were 'correct' because that fundamental moral rule and decision was so clear."

"I learned about the importance of setting rules, especially if you are on a moral quest. Rules provide checks and balances, and they help guard against bias;" "Rules are a moral force."

"This is a different kind of leadership: dinner parties, back channels, all of those things helped with Graham's situation awareness. The number of people who warned Graham that she was personally at risk was striking; she was plugged in and knew how to benefit from it."

"This is what leadership looks like when you select well. You can rely on people, can trust them (and do trust them) to do the right thing."

"I learned what not to do. Graham was too distant and removed from the most important decision-making; a good leader would be more involved."

Has Graham demonstrated moral leadership?

Most students who respond to this question assert that Graham's actions do qualify to be considered as moral leadership. They use different evaluation criteria, however, and their different rationales are instructive, indicating how far their thinking may have progressed.

Some appeal to frameworks used in the course. Graham demonstrated moral leadership because her actions by and large met the standards that have been discussed: moral ends – *yes*; moral means – *yes*; moral motives – typically scores a *maybe*.

Students frequently challenge Graham's description of her relationship with Richard Nixon, claiming that she was more biased against him than she acknowledges. They note that it would be reasonable for Graham to "hate" Nixon in light of the threats leveled against her and the rather peculiar combination of disdain and concern that she inspired in the Nixon White House. However, these accusations are not that troubling, and students appear to be satisfied with a judgment of mixed motives, claiming that Graham's support of the Watergate investigation was based on far more than ill will against President Nixon.

Others extend this argument. Like other moral leaders, Graham doesn't just act on her own behalf. The dominating motives that kept her going through the Pentagon Papers, and especially Watergate, were the interests of her journalists and a concern for the truth. "These are hallmarks of moral leadership – a concern for others' interests, and a commitment to moral principles." Students also find evidence of moral leadership in how Graham worked with others. "She not only acted on their behalf, she involved them in her decision-making." That is interest in others made real through action.

Finally, some students return to the concept of a moral code. Graham had a clear and well thought through understanding of the nature of the business she led: what its duties were, and to whom they were obligated. This clarity allowed her to demonstrate one other aspect of moral leadership: consistency. The consummate publisher, Graham did what effective publishers do – promote the good of society by defending freedom of the press and by supporting the long and often controversial search for truth.

Pentagon Papers: risk analysis

Pentagon Papers: evaluation of Graham's leadership

Differences: Watergate and Pentagon Papers

Watergate: evaluation of Graham's leadership

Figure 15.1 *Katharine Graham:* Personal History *roadmap*

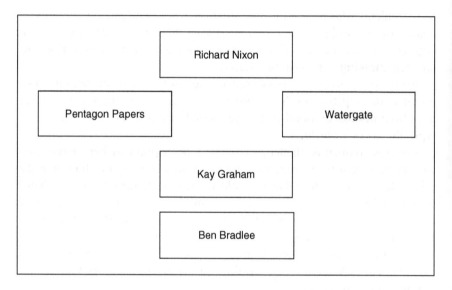

Figure 15.2 *Katharine Graham:* Personal History *board plan*

NOTES

1 Katharine Graham, *Personal History*, New York: Vintage Books, 1998, p. 450.

2 Ben Bradlee, *A Good Life*, New York: Touchstone Books, 1996, p. 323.

3 Graham, op. cit., p. 505.

4 Recent female leaders include Angela Merkel of Germany, Ellen Johnson-Sirleaf of Liberia, Michelle Bachelet of Chile, and Han Myung-Sook of South Korea: "Women Leaders Take Hold on Power Across the Globe," *Agence France-Presse*, January 16, 2006, and "South Korea Gets First Woman Prime Minister," *Agence France-Presse*, March 24, 2006.

5 Female CEOs of Fortune 500 companies include Meg Whitman of eBay, Inc., Carly Fiorina of Hewlett-Packard, Anne Mulcahy of Xerox Corp., and Andrea Jung of Avon Products, Inc: "11 Fortune 500 Companies with Female CEOs,"

The Associated Press, August 14, 2006 and Andrea Orr, "Hewlett-Packard Picks Lucent Exec as CEO," *The Houston Chronicle,* July 20, 1999, p. 20.

6   Ibid., p. 448.

7   Ibid., p. 450.

8   Bradlee, op. cit., p. 315.

9   Graham, op. cit., p. 446.

10   Bradlee, op. cit., p. 312.

11   Geoffrey R. Stone, *Perilous Times: Free Speech in Wartime,* New York: W. W. Norton & Company, 2004, pp. 5–6.

12   Bradlee, op. cit., p. 315.

13   Ibid., p. 316.

14   Ibid., p. 316.

15   Graham, op. cit., p. 457.

16   Ibid., p. 456.

17   Ibid., p. 454.

18   By the most common reckoning, "Watergate" lasted two years: the break-in to the offices at the Watergate building of the Democratic National Committee occurred on June 17, 1972, and Richard Nixon resigned the US presidency on August 8, 1974. But, for Graham and others at the *Post,* the Watergate ordeal wasn't over until July 1975, when the US Federal Communications Commission rejected the last of the license challenges that had been mounted against the *Post*'s TV stations by Nixon supporters.

19   Ibid., p. 498.

20   Ibid., p. 469.

21   Graham, op. cit., p. 471.

22   Ibid., p. 505.

23   Ibid.

Chapter 16

American Ground: Unbuilding the World Trade Center

Assuming leadership

THE CITY GOVERNMENT ran the show. The agency charged with managing the physical work was an unlikely one. It was the Department of Design and Construction (DDC), an obscure bureaucracy 1,300 strong whose normal responsibility was to oversee municipal construction contracts – for sidewalk and street repairs, jails, and the like – and whose offices were not even in Manhattan but in Queens. The DDC was given the lead for the simple reason that its two top officials, a man named Kenneth Holden and his lieutenant, Michael Burton, had emerged from the chaos of September 11 as the most effective of the responders. Now they found themselves running a billion-dollar operation with the focus of the nation upon them.

Nearly everyone at the site was well paid. The money for the effort came from federal emergency funds, and it flowed freely. But despite some cases of corruption and greed, money was not the main motivation here – at least not until almost the end. Throughout the winter and into the spring the workers rarely forgot the original act of aggression, or the fact that nearly 3,000 people had died there, including the friends and relatives of some who were toiling in the debris ... Whether correctly or not, the workers believed that an important piece of history was playing out, and they wanted to participate in it – often fervently, and past the point of fatigue. There were some who could not stand the stress, and they had to leave. But among the thousands who stayed, almost all sought greater involvement rather than less.

. . .

The problems that had to be solved there were largely unprecedented. Actions and intervention were required on every level, often with no need or possibility of asking for permission. As a result, within the vital new culture that grew up at the Trade Center site even the lowliest laborers and firefighters were given power. Many of them rose to it, and some of them sank. Among those who gained the greatest influence were people without previous rank who discovered balance and ability within themselves, and who in turn were discovered by others.[1]

AMERICAN GROUND: THEMES AND QUESTIONS

Emergent leadership: earning the right to lead

American Ground concludes the Moral Leadership module, and the course. It is, in many ways, the perfect ending – **moving from the domain of hierarchical leadership to *emergent leadership*, the kind of leadership that students might be expected to demonstrate long before they reach a position of highest responsibility – or, indeed, even if they never do so.** The book chronicles the story of the "unbuilding" of the World Trade Center, the enormous (and, until this account, relatively unknown) nine-month ordeal of stabilizing the World Trade Center's seventeen-acre site following the terrorist attacks on September 11, 2001. The main elements of the task were clearing the site of 1.5 million tons of rubble – concrete, debris, and steel – which were all that remained of the twin towers and other Trade Center buildings, and doing this, moreover, within the context of a search for victims, first those who might still be alive, and then the nearly 3,000 dead (a number, of course, not known for a long while).

The unlikely heroes of this unlikely tale are city bureaucrats and engineers, firefighters and demolition experts who combined to form a loose but highly effective leadership group. First and foremost, this is a story about *earning legitimacy.* Responsibility for the site was supposed to flow to the New York City Mayor's Office of Emergency Management. Unlike previous protagonists of the Moral Leadership module, **the leaders of the unbuilding project did not have procedural legitimacy: they were never fully authorized in their role.** The text, and the class, pose the question: **How did this group of individuals earn the right to lead?**

Exercising authority

The answers to this question recall and deepen many of the themes of the module and of the course. Machiavelli would appreciate the first answer. One of the characteristics that set the World Trade Center "unbuilders" apart was

269

their ability to make decisions, to *exercise authority* in the face of the enormous uncertainty – physical, social, organizational, emotional, moral – that was the defining context of the World Trade Center site:

> [Ken Holden, of the DDC] said, "As I kept explaining to FEMA later, this is not Oklahoma. We had the equipment. We had the connections. We could handle it. We just went in and did what we had to do. And no one said no."
> "Did anyone say yes?"
> "No. But then again, we weren't asking."[2]

Technical legitimacy

The willingness to make decisions stemmed, in part, from a deep expertise, shared among the leaders who emerged from the thousands who came to the site to help out. The World Trade Center leaders illustrate **technical legitimacy, a recognition by others that the individual possesses a powerful ability to draw upon knowledge, experience, and skill to make judgments necessary to the structure and management of work.** Astonishingly, not a single death occurred among the thousands of volunteer and paid workers who unbuilt the site, and the work proceeded faster and with greater productivity than any would at first have predicted.

American Ground deepens the students' view of the enormous value of technical expertise, and the breadth of roles played by the World Trade Center leaders shows what leadership and technical legitimacy look like across a wide spectrum of careers. This is project management on a scale that is hard to imagine but easy to learn from, and students gain much from analyzing the organizational and communication processes that are created to manage in the face of unending uncertainty the three thousand workers from city and federal agencies, private construction and demolition companies, and the "badges" – the New York City firefighters and police who populated the Trade Center site.

Moral legitimacy

But the unbuilders of *American Ground* were not just faced with a technical challenge of unprecedented complexity, uncertainty, and scale; they also faced moral challenges of similar dimensions. The first attack on the World Trade Center in 1993 set a pattern that was expected to repeat: an hours-long evacuation of the gigantic complex from which thousands would emerge alive. And, indeed, some fifteen thousand workers did manage to escape from the September 11th wreckage. But after that point there were only 18 survivors found in the entire unbuilding process, a devastating reality that set in slowly, and that turned the challenge from a search for survivors to a search for the remains of what turned out to be nearly three thousand dead.

How the unbuilders managed this challenge is at the heart of the story, and the **moral legitimacy of the WTC leaders depended on the ways in which they balanced the physical requirements of the unbuilding with two moral "ends": the safety of the workers on the site, and a respectful search for the remains of the victims.** These two ends required very different means, and students see the contrast between the seemingly intuitive understanding that Trade Center leaders showed to worker safety issues[3] and the much harder-won understanding they eventually obtained of the moral and emotional terrain of the victim recovery process.

Leaders' motives

American Ground also closes out an issue that emerged in the first class of the course. In *Endurance*, students began their search for ways to understand **the role of motivation in moral leadership.** Ernest Shackleton's search for fortune and renown made it hard for some students to credit his leadership with the designation of *moral* leadership. *American Ground* presents students with a similarly ambitious leader, one of the four who figure prominently in the book, the most visible, the public "Czar" of the Trade Center site. For some students, this far more realistic portrait of ambition coupled with recognizable skills and abilities *and* a concern with moral ends and means allows a breakthrough. Students come to recognize that motives are inevitably mixed. **They become more able to see the goal of moral leadership as one that can be obtained by people in the real world, in the course of living ordinary lives, even if these lives intersect with some extraordinary times and challenges.**

STUDENT ASSIGNMENT

READING: *American Ground: Unbuilding the World Trade Center*, by William Langewiesche.

1   This is an astonishing story of emergent leadership. In your view, how did the leadership team acquire their status?

2   What moral dilemmas did this team face? How did the dilemmas evolve over time? How well do you think the leaders handled them?

3   What is the relevance of this story for you?

CLASS PLAN OUTLINE: DISCUSSION BLOCKS

1 What Were the Most Difficult Aspects of the Leadership Challenge Faced by Trade Center Leaders? (20′)

2 How Did They Earn Their Legitimacy – Their Right to Lead? (30′)

3 Evaluation of Trade Center Leaders' Performance (25′)

4 What Lessons Do You Take from This Story? (20′)

5 Final Discussion (10′)

CLASS PLAN OVERVIEW

American Ground is a contemporary story, a strength and one of the primary purposes for including it in the course. Our students are being molded by terror attacks in various parts of the world in much the same way that the Vietnam War, or the First or Second World Wars shaped prior generations. This is the reality students confront, and they are aware of the need to come to terms with it, even as many acknowledge that it is too soon to appreciate all of the ways in which their outlook, and the norms and laws of the countries they live in, are being shaped by terror attacks and people's reactions to them. But currency brings with it some definite challenges. The class plan is designed to address some of them.

The first of these is the challenge posed by personal relationships that students may have with events of September 11th or with other recent occurrences of terror strikes. Some students may know people who were killed or wounded in one of these attacks. Others may have lived through an attack themselves. Or (as is most common) they may at least distinctly remember where they were and what they were doing when they first got news of the attack.

For these reasons, the class opens with a brief discussion in which students are invited to share their connection to the events of September 11th; instructors will want to add other locally salient situations. This creates important context for the students as a group. They know where sensitivities may lie, and can use this knowledge to manage their own comments and the questions they ask each other.

But where the first challenge focuses on the nearness of students to the events of September 11th, the second challenge is focused on the need to impose distance from them. The purpose of this class is to analyze a unique leadership challenge that was created as a consequence of a specific terror attack, not to debate student opinion on the morality (or even efficacy) of terror attacks on civilian noncombatants – a topic they argued in the class on *Truman and the Bomb*.

The opening discussion thus focuses on helping students imagine events at "Ground Zero" – the World Trade Center site – and is designed to move students from their own perspective to the situation facing the Trade Center's unbuilders. This may require some reliving on the part of some students, but works quite successfully, in the main, in moving students into the story.

The middle blocks of the discussion take off from this starting point, and are straightforward. Students explore various explanations for how the right to lead was earned by those in charge of the unbuilding effort, and evaluate how well the leaders managed the physical and moral tests they faced.

Here, too, the faithful depiction of events presents a challenge. Langewiesche describes the surprising collection of leaders who emerged to manage the site, and students must familiarize themselves with four main leaders and others who play a prominent role. The multiplicity of characters has not proved problematic, but you may want to give students some assistance by putting on the board data about the main leaders. (See Table 16.1: The World Trade Center's "Unbuilders," for details, and Figure 16.2: *American Ground* board plan.)

A final challenge is working with events that have taken on near-mythic proportions. Many students have pre-existing opinions about what happened at the World Trade Center as a result of the widespread news coverage of the event and its aftermath. Langewiesche presents a novel and at times dismaying account of the actions taken by groups (such as the New York City Fire Department) whose reputation stands at odds with events reported by him. In addition to allowing students to draw final lessons, the next-to-last discussion probes the ambivalent reactions that some students have, allowing a more nuanced discussion to unfold in which students explore the impact this contradictory evidence has on their assessment of the situation and players in it.[4]

There is also an optional final discussion that I have used to provide students with an opportunity to talk with each other about the ways in which they have experienced "The Moral Leader" – for most of them, a unique course.

A way of opening the discussion

Since this is our last class, after American Ground *we'll have a final discussion on a different topic – I'll tell you more about it later. But now for* American

Table 16.1 The World Trade Center's "Unbuilders"

Name	Role at World Trade Center	Organization	Responsibility
Mike Burton	Trade Center "Czar;" oversee practical details of the cleanup[1]	Department of Design and Construction (DDC): build and repair New York City municipal infrastructure	Second-in-command; "DDCs doer"[2]
Ken Holden	Burton's boss; behind-the-scenes leader; runs interference with Mayor Giuliani	DDC	Commissioner[3]
Peter Rinaldi	Supervise consultants brought in for specialized belowground engineering;[4] "the one man everyone turned to for an opinion"[5]	Port Authority of New York and New Jersey	Oversee engineering for all Port Authority tunnels and bridges[6]
Sam Melissi	"Saint Sam the Fireman;" mediator between warring factions[7]	New York Fire Department	Fireman; served on specialized collapsed-building team[8]

Notes
1 William Langewiesche, American Ground: Unbuilding the World Trade Center, New York: North Point Press, 2002, first paperback edn 2003, p. 66.
2 Ibid., p. 93
3 Ibid., p. 65
4 Ibid., p. 26
5 Ibid.
6 Ibid., p. 25
7 Ibid., p. 23
8 Ibid., p. 97

Ground: *William Langewiesche's book was initially published as a series in the* Atlantic Monthly *magazine in the US; it was a sensation when it came out, since it documented a facet of the World Trade Center attacks and their aftermath that was virually unknown. Focusing on leadership by ordinary people, it is a perfect book with wichto end our course.*

1 CONTEXT SETTING: THE LEADERSHIP CHALLENGE (20')

This discussion is designed to move students from their own personal connection to events at the World Trade Center, or similar events elsewhere, into the situation that the Trade Center leaders confronted.

Questions driving the discussion are in bold

Because this work is contemporary, some of you may have a direct connection to the events of September 11th.[5] In the interests of sensitivity, does anyone have any personal relationship to these events (or others like them) that we should know about?

Students are grateful that this question is asked, since by this point in the course they know each other fairly well and are eager not to trespass on each other's feelings. Not surprisingly, students vary greatly in how much they want to talk about the exact nature of their involvement with September 11th. Some students have been very candid about the loss of close friends or relatives, while others simply note that they have a connection but not one they are comfortable discussing. The students who appear to have the easiest time are those who were present that day (or knew people who were) but who suffered no loss, and for whom the event could be described in purely physical terms. These students have noted the peculiar light (the sunlight fell differently after the Trade Center towers toppled), the heat, the smell of death and smoke, the chaos, the gray ash that covered everything, and the rain of papers, photos, and personal belongings from the offices that were destroyed.

Let's picture the World Trade Center site on September 11th and 12th. What was the situation that confronted Mike Burton, Ken Holden, Peter Rinaldi and others who arrived at the start?

Students are then asked to add to these personal stories other details that are important to creating a realistic picture of how the Trade Center site must have looked to the would-be unbuilders. They may need to be prompted about some of the most obvious attributes: the physical danger of falling buildings; intense fire; fifteen thousand office workers coming out of the rubble while hundreds of firefighters and police rush back in. Students note that the Trade Center site was defined by its perimeter: it was a self-contained unit that was experiencing its own hell, and thus quite different from the rest of the city. Inside was massive confusion, in which it was not clear who was in charge, or what they were in charge of. The internal confusion was matched by a broader external confusion and uncertainty that the leaders would have to consider. What did the attacks mean? What was happening? Was another attack coming?

Students don't just focus on what the Trade Center site must have looked like to Mike Burton, Ken Holden, Peter Rinaldi, and others, but on who was doing the looking. Many agree with observations made in the text that most of the unbuilding leaders were helped by not having a direct personal connection to any of the site's victims. Unlike the firefighters and the police, they were not rescuing their own dead or wounded, and this, the students believe, helped them see the WTC situation clearly and objectively. They also note that most of the lookers were engineers, able more than others to imagine what might be going on with the physical structure of the Trade Center site.

What do you think the unbuilders expected? What would happen? What would they need to do?

You will want to ask students to imagine the initial expectations of the unbuilders. History is important, and it is clear from Langewiesche's account that nearly everyone expected the attack on 2001 to follow the general outline of events that occurred after the initial attack on the World Trade Center in 1993. Six people died in that attack, and thousands had to be helped from the building, but – critically – the buildings survived. So what would have been expected in 2001? Lots of survivors would need to be rescued; and the rescue efforts would be successful. Someone would be in charge. People could be counted on to know what to do – the firefighters, the police, and other first responders. And, most of all, the buildings would hold.

In your view, what were the most difficult aspects of their leadership challenge?

The final question asks students to lay out what they believe to be the most important leadership challenges facing the Trade Center leaders. Some students focus on the management of uncertainty, the sheer scale of the problem, and how much wasn't known about it. Others consider the personal aspects of the challenge: "how to handle the emotions of it all, yours and everyone else's." Some focus on the organizational challenge: "You need to determine who is in charge, and who you are in relation to them." And, for others, the challenge is "To just act. The longer they waited, the more the situation would fall apart."

2 HOW DID THEY EARN THEIR LEGITIMACY – THE RIGHT TO LEAD? (30′)

Students enjoy answering this question, the core question posed by Langewiesche's account. *American Ground* is inspirational for many students who see in its flawed and (therefore) human actors the promise that they, too, could step up to a moral leadership challenge if faced with one. But stepping up, while important, is not enough. The WTC unbuilders were trusted not just because they volunteered to lead, but because of what they brought to the leadership task. The multiple actors enable students to flesh out the characteristics of legitimacy that they have been working with in prior classes. And these characteristics, in turn, reinforce the themes of the last module of the course.

As you know, authority over disasters in New York City was supposed to be the province of the OEM – Office of Emergency Management. Burton and Holden's department (the DDC) had no formal authority over the World Trade Center site, yet Holden, Burton, and others (such as Peter Rinaldi and Sam Melissi) none the less emerged as its leaders. How did they do that? How did they obtain their leadership status?

Exercising authority

Students usually begin with the leaders' willingness to exercise authority, and the leaders earn high marks for initiative, a vital factor and antidote to the uncertainty and paralysis that often accompanies an emergency. The opening scenes of the disaster show Burton and Holden in motion nearly from the start, calling up construction companies, planning for equipment needs and anticipating logistical problems. Burton's "talent for making up his mind"[6] is evident, as is his willingness to be responsible for the actions he takes. All of these capabilities are reminiscent of Machiavelli's advice to the prince that in the face of uncertainty it is "better to be impetuous than circumspect."[7] Students point to the self-reinforcing cycle of early decision-making: if the first decision works out, then leaders are often trusted to make another.

Little procedural legitimacy

But at the World Trade Center a willingness to exercise authority had to be translated into a willingness to make decisions despite a lack of formal or hierarchical authority. Students point out that the procedural legitimacy of the two leaders was weak (said one, as a city agency they had a "tiny bit of procedural legitimacy"), and none of the four principal leaders (including Rinaldi and Melissi) had official roles at the Trade Center that in any way corresponded to the power and influence they exercised.

American Ground shows students that technical and moral legitimacy can overcome a deficiency in procedural authority. This is particularly relevant – and heartening – for students who are at the beginning of their work lives, because few organizational roles carry with them all of the power that is needed to accomplish their goals.

Technical legitimacy

Students readily address the technical legitimacy of the four leaders (and others who are featured), defining the elements that were instrumental in providing a foundation for their leadership. Some read the description of the responsibilities of the Department of Design and Construction carefully, and point out that Holden and Burton were in a position to "do something as logistical" as removing 1.5 million tons of debris from the Trade Center site. Others point to their contacts in the construction industry and knowledge of key players and required skills: the Trade Center would need demolition experts, and those with experience in high-rise, underground, and underwater construction.

Students will also note that many of the leaders shared a common background as engineers. Trained in methodical problem-solving – the characteristic approach of that profession – they were able to apply lifelong skills and aptitudes. (Langewiesche is much taken with the contrast between the engineering mentality and what he sees as opposing human instincts; descriptions like the following recur through the text: "Rinaldi was human, but also always an engineer."[8])

One student likened the leaders' diagnostic skills to the popular movie *The Matrix*, pointing out that where ordinary people might see steel beams and crumbled buildings Peter Rinaldi and Mike Burton saw structural problems and the workings of materials science – what might stand and what might fall.

Part of expertise is acknowledging what can and can't be known: "Burton said, George, what assurance do you have that the fill is not causing the collapse?" Tamaro [an underground specialist and a "renowned engineer"[9]] said, "Why don't you ask me when I am going to die?"[10]

Situational leadership

The leaders demonstrated the ability to match their leadership to the peculiar circumstances of the Trade Center site.

Burton of the DDC was the organizer – excellent at driving results and identifying and solving problems. Holden, DDC commissioner, worked behind the scenes, securing resources, and protecting the others from the (at times) appalling demands of Mayor Rudi Giuliani. Rinaldi, part of the Port Authority (the "owners" of the World Trade Center), led technical matters in a way that was uniquely adapted to the requirements of the situation.

> Rinaldi was nominally in charge, but he neither gave commands nor asserted himself by taking the lead. I think by then he had already discovered what some others never did – that the imposition of conventional order on these ruins was a formalism or a fiction, and unnecessary. Progress was made instead in the privacy of a thousand moments, on loose, broad fronts, by individuals looking after themselves and generally acting alone.[11]

Moral legitimacy

Students also address the sources of the leaders' moral legitimacy. Burton, Holden, and Rinaldi were seen as capable and honest brokers. Because they were not principally involved with the recovery of the remains of friends or colleagues they rode above the tensions that marked relationships among the firefighters, police, and civilian contractors. Like others on the site, they pursued what was universally perceived as a moral end:

> Despite the apocalyptic nature of the scene, the response was unhesitant and almost childishly optimistic: it was simply understood that you would find survivors, and then that you would find the dead, and that this would help their families get on with their lives, and that your resources were unlimited, and that you would work night and day to clean up the mess, and that this would allow the world's greatest city to rebuild quickly, and maybe even make itself into something better than before. From the first hours these assumptions were never very far away.[12]

Of the four leaders, only one is specifically identified in the text as a *moral leader*. Saint Sam, as the fireman Sam Melissi is called on the site, was renowned for the dedication he showed to the process of recovering the victims of the attack.

[His] profoundly altruistic impulses ... over time became widely recognized, eventually giving him a moral authority that no one else at the site came close to matching. The authority translated into the power to make suggestions that others were willing to follow ... The power surprised and plagued him to the end; he did not think of himself as a leader, and in other circumstances he probably would not have been one.[13]

We've had four leaders whose legitimacy, arguably, stemmed from their perceived moral authority – Ernest Shackleton, Thomas More, Kay Graham, and now Sam Melissi. Do they share any characteristics in common?

This question allows students to broaden and deepen their understanding of moral legitimacy. "Each stands up for what they believe in – each acts on principle: Shackleton, to save his crew; More, to stay true to his religion; Graham, to defend freedom of the press; Melissi, to protect the memory of the firefighters."

Students debate whether moral leadership requires self-sacrifice: "Each of these leaders sacrificed their own well-being for that of others." A student responded, "Not completely. If they hadn't done what they did – been true to their beliefs – they would have sacrificed themselves – even the most important part of themselves."

When you look at these four: is being a moral leader and having moral legitimacy an unmitigated good? Is this something *you* aspire to?

"When I started this class, I would have thought that's what I'd aspire to, but now I think I don't; you have to give up too much." "But that's exactly what I'd like to be known *for* – for *moral* legitimacy. I'd much rather have people listen to what I say because they respect my values and principles than because I went to an elite school and earned technical legitimacy from my skills." "I agree. The question that was asked is exactly the right question: Is this something *you* aspire to? For each of us, if we found that principle we believed in as much as More believed in his religion, it would be exactly what we'd want to do."

"I'm concerned that moral legitimacy raises the bar too high. You'll be scrutinized, and if you are not consistent it's harder on the person than if it was just business that they were seen as managing." "I agree – it's so subjective. I'd rather make my mark with procedural and technical legitimacy; moral legitimacy needs to change with situations and is very hard to maintain." "But at least you get to sleep at night – that's the greatest gift of all." "I don't know – you'd like to think you'll sleep well, but so many of the characters we've seen did not sleep well. If we've learned anything, it's that moral choosing is hard."

3 HOW WELL DID THEY DO? (25')

The discussion of the leaders' legitimacy leaves students in a bit of a lull, since the analysis appears to support a relatively (and nearly uniformly) positive view of their performance. This next block is designed to dig deeper, examining specific leadership challenges, particularly those with moral or ethical stakes. The picture of the leaders that emerges is more mixed than the one that preceded it.

We know the unbuilders did very well on the physical aspects of clearing the site. Completed in nine months – months earlier than official estimates – 1.5 million tons of rubble were removed from the World Trade Center's 17 acres. They spent less time, and less money, than had been expected. And, critically, the site was stabilized within its slurry wall. If those were the physical challenges, what were the moral challenges the leaders faced?

The unbuilders were enormously successful at the engineering aspects of their task, but that was only half of what they needed to manage; the evaluation of the leaders' performance takes place within the context of their moral challenges. The first and most visible of these was the challenge of balancing the activities related to clearing the site with those required for the search and recovery of the bodies of victims. A second, related challenge was maintaining the safety of the workers in the unimaginably dangerous and uncontrollable terrain of the bombed site. Students often begin with the balance that needed to be struck between the physical unbuilding, conducted by civilian contractors, and the victim search and recovery process, the province of the firefighters and the police.

How well did the leaders handle the victim recovery process?

Students are usually impressed with the processes put in place to recover remains of victims during the unbuilding.[14] In total, 1,209 victims were identified by the Medical Examiner's Office during the ten months of the site unbuilding. Of these, only 293 were from (almost) whole bodies. The remainder was identified from 19,693 body parts.[15] As evidence of the effectiveness of the unbuilding process and its leaders, students point out that only 78 of the 1,209 victims were discovered in the remains sent eventually to a debris-processing center at Fresh Kills.

281

Yet Mike Burton, Trade Center Czar and main driver of activity on the site, came under heavy fire, especially from widows and family members of firefighters still missing. Their criticism may have been warranted, since Burton was described as nakedly "climbing his mountain of success,"[16] "pushing for speed,"[17] and intent on completing the project "below cost and ahead of schedule – however arbitrary those targets may have been."[18] Criticism culminated at a public meeting called by firefighters on behalf of the dead firefighters's families.

How did you understand the "widows' meeting"? What was going on at it?

This meeting, later referred to as the "widows' meeting," proved a turning point for Burton and Bill Cote, long-time friend and close aide on the site who attended with him. Furious at what they perceived as an all-out attempt on Burton's part to complete the unbuilding project at the expense of victim recovery, the widows jeered at Burton, referring to him repeatedly as "Mr Scoop and Dump" and refusing to allow him to explain his methods or the priority he felt he had placed on finding the bodies of the dead. Shaken by the meeting, Burton and Cote retreated to a nearby bar to discuss their reaction.

> "[They were] troubled by the realization . . . that there were people who found their actions were wrong, even wicked. It made them question the doggedness of their approach, and reminded them of a simple imperative they were trying to forget: that the unbuilding was more than just a problem of deconstruction, and that for the final measure of success they would have to take emotions into account."[19]

How do you evaluate Burton's and Cote's response to the widows' meeting?

Some students are struck – positively – by the response of Burton and Cote to the meeting. They observe how easy it would have been to dismiss the widows' and other family members' complaints as hysterics or grandstanding. Burton's and Cote's willingness to allow themselves to be persuaded of the importance of emotions is seen as a sign of moral growth and development. One student pointed out, "Speed was not just important to the victims. Working on the pile was hard and emotionally draining; the leaders were right in pushing speed for the sake of workers on the pile."

Others are more critical, citing the meeting as evidence of how long it took Burton to appreciate the human toll of the victim recovery process on family members: "This is a rights-based issue. Burton didn't see the widows as having rights that needed to be protected." But even students critical of his actions could empathize with the difficulty Burton faced at the meeting: "This was really hard. Picture six thousand Antigones screaming at you to recover their dead!"

How well did the leaders handle worker safety?

These rather positive assessments are offset by students' evaluation of the handling of worker safety by Trade Center leaders. Students often begin on a positive note: there were no deaths, and even few major injuries among the nearly three thousand paid and volunteer workers on the Trade Center site. If they have not made this point previously, students will point out (or can be asked to describe) the characteristics of the attack site that impacted workers: the dangerous mountains of rubble that shifted without warning, the fires and potential flooding of the site, more than half of which was under sea level; the need to explore areas where it was impossible to anticipate hidden risks; and the general uncertainty that accompanied the deconstruction and victim recovery activities.

The safety challenge was magnified by the attitudes of the workers themselves, especially the firefighters, described by Langewiesche as "standing for hours in the heaviest smoke and dust, refusing as a matter of pride to wear the respirators that dangled around their necks. They seemed to have surrendered to an attitude of reckless self-abandonment. To varying degrees the police and construction workers had surrendered to it too."[20]

Students debate how well the leaders protected the workers from the inherent risks of their work. Some commend Burton for understanding (as Langewieshe puts it) "that conventional standards of safety simply did not apply to these ruins,"[21] and for being willing to make decisions when needed and to take responsibility for them.

> To the fireman he said, "Listen. You've already been in the building. You've already risked your life once. It would take us a week in daylight to tell whether the building is safe or not. If you climb the stairs on the far side, it's probably okay. That's a guess. But it won't be any riskier than where you've already been."[22]

Some students see this as moral terrain – making decisions on behalf of others, and being willing to accept the burden of responsibility. But, given the vast scope of the project, opportunities for direct decision-making were not that frequent, and the unbuilders developed what students describe as one of two ways of managing.

The first is normative to business students, trained in the value of planning, control, bureaucracy, and rules. The second was normative to the Trade Center site. It is based on understanding "[t]hat risk was the very nature of the Trade Center operation,"[23] For the improvisation and creativity that was required, workers had to be responsible for themselves. Students assert that a leadership style premised on personal responsibility, rather than rules-based control, also matched the motivation of workers on the site, who volunteered to be there, and found personal and moral value in the work.

But some students are appalled, asserting that unnecessary risks were taken with the lives of workers. With the benefit of hindsight, some question what all the rush was about – particularly since the planning for a new World Trade Center complex, mired in controversy, is still not complete years later. Others argue that the positive assessment is possible only because the consequences were positive. Had workers died or had there been more serious injuries, the leaders' laissez-faire approach to safety would have seemed callous and irresponsible.

Students who are familiar with reports of health problems that have emerged among Trade Center workers submit that we may end up judging the leaders very differently in the future if (as appears to be the case for some workers, see note 3) results emerge of worker illness due to exposure to asbestos and other toxins imbedded in debris and stirred up by constant activity on the site.

4 WHAT LESSONS DO YOU TAKE FROM THIS STORY? (20')

The last discussion brings many themes together from the text and the course. As the final substantive discussion, it is appropriate to ask students to step back and take stock: What have they taken from this text, and, more broadly, what relevance does the story have for their lives? As a segue into this discussion, you'll want to provide an opening for students who are troubled, as many are, by some of the details of Langewiesche's account, particularly in relation to the firefighters.

American Ground was widely praised, but was also quite controversial, in large part because of the stories that Langewiesche relates about theft on the part of the firefighters, and his focus on the "Battle of the Badges." Does this book bother anyone? Why?

Students often discuss the leadership challenge, presented by Langewiesche as a conflict in "tribal allegiances" between the firefighters and the police who worked at the site. The tensions between the groups was driven in the main by actions of the firefighters, who became early and prominent heroes of the September 11th story, representing to many Americans an inspiring and reassuring example of self-sacrifice and dedication to public safety. But on the site the behavior of the firefighters was often at odds with this depiction, and many showed single-minded commitment to unearthing the bodies of their own fallen colleagues, while displaying insensitivity to the far greater numbers of civilian dead whose bodies were the focus of police excavation efforts.[24] Langewiesche also reports acts of looting and theft on the part of firefighters (and some civilian contractors).

Students sometimes criticize Langewiesche's motivations in writing *American Ground*, citing his initiative in writing Burton to be allowed to chronicle the unbuilding, and his exclusive access to the site during that period, as evidence of mixed motives that may have led him to exaggerate the wrongdoing of firefighters, and the effectivness of Burton and other leaders. Those familiar with some of the rebuttals to events in the book, addressed in Langewiesche's afterword, may also question the validity of his reporting. These criticisms arise in the context of student evaluation of Langewiesche's account of firefighter activity, and the conflicts between the firefighters and the police who worked at the site.

Some students are disappointed and others are downright angry that the high regard with which they held the firefighters may have been misplaced. This prompts a debate. As one student argued, "I really thought it was unnecessary for Langewiesche to write all the details that made the firefighters not heroes. We needed them to be heroes. Why would he do that?" Another responded, "It's important for the history of the event to be true and cover all perspectives." Another added, "I need the information. I want to be able to choose for myself whether they are or are not heroes." And a fourth summed up: "I just replaced one set of heroes with another. I don't think the firefighters are heroes anymore, but I now have this whole other set of unsung heroes who did amazing things day after day."

Let's step back from the details here: What lessons do you take from this story?

I've provided detailed questions that reflect recurring themes from the text, but students often do quite well just by being prompted with the simple question of what lessons they take from the story. You may want to put students into buzz groups – perhaps even ones that are not accustomed to – to give them an opportunity to step back and think about the discussion as a whole.

What are your thoughts – now – on moral leadership and its requirements?

Many of the students' lessons relate to their evolving understanding of moral leadership and its requirements. Drawing on Machiavelli and the theme of exercising authority, some students point out a requirement of moral leadership – initiative – a willingness to lead when others can't or won't. "I've learned that the real hierarchy is not that important. I saw that you can just step up to the plate and become a leader, even just by using moral legitimacy, and people will follow you." Another student observed, "In the course we frequently talked about the importance of emotion, but in the case of the Trade Center leaders, it appears that there are circumstances in which cutting yourself off from emotion may be necessary to be able to lead."

Students also stress the importance of preparation. *American Ground* reminds some of them of *Endurance,* and even of *The Secret Sharer*: it seems that opportunities to exercise moral leadership often come as emergencies. "By that time," one agued, "it's too late to prepare; you simply act on instinct, from whatever foundation already exists. You have to refine your leadership principles and instincts before they are called for, to have them when they are needed."

One of the questions that has dogged us throughout the course is the question of motivation. We said that moral legitimacy is conferred when a leader pursues moral ends, through moral means, for moral motives. How do you think about leaders and their motives?

Students return one last time to the topic of motivation. They acknowledge Mike Burton's evident ambition, but many seem to finally come to an accommodation with the concept of mixed motives. As one student put it, "We shouldn't let the fact that success and moral goals sometimes overlap be a reason to blame a leader."

Students propose that immoral (or amoral) motivation would exist if the leader were only taking action for the sake of personal recognition. One offered a test case: If leaders would not be recognized for their actions, would they still take them? In the case of the Trade Center leaders, this student was confident that they would – and, since this is true, he credited the leaders with exercising moral leadership.

5 FINAL DISCUSSION (10')

"The Moral Leader" is a special kind of course, focused as much on student discovery and self-cultivation as on formal learning. Students typically develop close relationships with each other, stimulated by the nature of the texts they read and the discussions they have about them – candid discussions that often move the students quite deeply. Like me, you may want to give students a chance to close this chapter with each other, to acknowledge some of the feelings they have had during the course, and to express the appreciation that many of them feel for the contributions that others have made. You will know your own students well enough to decide whether such a discussion would be helpful to them; I have found that it is a risk worth taking.

The discussion question has been carefully crafted (through trial and error) to allow the discussion to stay at the level of the group; it does not require students to make comments about individuals (and in fact discourages them from doing so, since inevitably some students would be singled out and others wouldn't), or to take time to thank (or critique) the instructor. This, too, is a lesson about moral leadership for the students – a lesson about acknowledging a shared experience, and in having the courage to say some of the positive things – out loud – that they may have been thinking.

A way of introducing the discussion

Throughout the course, I have reflected on how much I enjoy our discussions. I know, from comments that many of you have made to me, that I am not alone in this. I think it's appropriate at the end of a course like "The Moral Leader" to give you a chance to reflect on – and tell each other – something about the experience of the class and what it has meant to you. So please take a minute or two to think about our class and be prepared to answer this question: What would you like to tell your classmates about your experience of being in this course?

"I thought it was really important to be required to put my thoughts about morality into words. It's easy to think that what you believe is self-evident but it's not, and you learn that by having to articulate and defend it to others."

"I like knowing that I'm not alone in thinking about these things – I used to think I was. I'll know when I face situations in the future that I thought about them for a while in here."

"I grew up very conservative; I've learned so much from the viewpoints that everyone has shared."

"Even though we almost never talk about business, this is the most relevant class to what I'll be doing next year."

"I liked the fact that things aren't sugar-coated in the course. In our other classes, things always work out – the companies almost always come out fine. Here, things often don't work out and we had to struggle with that. We grew more in this class because of it."

The leadership challenge

How did they earn the right to lead?

How well did they do?

Your lessons from this story

Figure 16.1 American Ground *roadmap*

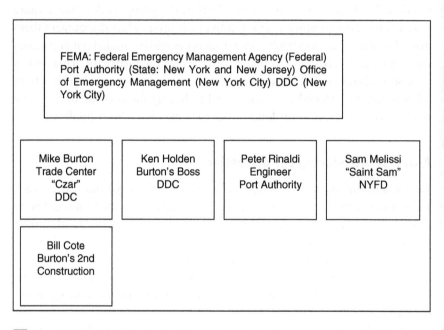

Figure 16.2 American Ground *board plan*

NOTES

1 William Langewiesche, *American Ground: Unbuilding the World Trade Center,* New York: North Point Press, 2002, first paperback edition 2003, pp. 9–10.

2 Ibid., p. 95.

3 Since the publication of Langeweische's account, some workers have begun to suffer from long-term health effects resulting from exposure to toxins imbedded in Ground Zero debris. Lawsuits have been filed on behalf of Ground Zero workers against the city of New York. Langewiesche captures the problems leaders faced in enforcing compliance with worker safety precautions, and students can – and do – judge for themselves how Trade Center leaders may have contributed to worker health problems. For a review of actions taken at

the time to protect workers and of worker claims, see "Use of Air Masks at Issue in Claims of 9/11 Illnesses," by Anthony DePalma, *The New York Times*, June 5, 2006.

4   Langewiesche's afterword to the paperback edition of *American Ground* provides a detailed description of the controversies that emerged from some of his reporting and his own (few) corrections and analysis. You can refer it to students who seem particularly concerned about the truthfulness of his accounts.

5   There were three attacks on September 11th: the attack on the World Trade Center's twin towers; an attack at the Pentagon in Washington, DC; and the failed attack that ended with a third plane crashed near Shankstown, Pennsylvania.

6   Langewiesche, op. cit., p. 93.

7   Niccolò Machiavelli, *The Prince*, New York and London: Penguin Books, 1999, p. 82.

8   Ibid., p. 39.

9   Ibid., p. 121.

10 Ibid., p. 129.

11 Ibid., pp. 26–27.

12 Ibid., p. 8.

13 Ibid., p. 22.

14 The processes evolved over time. See p. 133 for a description of the three-stage process for screening debris for human remains that followed the initial period of site stabilization. Two screens (physical inspection of material, examined for remains) were done on the Trade Center site, followed by a third screen, itself a three-stage process, conducted at Fresh Kills: first, extraction of metal pieces; then debris less than 6 inches raked by hand; finally, smaller parts of less than 0.25 inch were sifted and then inspected on a conveyor belt. These processes yielded 5 body parts per day that collectively identified 78 people. Students use these numbers to point out the effectiveness of the on-site process of victim identification at the Trade Center, since of the total 1,209 victims identified only 78 (or approximately 6%) were found at Fresh Kills.

15 Langewiesche, op. cit., p. 135.

16 Ibid., p. 164.

17 Ibid.

18 Ibid.

19 Ibid.

20 Ibid., p. 71.

21 Ibid., p. 93.

22 Ibid.

23 Ibid., p. 191.

24 The numbers are instructive: 343 firemen were killed, but that number was dwarfed by the 658 deaths of the financial services firm Cantor Fitzgerald, and the more than 2,000 others who also died at the Trade Center.

Adapting "The Moral Leader"

You may now be persuaded that learning through literature helps deepen students' learning, and I hope you are encouraged to experiment with it in your own circumstance. But you may be unable to do so for an entire course or program. This appendix suggests several ways to adapt the texts and approach used in "The Moral Leader". While it hardly addresses all of the possibilities, enough are provided that your own ideas can be sparked.

THE "MORAL LEADER" APPROACH

You will want to begin by considering what distinguishes the approach used in "The Moral Leader" from other kinds of learning.

Personal discovery

The approach is dedicated to *personal discovery* on the part of students. Even as sessions inserted into other courses or programs, learning through literature requires respect for student exploration, a desire for students to take the literature and, quite literally, to make it their own. For this to happen, instructors must be willing to follow discussion as well as to lead it; to be flexible, and surprised, at the turn that sessions may take. Each group of students, and each student, experiences and interprets the texts in individual, often very distinctive, ways. At the same time, the stories evoke certain themes and questions with regularity, and the material itself is so evocative that many of the themes "naturally" arise; an important aspect of this approach is trust in that happening.

Describe, analyze, judge

Personal discovery is enhanced by reading and facilitation that largely follow the framework of *describe, analyze, judge* – an ordering that enables students to build from their description, analyses, and arguments to their assessments slowly and somewhat methodically. Fidelity to this process is not just a matter of reliable pedagogy; it stems as well from a belief that we are teaching students that good judgment comes only after the hard work of description and analysis. With these thoughts in mind, you may want to consider providing students with some guidance on how to prepare to work with literature, similar to the advice on "Reading the Materials" that is described in Chapter 3 of this guide and in the student textbook.[1]

The "Moral Leader" point of view

"The Moral Leader" represents a particular vantage point from which to explore, study and learn from literature. (Many others are possible.) The lesson plans in this guide follow the purpose and interests of the course – examining leadership and moral decision-making. For those interested in using the classes in chunks or as individual sessions, the question you will want to answer is how framing the study of the texts from a Moral Leader point of view will stimulate, surprise, enhance, and further the interests of your own courses and programs. I believe that adaptations of the materials to other purposes can do all of these things and more, if well matched.

USING A MODULE

As you have seen in the class plans, learning cumulates through "The Moral Leader," with student discussions in the last module on Moral Leadership using concepts that were introduced in the modules on Moral Challenge and Moral Reasoning. There is, none the less, an opportunity to insert any one of the modules into an existing course of your own. The modules have been designed to be coherent and largely self-contained, exploring a specific set of themes and questions that provide students with a clear set of lessons that they *experience* through the literature.

The module on Moral Challenge, for example, provides a rich opportunity to help students understand the central idea that not all moral challenges are alike, and that these differences have practical implications for the strategies used to address them. The module on Moral Reasoning would allow you and the students to survey common moral perspectives and then to explore other kinds of reasoning that people use when they think through a moral problem. The module on Moral Leadership investigates how moral leadership differs from leadership of any other kind, and why students judge some, but not all, actions of even very effective leaders as demonstrating *moral* leadership.[2]

Beyond the depth of coverage that you can achieve, the advantage of adapting an entire module is that it gives students a better chance to develop skills that are built into the approach.

291

USING SMALL CHUNKS OR INDIVIDUAL SESSIONS

You may be interested in adapting just one or two of the texts and class plans, inserting, as a colleague of mine put it, "jewels of learning" into the flow of a course or program. The following charts illustrate possible pairings of texts and themes from "The Moral Leader" with other topics. These are just suggestions to stimulate thinking; with your understanding of your own courses and programs, you will do a much better job of laying out the possibilities.

Moral Challenge Text Pairings

Text and setting	Central theme	Business topics	General topics
Endurance, by Alfred Lansing Antarctic, 1914	Survival: the challenge of right versus wrong	Leading teams and organizations Goal setting and coaching	Science and culture of exploration Imperial expansion Celestial navigation
Antigone, by Sophocles Ancient Greece	The challenge of right versus right	Negotiation and dispute resolution Personal ethics	Political leadership Sociology of resistance Justice Tragic drama and human conflict
Blessed Assurance, by Allan Gurganus 1940s America	The challenge of a moral dilemma	Marketing and product policy Diversity and business Inclusive leadership	The African-American experience The American South Race relations Psychology of decision-making Ethics and economics
Things Fall Apart, by Chinua Achebe Early twentieth-century Nigeria	The challenge of new principles	Global context of management Business leadership in changing times Managing across cultures	The African experience Nationalism and imperialism Cultural change and transitions

Moral Reasoning Text Pairings

Text and setting	Central theme	Business topics	General topics
Trifles, by Susan Glaspell Early twentieth-century rural America	Reasoning from moral theory	Managerial decision-making Small-group dynamics	Women's history The American heart-land Criminal investigation
"Moral Theories," from *Principles of Biomedical Ethics*, Tom L. Beauchamp and James F. Childress			Moral reasoning
The Sweet Hereafter, by Russell Banks Contemporary America	Reasoning from personal perspective	Mediation and consensus building Corporate law and liability	Community power Legal ethics Changing perspectives Psychology of family dynamics
The Remains of the Day, by Kazuo Ishiguro Britain between world wars	Reasoning from a moral code	The profession of management Agency theory Work–life balance	Class and culture Professional ethics History of work
A Man for All Seasons, by Robert Bolt Sixteenth-century England	Reasoning from multiple moralities	Principled leadership Power and influence Managing change	Religious belief and moral action Portrayal of history in film History of religion

Moral Leadership Text Pairings

Text and setting	Central theme	Business topics	General topics
The Prince, by Niccolò Machiavelli Sixteenth-century Italy	Exercising authority	Entrepreneurial leadership Leadership theory and practice Business ethics	Political theory The Renaissance Literature: The mirror of princes
The Secret Sharer, by Joseph Conrad 1890s off the coast of Siam	Earning legitimacy	Leadership development Leading teams and organizations	Government The responsibilities of public action Naval studies
Truman and the Bomb, compilation Japan, Second World War Excerpts from Just and Unjust Wars, by Michael Walzer	Balancing benefits and harms	Leadership and decision-making Managing innovation	The American presidency The atom bomb in history and culture War and political theory
Personal History, autobiography of Katharine Graham 1970s America, recalled Excerpt from A Good Life, autobiography of Ben Bradlee	Taking a stand	Principled leadership Power and influence Business ethics	Investigative reporting Women's leadership Professional ethics The Vietnam War
American Ground: Unbuilding the World Trade Center, by William Langewiesche Post-September 11th USA	Assuming leadership	Technical leadership Project management Managing operations	The sociology of organizations The ethics of public service Engineering as a profession

NOTES

1 "Reading the Material" is also available as a standalone note, developed to be used with the "Moral Leader" course, from Harvard Business School Press, Note# 9–065–027.

2 If you could devote a total of six sessions to a module on Moral Leadership, I would recommend beginning the module with a first class on *Endurance*, to frame the question: Is this moral leadership? The rest of the module's five classes would follow.

Defining morality and the "Moral Leader" class card

DEFINING MORALITY

I developed the "Moral Leader" class card assignment after having taught the course a few times. Here is how it came about. Two students approached me at the end of a class on *Blessed Assurance*, one quite intense and energized, and asked how I defined the term "moral." I noted Plato's famous definition of morality as the study of how one should live,[1] but it was clear that this description was too broad to be useful. I then forwarded an introduction to ethics and morality that I had found helpful (see "Additional background," below). Here is the reply I received from one of the students:

> I think [the article] does a good job of discerning what ethics are and how they are differentiated against custom and etiquette. It also does a good job of stating how there are different viewpoints in terms of what is right and wrong.
>
> However, the one question I still have after reading the document is where do morals get defined? When people say immoral or moral, whose definition are they going by? One argument is that morals represent a general set of beliefs that society, in general, believes to be the right way to do things. However, does that make that moral or immoral? Nietzsche argued that society doesn't really know anything and that morals should come from the individual self and personal reflection on the self in terms of moral development. The ultimate challenge I see still is that in any discussion of whether something is moral or not is that everyone might have different views because their definition of moral is different. For example, today some believed that Jerry [from *Blessed Assurance*] was immoral because of his actions, while others believed he was working for a

shady operation, but what he did specifically was not immoral because he was just doing his job.

Does my question make sense?

"The Moral Leader" takes an inductive approach to the definition of morality. As I learned in the exchange with that student, students don't need pre-defined terms and concepts. They come to the course with some notion of morality – understanding, for example, that it covers the territory of right and wrong action, and raises questions about the basis on which such judgments should be made. Instead, students are given the chance gradually to evolve their own *workable* definition of morality, a definition of morality-in-use that reflects the judgments they make and those they have reflected on, used by the characters studied in the stories, augmented by debates in class, conceptual overviews in the student textbook, and the two substantive readings on moral philosophy offered during the course.

This approach, consistent with the course's intent, is based on the belief that students will be more likely to learn deeply (personally, in ways that matter to them) and may even be able to translate learning into future reflection and decision-making if they can formulate, test, revise, and refine personal definitions that begin where *they* begin and end where they can take them.

The "Moral Leader" class card is designed to uncover students' mental models or incoming definitions of the conceptual frameworks that underlie the course. You will see from the student examples following the class card assignment that students vary greatly in their starting point for learning.

ADDITIONAL BACKGROUND

This guide's class plans analyze the moral elements of each of the readings and describe, in detail, how to lead discussions of the moral decisions the characters face. The excerpts from *Principles of Biomedical Ethics* (for class five), *Just and Unjust Wars* (for class eleven), and the module overviews in the student textbook all provide further conceptual grounding. Both texts are wonderful to read in their entirety; as applied ethics (that is, ethics particular to a specific domain) they offer fascinating and especially well fleshed out examples of moral reasoning grounded in the practical realities of (respectively) biomedical situations and the conduct of war.

While by no means necessary, you may find it reassuring to acquaint yourself with a few other established definitions of morality and ethics. Louis Pojman has written a particularly lucid and comprehensive short introduction (which I had forwarded to the student), "What Is Ethics?,"[2] as has Deborah

Rhode, "Traditions of Moral Reasoning," in her excellent text on legal ethics.[3]

The "Moral Leader" class card frequently stimulates questions; one of the most common concerns the difference between "morality" and "ethics," and you may have noted that throughout this guide, and in the course, I have made no attempt to distinguish between these terms. The following definition from *The Oxford Companion to Philosophy* lays out why this approach is followed by many who wish to engage in practical discussions of these topics:

> **ethics and morality:** "Morality" and "ethics" are terms often used as synonyms: an ethical issue just is a moral issue. Increasingly, however, the term "ethics" is being used to apply to specialized areas of morality, such as medicine, business, the environment, and so on. Where professions are involved, a governing body will typically draw up a code of ethics for its members. "Ethics" in this sense can be thought of as a subset of morality, being that aspect of morality concerned with moral obligations pertaining to the practice of a profession. On the other hand, some philosophers, from Socrates to Bernard Williams, use "ethics" in a broad sense to refer to reflective answers to the question "How should I live?" If we accept this broad sense of "ethics," then morality becomes a subset of ethics, being that aspect of ethics concerned with obligation.[4]

THE "MORAL LEADER" CLASS CARD ASSIGNMENT

This class card gives you a chance to reflect on the ideas we shall explore in "The Moral Leader." I think you will find the class card helpful now, and as a baseline of ideas to build on, refine, and revise as the course unfolds. There are no right or wrong answers, just the beginning of deliberation that will weave itself through our class discussions and culminate in your end-of-term paper.

Please answer the questions below and email your class card to me prior to our third session. I look forward to reading your reply.

Name:

1   How would you define Moral Challenge?

2   What do you think Moral Reasoning consists of?

3   What does Moral Leadership mean (or suggest) to you?

SAMPLE STUDENT RESPONSES

Student 1

1 How do you define Moral Challenge?

A moral challenge is a significant dilemma in which an individual is forced to make a decision that in some way challenges his/her values or brings into question longstanding personal ideologies. Where other types of challenges involve other people or other things, a moral challenge is largely an internal question – there is no mountain to conquer or project to complete, it is more a dilemma for your own psyche to grapple with. The decision often is complicated by there being no clear "right" answer, or if there is a right answer, the situation makes it difficult to choose. A true moral challenge leaves one changed for having dealt with it.

2 What does Moral Reasoning consist of?

Not very familiar with this concept! I would imagine that moral reasoning is the process by which one uses his/her own moral compass to wrestle with an issue. The challenge to be overcome is not necessarily a moral challenge or ethical dilemma but rather any issue that requires an individual to use a values-based decision-making thought process.

3 What does Moral Leadership mean (or suggest) to you?

Moral leadership is the act of taking a stand on a certain issue or in a certain situation based on one's values. One can provide moral leadership at any level of any group or organization by acting in challenging situations in a way consistent with one's values. Oftentimes this takes enormous strength of character because it involves speaking out or putting oneself on the line. Moral leadership can also be exhibited by helping others think through decisions/situations in using values as guideposts.

Student 2

1 How would you define Moral Challenge?

Moral challenges arise when what is comfortable, easy, or profitable conflicts with what is right. In a person's life, there will inevitably be several occasions when a choice presents itself: on one side lies personal benefit and on the other the "right" thing to do. It is my hope that in these circumstances, I will choose what I believe to be right.

The most difficult moral challenges are those situations which require a struggle even to determine what "right" is.

2 What do you think Moral Reasoning consists of?

Moral reasoning is the process individuals go through in their quest to discover what is right. Often times, this "reasoning" process is free of thought – for example, millions of people turn to the "word of God" as all the reason they need. Others attempt to quantify the ends of certain actions, and to follow the course that results in the most total happiness – to be utilitarian. Still more consult with friends, family, and ultimately their own hearts and minds to determine the right way to act.

My personal belief is that each of us has to arrive at what we consider right independently. Whatever that belief may be, it is our duty to act on it, to behave in the ways that we truly believe are right. This means that even though I may wholeheartedly disagree with another's interpretation of right and wrong, I must respect that person if she lives her life according to what she believes in.

3 What does Moral Leadership mean (or suggest) to you?

Moral leadership is the ability to influence the way others see their world – Moral leaders can change the way people look at right and wrong. In this way, I think of men like Martin Luther King Jr and Abraham Lincoln. But I also must think about Adolf Hitler and Osama bin Laden. Each of these men, through rhetoric, charisma, and firm commitment to cause altered the way large portions of society viewed right and wrong. Personally, of course, I have a deep respect and admiration for King and Lincoln and find Hitler and bin Laden utterly repugnant. My morals, what I consider good and right, could not be further removed from Hitler's. However, when I think of moral leadership, I think of those people who have the ability to alter what right and wrong mean in others' eyes.

Student 3

1 How do you define Moral Challenge?

I would define 'moral challenge' as a 'situation of acute hardship caused by or related to its unique or unexpected moral component'. This definition has a couple of key features:

- *Acute hardship*: I believe that many things (perhaps even most things) in life have a moral component, depending on how widely you define the word "moral". However, I think that most of these do not present a challenge, as we are sufficiently socialized to have our subconscious deal with them. It is the acute hardship we sometimes feel that is the hallmark of moral challenge.

- *"Caused by or related to"*: I include these words to indicate that many acute hardships do not have a large moral component. Contrast Shackleton weighing the lives of his men (moral challenge) to a situation where you were alone on the ice attempting escape (challenge, but not moral).

- *"Unique or unexpected"*: I feel that the challenge should be unique or unexpected for it to be truly challenging. If it is routine (for example the choice a criminal defense lawyer makes to not disclose damaging information about their clients), then my hypothesis is that that person has had the time to adequately prepare for and analyze the challenge.

- *"Moral component"*: This is the key here. The hardship must be of a moral or ethical nature. Examples might be where you have to deal with two competing moral imperatives that seem inconsistent with one another, or where you believe your moral choice will have negative consequences, or where you are uncertain of even what the right moral and cognitive framework is for the issue at hand.

2 What does Moral Reasoning consist of?

I think "moral reasoning" consists of "a considered approach to a moral challenge, based on an existing or new moral framework." This has some nuances I have thought about:

- *"Considered approach"*: I think it is possible to make more decisions or judgments very quickly if we are required to do so. However, I think this removes the "reasoning" component, so I believe a considered approach is essential.

- *"Moral challenge"*: Some kind of moral challenge (as discussed above) is necessary to separate moral reasoning from any other kind of reasoning, no matter how complex.

- *"Existing or new"*: I believe that the person doing the moral reasoning must be cognizant that they are doing so. This could happen in one of two ways. First, they recognize that the situation is similar to or analogous to previous situations, and so can apply an existing framework. Alternatively, they realize that the situation is new, but recognize the moral component, and develop a new reasoning method on the fly.

- *"Moral framework"*: I consider that the decision-making involved in this moral reasoning must be based on a moral framework, not just some haphazard set of ideas. In this sense, it is a set of rules for decision-making or some kind of framework for assessing novel situations.

3 What does Moral Leadership mean (or suggest) to you?

"Moral leadership" means to me a "situation where a person inspires following in others on the basis of an acceptable, consistent moral code." Again, individual elements of this have meaning for me:

- *"A person"*: Just as business leadership is not only exercised by the CEO, moral leadership is not just exercised by traditional notions of a "moral leader" such as Mandela, Gandhi etc. Any person can exercise it in the right circumstances.

- *"Inspires following in others"*: Perhaps this is a semantic point. However, I believe that unless the putative moral leader inspires others to follow their moral example, then they are just a moral individual, and not a moral leader.

- *"Acceptable, consistent"*: I believe that moral leadership must have its roots in some sort of decision-making code or framework. For me, it must pass two additional tests. It must be acceptable and at the very least not obviously immoral or amoral in character. It must also be consistent, as a set of moral guidelines that is not internally consistent would be difficult for others to follow.

- *"Moral code"*: I think that the moral code here can take many forms. At its most instrumental it could be an approach to solving a particular moral problem (for example, what is my stance on euthanasia?). However, more broadly, it could be a code of rules for how to conduct moral reasoning for both new and existing situations.

NOTES

1   "We are discussing no small matter, but how we ought to live." Socrates, in Plato's *Republic*, quoted in Louis Pojman, *Ethical Theory: Classical and Contemporary Readings*, 4th edn, Wordsworth/Thomson Learning, 2002, p. 1.
2   Ibid., pp. 1–7.
3   See also Chapter 2, "Traditions of Moral Reasoning," in Deborah L. Rhode, *Professional Responsibility: Ethics by the Pervasive Method*, 2nd edn, New York: Aspen Law & Business, 1998, for a review of moral theories from the standpoint of legal ethics.
4   *The Oxford Companion to Philosophy*, New York: Oxford University Press, 2005, p. 271. See also Thomas Mautner, *A Dictionary of Philosophy*, Cambridge, Mass: Blackwell, 1996, for definitions of ethics, p. 137, moral, p. 276, moral philosophy, p. 277, morality, pp. 278–279, and *The Cambridge Dictionary of Philosophy*, Cambridge: Cambridge University Press, 1999, for definitions of ethics and related concepts, pp. 284–289, and morality, p. 586.

The "Moral Leader" course paper

These are the instructions I present to students.

GUIDELINES FOR THE "MORAL LEADER" COURSE PAPER

The assignment for the course paper is to describe and analyze a situation involving the demonstration of moral leadership. Your paper should be approximately fifteen pages long, double-spaced. Don't worry if your paper turns out to be longer than this. I enjoy reading these papers and don't count words. Please submit your paper using your student ID number only, as I prefer to grade the papers blind, i.e. without knowing the authors.

Assignment

The purpose of the final paper is to help you clarify – and chronicle – your own understanding of moral leadership, particularly as it has evolved during the course. The assignment has three parts:

■ *A description of a situation* that you believe demonstrates moral leadership
■ *Analysis of why you believe this* – the reasoning behind your assumption, and your assessment of the decisions and actions of the protagonist
■ *Reflections and lessons* – implications you draw from the protagonist/ situation and the course that inform your understanding and your own, personal definition of moral leadership.

Selection of topic

The protagonist of your paper can be drawn from biographies, autobiographies, novels, drama, and works of history – but not from any readings covered in the course.

Students have written successful papers on texts as familiar as F. Scott Fitzgerald's *The Great Gatsby* and Henrik Ibsen's *A Doll's House*, on novels or biographies I never heard of until the student told me about them, and about a wide range of historical figures and situations, including Thabo Mbeke's stance on HIV/AIDs, and Anwar Sadat and the Middle East peace process. The two main criteria for selection are: (1) to choose works whose protagonist and situation interest you personally; (2) to select topics that can be effectively covered in a 15-page paper (see "Suggestions," below).

There is a bibliography of readings on ethics and literature to stimulate your thinking. I encourage you to let me know about the text or historical figure you want to use since some topics work better in the context of this paper than others. I am happy to respond to emailed inquiries and ideas, or to meet in person or talk by phone.

Suggestions

First, you should err on the side of *depth rather than breadth.* You will find it more rewarding to describe something, provide an analysis of it, and connect it to your own insights if you focus on one (or at most two) characters facing one or two decisions/actions/events/episodes that you believe demonstrate moral leadership. It is preferable to dig deeper into one or two situations than to attempt a broad sweep of multiple situations, especially those involving an array of characters.

Second, an important aspect of this paper is *showing how your thinking has been influenced* by the stories we have read, the themes that have been raised, and the discussions you've participated in. For example, in addition to reflecting on moral leadership, your analysis may include a discussion of the type of moral challenge the protagonist faces, or whether you see evidence of what you would consider to be moral reasoning. You may also find it helpful to contrast the decisions and actions of the protagonist with protagonists and situations read about during the course. Here, too, depth is preferable to breadth. This may mean drawing fewer lessons, but presenting each with greater detail and fuller analysis. It generally means drawing upon fewer rather than more works of literature.

Third, you will find the paper more valuable to the extent that *the lessons you draw are personal.* You should write this paper for yourself and make it an opportunity for reflection on aspects of moral leadership that matter to you. You have documented your incoming definition of moral leadership on your Moral Leader class card, and you may want to reflect on how your ideas about this concept have evolved through the course, the class discussions, and the process of writing your paper.

Finally, while fifteen pages may seem a lot at the outset, in fact it can be a challenge to fit everything in as you begin to write. *Space management is important* to make sure that you cover the points that you want to make in sufficient depth.

Moral Leader Paper Grading Template

Coherence: Analysis of protagonist/situation and definition of moral leadership

Nature of task: ambitious/original/novel	2	4	6	8	10
Nature of argument: ambitious/original/novel	2	4	6	8	10
Analysis is clear, well defended, sound	2	4	6	8	10
Reasoning is cogent, persuasive, complete	2	4	6	8	10
Overall quality of execution	2	4	6	8	10
Total score					

Integration of course themes / readings: Whether what happened in the course is meaningfully applied to the argument made. A degree of application running from parroting to transformation of the topic and student

Accurate/clear description of course themes	2	4	6	8	10
Appropriate use of themes and readings	2	4	6	8	10
New/novel interpretation/argument	2	4	6	8	10
Total score					

Authenticity / quality of reflection: Integration of student's own viewpoint and quality of "implications" section on personal learning / definition of moral leadership

Integration of personal concerns into analysis	2	4	6	8	10
Personal definition of moral leadership	2	4	6	8	10
Thoughtful, complete, novel reflections	2	4	6	8	10
Total score					

Bonus points

Esp. creative/innovative	2	4	6	8	10
Esp. well reasoned, insightful, well presented	2	4	6	8	10
Overall score					
Comments:					

RESOURCES FOR THE "MORAL LEADER" PAPER

Readings on ethics and leadership[1]

The list below is by no means exhaustive, but it contains a number of books, mostly works of fiction, that offer a variety of insights into issues of leadership and responsibility. Some of the books have been used in previous versions of this course; others were strong candidates for the course but were excluded because of their length.

Please let me know if you have any suggestions for other books I could add to this list.

Jonathan Alter, *The Defining Moment: FDR's Hundred Days and the Triumph of Hope.* This biography analyzes the background and early actions of US President Franklin Delano Roosevelt, who came to office in 1933 in the heart of the American Depression.

Louis Auchincloss, *The Rector of Justin.* A fascinating portrait of the life and work of the founder of a New England prep school – a story of entrepreneurship, idealism, shrewdness, and pragmatism.

Louis Auchincloss, *The Collected Short Stories of Louis Auchincloss.* For the most part, these are stories of men and women in the social and economic elite of New York City, written by a man who spent his life within this milieu and made a dual career as an attorney and a prolific author.

Howard Bahr, *The Year of Jubilo: A Novel of the Civil War.* A novel about the challenges of a returning Confederate soldier as he navigates the transition to civil life, a transformed town, and new and old loyalties and conflicts.

Russell Banks, *Cloudsplitter.* Author of *The Sweet Hereafter*, this is Banks' historical novel about John Brown, American abolitionist and leader of the failed attempt to capture a federal arsenal in Harper's Ferry, Virginia.

Tom Barbash, *On Top of the World: Cantor Fitzgerald, Howard Lutnick & 9/11.* 658 of 1,000 Cantor Fitzgerald employees died at the World Trade Center on September 11th, the single largest loss of any WTC business. A chronicle of CEO Howard Lutnick's actions in response to this organizational and personal crisis.

Albert Camus, *The Plague.* A story about the resilience of the human spirit in the face of almost overwhelming horror, as the bubonic plague sweeps through a quarantined city in Algeria.

Raymond Chandler, *The Big Sleep.* A classic American detective story, first published in 1939, which can be read as a story about the pursuit of professional excellence and the moral dilemmas arising from dedicated service to a client.

Terrence Cheng, *Sons of Heaven*. Many remember the Tiananmen Square massacre by the photograph of a single student who stands alone, facing a line of incoming government tanks. The identity of this student has never been determined. This novel is a fictional "back story" that creates a description of the student's life and motivations for the actions he took.

Joseph Conrad, *Typhoon*. A story of moral courage at sea, involving an unlikely hero – a quiet, unassuming ship's captain.

Theodore Dreiser, *The Financier*. The rise and fall, and subsequent rise, of a nineteenth-century financier – a counterpart in many respects to 1980s corporate raider Michael Milken.

F. Scott Fitzgerald, *The Great Gatsby*. The famous story of Jay Gatsby, a successful Roaring Twenties financier and his deluded quest for the good life.

Allegra Goodman, *Intuition*. Set in a prestigious medical research laboratory, this novel traces the accusations, and their consequences, that one of the laboratory's star young postdocs has been falsifying his research results.

Nadine Gordimer, *My Son's Story*. Gordimer is a Nobel Prize-winning South African writer who has chronicled that country's search to free itself from apartheid. This novel describes the evolution of a family led by an anti-apartheid activist, and the impact of his actions on his family and the cause.

Nadine Gordimer, *Six Feet of the Country*. A collection of Gordimer's short stories. The story "A Chip of Glass Ruby" has been used as a reading in prior versions of the "Moral Leader" course.

Jonathan Harr, *A Civil Action*. The non-fiction account upon which the recent movie was based. A fascinating story of moral leadership, in all its complexities, as seen through the efforts of a young lawyer bringing a class-action environmental suit against two large companies.

Nathaniel Hawthorne, *The Scarlet Letter*. One of the greatest American novels, this is the story of Hester Prynne, a Puritan woman convicted of committing adultery, her husband, and her lover, who is also an admired clergyman. Prynne, in many respects, some surprising, emerged as the moral leader in the story.

Joseph Heller, *Something Happened*. A black comedy, by the author of *Catch-22*, about success in corporate life and a fast-track executive adept at living on the surface of things.

Henrik Ibsen, *A Doll's House*. The classic play about a wife's moral choices and her actions of self-liberation, set in Victorian times.

Edward P. Jones, *The Known World*. This Pulitzer Prize-winning novel and "book of tremendous moral intricacy" (*The New Yorker*) describes the little-known history of African-Americans who were themselves slave-owners.

Tracy Kidder, *Mountains Beyond Mountains*. This book describes the work and life of Dr Paul Farmer, celebrated infectious-disease specialist and Harvard professor who devotes himself to fighting tuberculosis in rural Haiti.

Barbara Kingsolver, *The Poisonwood Bible*. The story of the quiet and heroic leadership of a mother who takes her children to the Congo, following her missionary husband, and then leaves him and Africa and reassembles a life from the wreckage of these decisions.

David Lodge, *Nice Work*. A serious and funny book about what two people learn from the collision of their very different worlds. One is a factory manager; the other a deconstructionist professor of literature.

David Mamet, *Glengarry Glen Ross*. A Pulitzer Prize-winning play about the brutal competition among a group of real-estate agents.

John Marquand, *Point of No Return*. A successful investment banker returns to his hometown and reflects on the choices that shaped his life.

Arthur Miller, *All My Sons* and *Death of a Salesman*. Two classic, powerful plays about identity and family.

William Shakespeare, *Macbeth*. A study of ambition, the murkiness of values, and the powerful seduction of shortcuts to success.

Michael Shaara, *The Killer Angels*. A great historical novel that tells the story of the Battle of Gettysburg in brilliant detail. It presents a wide range of leaders, moral and otherwise, including the remarkable Colonel Joshua Lawrence Chamberlain.

George Bernard Shaw, *Major Barbara*. A witty, complex, surprising play about an arms manufacturer and his idealistic daughter.

Anita Shreve, *The Pilot's Wife*. The story of moral challenges faced by the wife of a secret member of the IRA.

Leo Tolstoy, *War and Peace*. One of the great books, worth reading and rereading for a multitude of reasons, among which are Tolstoy's vivid and unforgettable portraits of men and women who change the world, on both the grand stage of life and in subtle, everyday ways.

Leo Tolstoy, *The Death of Ivan Ilyich*. The somber tale of an ambitious, successful man and his discovery of the vacuum his life had become.

John Updike, *Rabbit at Rest*. The final book in Updike's highly acclaimed trilogy recounting both the life of Harry Angstrom, a middle-class everyman, and the evolution of American society from the 1950s to the 1980s.

Gore Vidal, *Lincoln*. A long, masterful work of historical fiction that portrays not only the story of Lincoln's presidency but his thoughts and feelings, as well as those of the people Lincoln lived and worked with.

Tom Wolfe, *Bonfire of the Vanities* and *A Man in Full*. Two long, entertaining, often satirical portraits of American business life and society. The first views the world through the experience of a New York investment banker during the 1980s; the second through an Atlanta real-estate developer during the 1990s.

Historical protagonists

Some examples of historical figures that students have written papers on:

- Menachem Begin
- Neville Chamberlain
- Phoolan Devi
- Lyndon B. Johnson
- Robert F. Kennedy
- Cardinal Bernard Law
- Evita Peron
- Preston Manning
- Thabo Mbeki
- Helmut Kohl
- J. P. Morgan
- Anwar Sadat
- Oskar Schindler

NOTE

1   This bibliography builds on Joe Baadarracco's bibliography for "The Moral Leader" course and paper.

Bibliography

"11 Fortune 500 Companies with Female CEOs," *The Associated Press,* August 14, 2006.

Achebe, Chinua, *Things Fall Apart,* New York: Anchor Books, 1994.

Auer, J. Jeffrey and Ewbank, Henry Lee, *Handbook for Discussion Leaders,* New York: Harper & Brothers, 1954.

Bain, Ken, *What the Best College Teachers Do,* Cambridge, Mass.: Harvard University Press, 2004.

Baker-Smith, Dominic, *Introduction to The Prince,* New York: Everyman's Library, Alfred A. Knopf, 1992.

Banks, Russell, *The Sweet Hereafter,* New York: HarperPerennial, 1991.

Beauchamp, T. L. and Childress, J. F., *Principles of Biomedical Ethics,* Oxford and New York: Oxford University Press, 2001.

Berlin, Isaiah "The Originality of Machiavelli," in *Against the Current: Essays in the History of Ideas,* New York: Viking Press, 1980, pp. 25–79.

Blanchard, Kenneth, Zigarmi, Patricia, and Zigarmi, Drea, *Leadership and the One Minute Manager: Increasing Effectiveness through Situational Leadership,* New York: William Morrow & Company, Inc., 1985.

Bolt, Robert, *A Man for All Seasons,* New York: First Vintage International Edition, 1990.

Booth, Wayne C., *The Company We Keep: An Ethics of Fiction,* Berkeley, Calif.: University of California Press, 1988.

Bradlee, Ben, *A Good Life: Newspapering and other Adventures,* New York: Touchstone Books, 1996.

Bruner, Robert F., *Socrates' Muse: Reflections on Effective Case Discussion Leadership,* Boston, Mass.: McGraw-Hill Irwin, 2003.

The Cambridge Dictionary of Philosophy, Cambridge: Cambridge University Press, 1999.

Christensen, C. Roland, "Premises and Practices of Discussion Teaching," in C. Roland Christensen, David A. Garvin, and Ann Sweet (eds), *Education for Judgment: The Artistry of Discussion Leadership,* Boston, Mass.: Harvard Business School Press, 1991, pp. 15–34.

Coles, Robert *The Call of Stories: Teaching and the Moral Imagination,* Boston, Mass.: Houghton Mifflin, 1989.

Conrad, Joseph, *The Secret Sharer,* New York: Dover, 1993.

Course, A. G., *The Merchant Navy: A Social History,* London: Frederick Muller Ltd, 1963.

Cunningham, William A., Johnson, Marcia K., Raye, Carol L., Gatenby, J. Chris, Gore, John C., and Banaji, Mahzarin R., "Separable Neural Components in the Processing of Black and White Faces," *Psychological Science*, 2004, vol. 15, no. 12, 806–813.

Damasio, Antonio R., *Descartes' Error: Emotion, Reason and the Human Brain*, New York: G. P. Putnam, 1994.

DePalma, Anthony, "Use of Air Masks at Issue in Claims of 9/11 Illnesses," *The New York Times*, June 5, 2006, p. 1.

Falzon, Christopher, *Philosophy Goes to the Movies: An Introduction to Philosophy*, New York and London: Routledge, 2002.

Fiedler, Fred, *A Theory of Leadership Effectiveness*, New York: McGraw-Hill, 1967.

Freeland, Cynthia A. and Wartenburg, Thomas E. (eds), *Philosophy and Film*, New York and London: Routledge, 1995.

Garner, Bryan A. (ed.), *Black's Law Dictionary* 8th edn, St Paul, Minn.: Thompson West, 2004.

Garvin, David A., "A Delicate Balance: Ethical Dilemmas and the Discussion Process" in C. Roland Christensen, David A. Garvin, and Ann Sweet (eds), *Education for Judgment: The Artistry of Discussion Leadership*, Boston, Mass.: Harvard Business School Press, 1991, pp. 287–303.

Garvin, Joyce, "Undue Influence: Confessions from an Uneasy Discussion Leader," in C. Roland Christensen, David A. Garvin, and Ann Sweet (eds), *Education for Judgment: The Artistry of Discussion Leadership*, Boston, Mass.: Harvard Business School Press, 1991, pp. 275–286.

Graham, Katharine, *Personal History*, New York: Vintage Books, 1998.

Greene, Joshua D., Somerville, Brian R., Nystrom, Leigh E., Darley, John M., and Cohen, Jonathan D., "An fMRI Investigation of Emotional Engagement in Moral Judgment," *Science*, 2000, vol. 293, 2105–2108.

Gurganus, Alan, "Blessed Assurance: A Moral Tale," in *White People*, New York: Vintage Contemporaries, 1990, pp. 192–252.

Hersey, John, Hiroshima, New York: Alfred A. Knopf, 1998.

Hersey, Paul, *The Situational Leader*, New York: Warner Books, 1984.

Highsmith, Patricia, "Reminiscences of a Gentleman's Gentleman," Interview of Kazuo Ishiguro, *LA Times*, October 1, 1989, p. 3.

Hilliam, David, *Kings, Queens, Bones, and Bastards: Who's Who in the English Monarchy from Egbert to Elizabeth II*, Stroud: Sutton Publishing, 1998.

Ishiguro, Kazuo, *The Remains of the Day*, New York: Vintage International, 1988.

Jackall, Robert, *Moral Mazes: The World of Corporate Managers*, New York: Oxford University Press, 1988.

Klein, Gary, *Sources of Power: How People Make Decisions*, Cambridge, Mass.: The MIT Press, 1998.

Langewiesche, William, *American Ground: Unbuilding the World Trade Center*, New York: North Point Press, 2002, first paperback edition 2003.

Lansing, Alfred, *Endurance: Shackleton's Incredible Voyage*, New York: Carroll & Graff, 1999.

Lemprière, J., *Bibliotheca Classica* or *A Classical Dictionary*, 3rd edn, London, 1797.

McCullough, David, *Truman*, New York: Simon & Schuster, 1992.

Machiavelli, Niccolò, *The Prince*, New York and London: Penguin Books, 1999.

Mautner, Thomas, *A Dictionary of Philosophy*, Cambridge, Mass.: Blackwell, 1996.

Orr, Andrea, "Hewlitt-Packard Picks Lucent Exec as CEO," *The Houston Chronicle*, July 20, 1999. p. 20.

The Oxford Companion to Philosophy, New York: Oxford University Press, 2005.

Nussbaum, Martha C., *Love's Knowledge: Essays on Philosophy and Literature*, New York: Oxford University Press, 1990.

Plous, Scott, *The Psychology of Judgment and Decision Making*, New York: McGraw-Hill, Inc., 1993.

Pojman, Louis, *Ethical Theory: Classical and Contemporary Readings*, 4th edn, Wordsworth/Thomson Learning, 2002.

Pojman, Louis and Vaughn, Lewis (eds), *The Moral Life: An Introductory Reader in Ethics and Literature*, New York: Oxford University Press, 2006.

Porter, Burton F., *Philosophy through Fiction and Film*, Upper Saddle River, NJ: Pearson Prentice Hall, 2004.

Project Implicit: https://implicit.harvard.edu/implicit.

Rhode, Deborah L., *Professional Responsibility: Ethics by the Pervasive Method*, 2nd edn, New York: Aspen Law & Business, 1998.

Ruffo Fiore, Silvia, *Niccolò Machiavelli: An Annotated Bibliography of Modern Criticism and Scholarship*, Westport, Conn.: Greenwood Press, 1990.

Sherwin, Martin J., "The Atomic Bomb and the Origins of the Cold War: vs Atomic-Energy Policy and Diplomacy 1941–1945," *The American Historical Review* 78, 1973, 945–968.

Social Justice Research, 2004, vol. 17, no. 2.

Sophocles, "Antigone," in *The Theban Plays*, translated by E. F. Watling, New York and London: Penguin Books, 1947, pp. 126–162.

"South Korea Gets First Woman Prime Minister," *Agence France-Presse*, March 24, 2006.

Steiner, George, *Antigones*, New Haven, Conn: Yale University Press, 1984.

Stimson, Henry L. and Bundy, McGeorge, *On Active Service in Peace and War*, New York: Harper & Brothers, 1947.

Stone, Geoffrey R., *Perilous Times: Free Speech in Wartime*, New York: W.W. Norton & Company, 2004.

Sucher, Sandra J., *The Moral Leader: Challenges, Tools, and Insights*, Oxford: Routledge, 2008.

Sucher, Sandra J., *Reading the Material*, Cambridge, Mass.: Harvard Business School Press, HBS Note #9–065–027.

Truman, Harry S., *Memorirs by Harry S. Truman, Vol. I: Year of Decisions*, Garden City, NY: Doubleday, 1955.

Walzer, Michael, *Arguing About War*, New Haven, Conn.: Yale University Press, 2004.

Walzer, Michael, *Just and Unjust Wars: A Moral Argument with Historical Illustrations*, New York: Basic Books, 1977, 2000.

Wolf, Sidney M., *The Accountant's Guide to Corporation, Partnership, and Agency Law*, New York, Westport, London: Quorum Books, 1989.

"Women Leaders Take Hold on Power across the Globe," *Agence France-Presse*, January 16, 2006.

Index

Note: *italic* page numbers denote references to figures/tables.

For Product Safety Concerns and Information please contact our
EU representative GPSR@taylorandfrancis.com Taylor & Francis
Verlag GmbH, Kaufingerstraße 24, 80331 München, Germany